On the Bones of the Serpent

Debbora Battaglia

On the Bones

of the Serpent

Person, Memory, and Mortality in Sabarl Island Society

The University of Chicago Press   *Chicago and London*

DEBBORA BATTAGLIA is assistant professor of anthropology at Mount Holyoke College.

The University of Chicago Press, Chicago 60637
The University of Chicago Press, Ltd., London

© 1990 by the University of Chicago
All rights reserved. Published 1990
Printed in the United States of America
99 98 97 96 95 94 93 92 91 90   5 4 3 2 1

⊗ The paper used in this publication meets the minimum requirements of the American National Standard for Information Sciences—Permanence of Paper for Printed Library Materials, ANSI Z39.48-1984

Library of Congress Cataloging-in-Publication Data
Battaglia, Debbora.
   On the bones of the serpent : person, memory, and mortality in Sabarl Island society / Debbora Battaglia.
      p.   cm.
   Includes bibliographical references.
   ISBN 0–226–03888–2 (alk. paper).—ISBN 0–226–03889–0 (pbk. : alk. paper)
   1. Sabarl (Papua New Guinea people) 2. Sabarl (Papua New Guinea people)—Funeral customs and rites.   I. Title.
DU740.42.B39   1990
393'.1'09953—dc20
                                                                        89–35896
                                                                        CIP

To B. B. and B. B.

Contents

Acknowledgments

An ethnographer should be accustomed to living with sins of omission, but mine always haunt me. I began this study at the age of twenty-six, when my debts were easy to list; a decade later, the situation seems a lifetime more complex. Of course my overwhelming debt is to the people of Sabarl Island, and in particular the residents of Maho village, who shared with me their often extraordinary strength of character and their delicacy in matters of the human heart. Certain people there "looked after" me and my interests, and to them I owe the survival of my spirit for the work: Simon Sulei and Diane Meliae, whose daughter Debi is my namesake, Anastasia Kumaoko, Jane Mulawa and Mark Baiyola, Luke Moia Olana and Margaret Nabowa, Fred Naige and Noella Mary, Andrew Endor, Domonic Wasilolo and Bernadette Tovin, Soter Gauloia, Ita, Nancy Ema, Pepetua Weniye, Sylvester Gamayogi and Filomena Yabobo, Elizabeth Toulo and Tony Nedibai, Lucila Danole, Julia. Along with so many others, they helped make me a more open person. I am also indebted to the Sacred Heart mission at Nimowa for hospitality generous beyond words. Everyone who knows him in this part of the world considers Father Anthony Young a special friend and spiritual resource, and I am no exception. Father Sam Nounou was a source of wisdom on the subject of Sabarl values and a model of gentility and morality throughout the Saisai region. Sister Margaret and, later, Sister Brenda Nash made a home for me away from home. Special thanks also to Diana and Chip Nichols for so graciously taking me in and looking after me at Panagwamola, and to their beautiful children.

Of course, ethnography never ends in the field. I have been nurtured intellectually, and by way of an abiding friendship, by Marilyn Strathern (who will blush to read this). A truly rare soul, I thank her for her contagious intensity of purpose and for her faith—not to mention her editorial skills. I thank Jack Goody for bringing me into the family, and my family of friends at Cambridge, for their patience as I was working things out in the early years of writing. Roy Wagner was an intellectual guide long before he knew it, and he remains a gentle presence in my thinking and work. For encouraging me over the years, often in spite of our theoretical differences, I am grateful to Annette Weiner, Michael Young, Donald Tuzin, Deborah Gewertz and Frederick Errington, Fred Myers and Faye Ginsburg, Rena Lederman, and Edward Schieffelin. Silipokapulapola Digim'rina was a superb field assistant on Sabarl in 1986.

I thank my dear husband, Bruce, for his unconditional support and for his genuine and touching concern for the welfare of my psyche—and for Brandon. I thank Victoria Ebin just for being, somewhere.

And to my mother and father, who nurtured my spirit of adventure and taught me that *almost* anything is possible, and to my brother and sister, I thank you for the "roots" of this Sabarl story.

Introduction

Approaching Remembrance

The Sabarl tell a story from the "beginning of time" (*sauga tawa lelei*) about a great sea eagle who challenges a giant serpent to a mortal test of strength. The eagle tricks the serpent into leaving its hole at the edge of the sea, then snatches it up in its beak and circles the sky until the serpent dies and decomposes. The rotting flesh falls into the water and forms a ring of islands. Then, when only the skeleton remains, the eagle tosses it away, creating Sabarl: the "bones" of the serpent.

Sabarl Island is in fact shaped much like a writhing snake, some four miles long by half a mile wide, with two small island "eyes" floating off one end. It is part of a string of metamorphic, coral, and volcanic islands known as the Calvados Chain, which forms the southerly section of the ring of lands created by the eagle and the serpent, with Misima and adjacent islands barely visible fifty miles to the north. The ring itself is part of the Louisiades—a great archipelago extending over three hundred miles southeastward off the southern tip of the New Guinea mainland and marking out the reefy seas of one of the world's largest lagoons.[1]

It is somewhat disconcerting, if you know the story, that modern air lanes more or less trace the route of the mythical eagle's flight. My first memorable glimpse of Sabarl was through the plastic windows of a small airplane. It appeared between patches of clouds that broke the line of the atoll into fragments of brilliant beach and coral cliff, dark tropical bush, thatched roofs in clusters, human figures, more beach, lagoon shallows, canoes like matchsticks, reef—and then only the impasto of deep sea and, in the distance, other islands, more hilly, seemingly more substantial. I was unaware at the time that the land I was trying to make visual sense of would be the site of my ethnographic

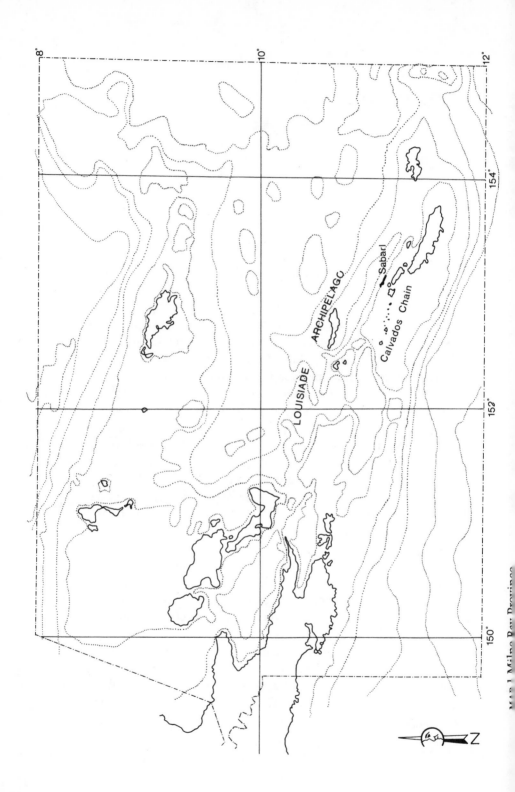

MAP 1 Milne Bay Province

LOUISIADE ARCHIPELAGO

Calvados Chain

Sabari

N

fieldwork, but I was very much aware of the personal effort involved in forming a coherent impression—even at that distance.

Ten years later, as I sit down to write something of my understanding of Sabarl society and culture, filtered as it was and (in the retelling) is through my own history, selecting and emphasizing those fragments that Sabarl people regard as "authentic" cultural images and voices—their own distinctive cultural process—I have come to regard this early attempt at perceiving Sabarl as a kind of emblem of the problem of ethnographic representation in general. For at the time of my first visit, rather newly exposed to French and British structuralism and the powerful movement in anthropology to seek out deep and total structures in human societies, I conceived of culture as a closed system of signs that human beings everywhere and at all times imposed on the seamless reality of the natural order. Moreover, I was in search of the underlying logic of the language of culture, particularly as this was expressed in visual imagery—a code I imagined I could crack from a lofty logical perspective. But eventually that view would change as I was confronted each day in the field (and still am, of course, at each sentence) by the inescapable reality of the limits of my understanding of Sabarl culture considered as process—messy, open ended, unfinished—as well as by the practical limits Sabarl people themselves set on attributing significance to their social actions. The pragmatic approach I have taken to representing Sabarl meaning making grows out of this seemingly paradoxical, shared sense of the limitations and ongoingness of the reproduction of cultural knowledge.

*

Cultural process is defined by a single problematic reality: that reality itself is culturally organized and disorganized, not discovered; that the meanings we give to our perceptions and experiences are constructed (rather than passively observed); that these meanings are alternately deconstructed as we recognize new differences and ascribe them significance.[2] I can never objectively describe cultural phenomena as I might natural ones, can never truly represent them except in fragments, since I can never know others and understand their otherness except partially and "intersubjectively," just as Sabarl themselves negotiate their own understandings of self through others.[3]

In thus making their way through life, Sabarl tend not to steer by some mythical charter of total or absolute knowledge. There are no all-knowing "seers" with privileged status in Sabarl society (at least among the living), no divinities personified as chiefs or kings or priests, and Sabarl people have little use for the concept of God. Rather,

Sabarl tend to exhibit a resigned certainty that things and people are knowable only in part, in their different aspects as determined by perspective. Furthermore (and this is the nub of the problem for Sabarl), although this knowledge can be retained, it is subject to formidable forces of dispersal and disintegration and, as such, to the vicissitudes of retrieval and reconstruction.

Now, in sketching out this Sabarl position on the impossibility of fixed or stable knowledge, it seems that Sabarl have anticipated many of the assumptions of a "perspectivist" ("postmodern," "deconstructive," "poststructural") anthropology. Fundamentally, this position represents in the social sciences a critique of the notion of absolute knowledge—taking a more interpretive and relativistic approach to understanding others and otherness. It is an anthropology that at least in theory demands a humbler ethnography and a concern for "ethnographic congruency"—a perspective that scrutinizes the rhetoric of ethnographic representation in its desire for a counterhegemonic discourse, holding its authors to greater accountability.[4]

It was, however, not anthropological theory but Sabarl epistemology itself that moved me in the direction of perspectivism, and this point needs to be emphasized. For it seems that ethnography goes most badly wrong, is most dishonest and distorting, when analysis ignores the cultural themes and elaborations its subjects reveal in social practice. A perspectivist language and, more particularly here, an emphasis on deconstruction in acts of constructing society and constructing meaning, is appropriate for writing about Sabarl culture, not because it represents an advance on some other analytic strategy but because Sabarl tend in practice to emphasize such things as the dissemination and dispersal of knowledge and valued resources (rather than their accumulation and centralization), the fluidity and inversion of power asymmetries in social relationships, the workings of symbolic displacement (visual and verbal punning, allegory, the general sleight of hand of meaning) in aesthetic objects, and perhaps centrally, the ephemerality of human beings and their historical products.

Where human agency plays so salient and intentional a role in things falling apart, in the demise and reformation of systems, the words to describe and analyze the process are appropriately taken from a deconstructivist vocabulary. But the point is that this too, like the consciousness it promotes, is inherently limited and limiting. Only, I believe, as we confront the limits of our own discourse, privileging Sabarl voices along the way as best we can and learning at which junctures Sabarl ways of knowing and reproducing knowledge can alone lead us toward insight, do we reveal the differences that make people interesting. Approached in this way, ethnography's task is not and has never been, as Strathern notes, "to fill in the terms that indigenous conceptualizations lacked but to create spaces that the exogenous analysis lacked" (1988:11).

The deconstructive inflection in Sabarl culture gives Sabarl society a very different profile from societies where cultural artifacts are cast (more or less literally) in stone or else are left to fall apart naturally or disposed of before their decomposition can be witnessed.[5] It differs from cultures where meanings are ratified by ascendant authorities and permanency is inscribed in canons and monuments or where social hierarchies are conceived as permanently enshrined in the natural order. In such societies the chimeric aspect of meaning is underplayed and the cultural emphasis is placed on "official" meanings and "totalizing" myths. And here an emphasis on constructive imagery by the ethnographer (for example, discussions of schema and coherent "models of and for" social action) is more resonant and is likely to yield insight. Without suggesting here a typology of constructivist and deconstructivist societies (since by definition the elements of each will be present in and constitute the other), it is nonetheless useful to return to the distinctions between these dialectical and "dialogical" ideologies and to the tensions they create in social practice.

The "roots" (to use the Sabarl idiom) of my thinking will become clearer as we consider some of the basic points of Sabarl epistemology.

MARKS AND THE RELATIVE VALUE OF WORDS

I was talking one day with a woman who was known for her skill in weaving intricate personal baskets, called *tiltil*. The decorative motifs woven into these baskets are chosen from a relatively small vocabulary of conventional images: a stream of "fresh water," the "moon," the "moon's shadow," "money" (a recent introduction). Though it is seldom that a new motif appears (I asked a girl if she could weave me the sea, and she replied, "We don't know how to weave salt"—there was no model for it, it would be inappropriate), women see the baskets as a kind of blank canvas where, if they wanted to, they could one day experiment with new images.

We had been discussing this creative process when I asked my consultant whether she could teach a blind girl to weave a particular image—say, a tree—that the girl had never seen. Her immediate response was no. But then she added that the girl could "imagine" or "conceive the idea of" (*pintue*) a tree and weave the image: "Afterward her friends would tell her its name."

Two points in this exchange are worth noting, since they introduce larger themes that will concern us later. The first is that this Sabarl woman found it (culturally) natural to add a social sequel to the scenario I described. She completed the action of a woman's weaving her private idea into a basket by adding the element of sociality—others who witnessed her creation and translated it for her (rendered it significant) and in doing so brought themselves into her story. In other words, the fact of a representational image,[6] properly "framed" in a familiar cultural artifact, both elicited a dialogue and presupposed an ongoing context of social interaction. In fact, without this further development our own dialogue would have ended—which is something neither of us wanted. The "story"[7] of the basket likewise wove us into a relationship *with a future*.

The second point has to do with the priority of visual imagery in Sabarl discourse, in this context but also more generally. It seems that before the name was the image, whether sensorially perceived or conceived in the "mind's eye." For Sabarl, concrete representational "marks" (*mui-*) and other figural or "imagistic" forms, as distillates of images and artifacts "for witnessing"[8] without the intervention of words, are valued as incontrovertible evidence of *nuwatu:* an organized "mind" or "thought," corresponding roughly to our notion of cognition—and as we shall see in a later chapter, a characteristic of Sabarl personhood.

Material images elicit this potential connectedness, whether they appear as patterns in the natural environment or are carved into wood, woven, painted, or assembled, danced, sung, or otherwise acted out. Whoever the author or authors, whether present-day or past (historical or mythical) beings, what is important is the impression of connectedness that arises in the act of "reading" (making sense of) the sign, between the image as an extension of its imagined producer and the perceiver. And because these images are situated in the palpable world and are "eyewitnessable" (*matana ihewa*), which is the ultimate *indigenous* criterion of verification, the mark is ascribed the "weight" of a vehicle of a past or potential truth (a "truth that is always absent"; Vance 1979:375) and is endowed as such with the status of public record.

The notion of connectedness is easier to grasp when we consider that for Sabarl figural markings have the status and function of "writing" (*luluwoli*). Sailing or punting past cliffsides, one can make out the images of flatfish, pots, canoe prows, baskets, male and female genitalia, in which Sabarl see the petrified "handmark" (*nimana muina*) of Enak the Creator (also known as God). Observing that the sun and moon take separate "paths" across the top of the world, people discern the traces of a story; they are eager to hear different versions of the moon's decision to separate from the sun. The eagle and the serpent "inscribed" the course of a primordial struggle onto the sea, which Sabarl travel today, like a map, in circular routes of prestige or subsistence trade that connect them with other islanders in struggles for fame or survival. They "cite" the bird's path when stringing beads into "lines" or sides of valuable necklaces with eagle-claw clasps, in their ideal or actual circular patterns of migration and their commitment to cycling home on the occasion of friends' and relatives' deaths—and they cite it when they talk about these things.

Cultural acts of "writing" can been seen from this perspective as a displacement of meaning onto different perceived markings—a cultural activity interwoven with the "fabric of traces." But more specifically, markings for Sabarl are figured as the leavings of social action. The artifacts of a previous productive condition, they are the raw material of something useful currently or to be useful in the future. (One narrative tells how veins of gold on Tagula,[9] a large island in the area, are the path of the feces of a great serpent.)

Yet, at the same time, writing creates what Sabarl describe as "holes in the net"—negative spaces between the markings of social action—and the precondition of erasures—spaces where markings once were. As we shall see, such "negative signs" may have all the power of positive signs to carry meaning and to arouse sentiments linked to a highly developed cultural sensitivity among Sabarl to separation and absence. Thus in the circumstances of each new performance and each new reading there arises a "dialectic of presence and absence" (Vance 1979:383), instantiated in subjective "dialogues" across time. Indeed, what follows in my account of Sabarl cultural experience might be called an ethnography of separation and absence.

This way of thinking about writing is considerably less prescribed than the view of what might otherwise be termed "embryonic writing" as a sequence of representational signs. Here we are dealing less with the human being's "unique hand with its unique thumb, coordinated . . . by ear, eye and brain" (Goody 1987:3), literally interpreted, than with the product of the "unique hand," figuratively, of a cultural animal—a manipulator of the symbolic tools of cultural production.

Following this broader usage, for Sabarl the "economy of inscription" has less to do with obeying "the motion of the hand working on the empty page" (Kristeva 1980:54) than with the movements of human life on the physical environment, as these movements are culturally projected, organized, and ascribed different values in social practice.

REMEMBRANCE

The importance to Sabarl of acts of marking and erasure has to do directly with the central place of remembrance and forgetting in ideation and cultural practice. Sabarl have no concept of "memory" as a faculty. The term *paganuwohasik*, "place/object of (or for) remembering," [10] is glossed as "memory," "remembrance," or "memorial." In Sabarl usage it conveys a sense of convergence and mooring, in space and in time, of different human perspectives. As a social action of literally "keeping in mind" (*nuwohasik*), "remembering" is significant to Sabarl primarily as a means of applying in the future something of value in the past or present—of thinking ahead and selectively projecting forward valuable knowledge.[11]

Image production in the name of memory focuses this value-production process, "fixing" it to an intersubjective space and time. It is interesting that Sabarl translate *paga* (place/object of) also as "custom"—referring to the cultural practices associated with a particular locale (an island, village, or hamlet) through which people experience a bond to an exemplary image of a "true," "pure," or "authentic" (*suwot*), pre-Westernized past.[12]

Compared with the mnemonic value of markings, Sabarl have little faith in spoken words as vehicles of "custom." Partly because they see themselves as relatively recent migrants whose ancestral origins are elsewhere in the archipelago (as discussed below), people talk as if the ancient narratives were somehow too fragile to survive the journey intact. Narrative style is tentative more often than not. I would hear that Sabarl (unlike some of their neighbors) are too far removed from mnemonic markers in the old world setting or have been in the present area too short a time to have learned its "stories" (tales, histories, legends, myths in local settings). Where narrative is concerned, a very weak sense of entitlement prevails. Yet this attitude extends beyond the bounds of narrative discourse, for the truth of any knowledge verbally conveyed is inherently suspect.

One evening on the beach I came across a small group of friends, seated around the last of a fire and speculating casually about the moon and its relation to the tides. Someone suggested that perhaps the moon fell into the sea "like a stone," so that the water rose highest when the moon was full. This apparently seemed plausible. Another idea, that there might be a hole in the ocean that affected the tides, was laughed off gently. These "ruminations" (*yowebwa*) lasted about an hour. The subject was topical because there was physical evidence of a pattern from a time in the world that was lost to the living but continued to influence their lives—a locus for recollection, and in its absence for speculation. Several people left for home intending to ask an elder about the matter.

Resolving contradictory versions of a story or making connections between seemingly different stories, discovering "one story" in many—in the local idiom, gathering different versions in "one place" (*habana hotie*, "focusing" or "organizing" them)—is for Sabarl both a challenge and a mark of intellect. Especially from women, one hears many tales about Dedeaulea, the beautiful woman in the moon. When a rock from the moon was exhibited in Port Moresby following the first lunar landing, a Sabarl leader who was visiting at the time returned home with an "eyewitness" (*matana ihewa*) account. Word spread that the moon was "only a rock," without a woman in it. But very soon people were asking how the rock got into the sky, how the woman got into it, and so on. In other words, "proper" stories and conventional explanations were regarded as part of a living truth that was out there somewhere in other people's memories, one of all possible aspects of an event and its evidence. People were always interested in new stories and new evidence, on the one hand for the different glimpses they afforded of some problem or point of contemporary interest, but on the other, for the opportunity to exercise reconstructive imaginative thought in the absence of official knowledge.

Returning to the problem of the moon and the tides, no one knew any "true stories" (*lihulihu suwot*) on the subject—that is, narratives taken as authentic and situated "in the beginning" (*sauga tawa lelei*) or in "ancestral time" (*hetutubumai wali sauga*) and passed down in "proper" form. Sabarl fashion proper narratives on the model of a growing plant, "directing" (*-logugui*) their words through the "root" of the story to its "trunk," its "branches," and finally the "new shoots"—the literary nodes from which new stories sprout.

This image of stories and their texts as *ideally* open ended and germinative is important. Only eyewitness accounts or words that are conventionally structured as still-growing texts have either credibility or interest value. At that, there are so many ways for words to go wrong—so many ways to misrepresent or "kill" the story. A good narrator was described as a person who could "select" (*pihasehase*) words carefully and put them into proper sequence (i.e., "roots" to "shoots"). But it was considered far more usual for people to "confuse" (*gonuwamut*) the facts, "make up" (*pintue*) things, let their "imaginations run away with them" (*igoyokapisi*), pass along "gossip" or "hearsay" (*gotabwayalu*).

In entrusting cultural knowledge to concrete, witnessable images over words, people are stating not so much a preference for permanence as a skeptical attitude toward the usefulness, or better, the reusability, of perceptions and experiences mediated by the words of others. Markings, more than "retrieval cues" for holding memories in mind (classically, Aristotle's concern in *De memoria*), are vehicles for the active reconstruction of remembrance, lending that inherently fluid process an aura of stability, addressing the problem of controlling the flow of construction and deconstruction that words are believed to make worse.

"Writing" *Segaiya* and Official Forgetting

For Sabarl, the creative focus of society and the most culturally elaborated form of "memory," as indigenously defined, is a series of inter-clan exchange feasts that honor individuals who have recently died. The general term for this series of feasts is *segaiya*. In the course of *segaiya* events, composed around focal rituals, exchanges, and distributions of wealth and food, people perform for the last time acts of social relation to the dead. Thus, on one level at least, *segaiya* actually elicits the story of the meaning and "value" (*mola-*) of the dead to their society. But at the same time a new, edited image of the person—a collective but ultimately "felt" memory of the dead as an absence delineated by the collectivity of relationships expressed and enacted concerning it—is being constructed "out of respect" for that persons's past contributions to society. It is this process that gives someone's memory a new and useful future as an ancestor. Remembrance, then, as a "productivity" (to use Kristeva's term) of memory, is a strategy for overcoming futility. Weiner notes this aspect for Trobriand mortuary feasts[13] when she states that "it is not easy to regenerate for the living the most social part of the person who has died so that the previous work of 'making' the person will not have been in vain . . . the attention to death . . . is a serious and time-consuming attempt to make some part of the dead person survive for the living" (1987:50).

Sabarl regard *segaiya* in general as their most impressive cultural text. But it is as an ephemeral "text enacted," forever under revision,[14] and not as some ancestrally forged work to be exactly repeated or recited each time someone dies.

In acknowledging the Sabarl regard for *segaiya* as a text, and taking this as the starting point of my own analysis, I am working also within a general anthropological tradition that takes the text as its object.[15] More specifically, I am concerned to show that, just as each text draws from a pool of prior discourse on that subject, each *segaiya* is a "permutation of texts," an "intertextuality." Each feast and feast series has an inherent historicity. It is part of a "historical family" of commemorative performances.[16]

Wherever textuality *as a form of productivity* is taken as the object of social study, research tends to become, in the words of Bakhtin, "inquiry and conversation, that is, dialogue . . . when studying man, we search for and find signs everywhere and we try to grasp their meaning" (1986:114). As an ethnographer, I have participated in the cultural "dialogues" (verbal, visual, gestural, musical, etc.) that constitute Sabarl social texts and have tried to make sense of them here in the terms of the people who produced them.

*

Before beginning a story, Sabarl will often quietly announce, *"Tahamtohon ega"*—"We are only rehearsing." I quickly learned that frequently there is only the rehearsal. If it is possible to read the present study as a kind of rehearsal, this will bring the reader much closer to a Sabarl perspective on the value of my words in print. In the chapters of part 1, I offer a reading of Sabarl notions of the person as a "guiding, generative formula that underlies and organizes significance" (Munn 1986:121), locating in physical and metaphysical constructs a referential map of the principles of social process. Part 2 is a collection of stories that develop a picture of relational personhood from social scenarios in which these principles are featured. Part 3 presents the *segaiya* sequence as a text of and for remembrance, showing how Sabarl weave historically situated memories and goals into an ideal image of sociality.

Social and Historical Background

Remembrance on Sabarl has much to do with the physical facts of archipelago life and with the local perception of insularity and a skeletal resource base as fearful problems. These problems for Sabarl exist on several levels. The first concerns physical survival. Long before I arrived on Sabarl I knew of the place by its local reputation.[17] Sabarl was a "hard place"—a coral frame, "only bones," with no fresh water or garden land to speak of, no sago (the staple starch), and very few coconuts. All these essential things were on other islands, miles away across a deepwater channel. I was told that seasonal winds could keep even very large outrigger canoes from reaching these islands, and that it was not unusual for people to be stranded on the beach for days, watching waterspouts form between them and fresh water and food.

Why so many people were living on Sabarl, more in fact than on any other island in the area, was a mystery of sufficient interest to draw me there.

At another level is the matter of social survival. For Sabarl this is conceived as a problem of remembering the rules of conduct that define a human being as a social person—someone capable of being an agent in the daily negotiation of social relations. The problem at this level has to do with the production of social order through the patterned exchange and distribution of valued resources—land, comestible and object wealth, and of course, other people—that are the artifacts or "evidence" (*mui-*) of social connectedness.

Finally, there is isolation in the ultimate sense of individuals confronting their mortality. For Sabarl this is the problem that elicits the most elaborate and circumscribing cultural response. People are concerned that they be "held in mind" (not be forgotten) by others who matter to them as sources of support and social growth—moral, economic, political, and so forth—others in whom and through whom they perceive and realize their own security and potential. To be forgotten is to lose that projective self, to become separated from an image of self in ongoing social context. It is this concern, transmuted by death, that is dramatized in commemorative feasts that, as we shall see, enact personhood itself as a relational phenomenon.[18]

Sabarl in Regional Context

An important cultural orientation of Sabarl persons is their place on the geolinguistic map of the archipelago created by the mythical bird and serpent. People of the Chain speak relatively simple "event-dominated" Austronesian languages:[19] Misima in the "lower" or western islands, Saisai in the "upper" or eastern islands, of which Sabarl is one. Misima is the lingua franca of the archipelago, and English is used in local schools. Pidgin is virtually unknown in these parts.

The Saisai speakers are further divided into two dialect groups: Sabarl (inhabiting Sabarl, Panabarli, Nigahau, and the eastern part of Kuanak) and Nimowa (inhabiting Nimowa, Piron, Dadahai, Wanim, Panatinani, and Panabusuna).

Mission territories align with the basic spatiolinguistic divisions: in the "lower" or western Chain, the United Church; in the "upper" or eastern Chain, the Roman Catholic Mission of the Sacred Heart. Until very recently, government activities have had little or no effect on village-level routine compared with that of the missions, which are associated with schooling, vocational training, access to money, and regular and emergency medical aid.

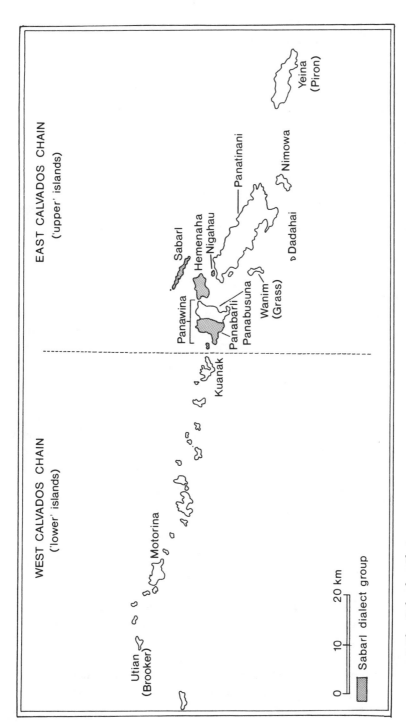

MAP 2 The Calvados Chain.

The "stories" of this book concern the eastern section of the Chain, that is, the Saisai language speakers of the "upper" islands, as I came to know them in 1976–77, with perspective added from field-work in 1979 and 1986. In 1976 these islands supported some 1,135 people in beachfront hamlets and villages. Maho, the largest village, had a population then of 202 (it had grown to just over 300 by 1986), and basically for this reason I chose it as my research base and focus of study (see tables 1–3).

Administratively, the Saisai were at this time part of the Misima Council District of the Milne Bay Province. However, in 1977 they voted with Tagula (also called Sudest or Vanatinai) and Yele (or Rossel) to split off from Misima and form the new and smaller Yeleyamba Council District. They have since split again from Yele, and it is clear that if the option existed decentralization would continue at least to the level of the language group.

The Saisai language group remains the broadest unit of cultural identity,[20] and marriage largely takes place within it. Although the subject here is the Sabarl dialect group, it must be understood to be socially and culturally enmeshed in the practice of Saisai values, and the Saisai "customs" through which cultural identity is performed. Thus, *segaiya* as practiced by Saisai is like a different language of remembrance to Tagula or Misima visitors, and vice versa.

Although Sabarl are affected by the rhetoric and to some extent the ideology of national-level politics, including the cash economy of the outer world, these influences are far less important than for other local groups. This is due partly to a preoccupation with subsistence that is at times overwhelming and partly to a fierce independence and contrariness of character that are part and parcel of an "islander" orientation to life.

NUTRITION AND HEALTH

By far the most pervasive concern of Saisai daily life is physical existence itself. Subsistence throughout the area is based on yam and sago cultivation. Sago (*Metroxylon sagu*) is worked year round. Yams (*Dioscorea esculenta* and *D. alata*), along with supplementary garden foods such as manioc, sweet potato, taro, banana, pineapple, and pumpkin, have only a single growing season. Gardens are planted and harvested during *bwaima*, the season of southeasterly winds (June through October) when ocean currents are relatively slow and the tides are low. As the season progresses beaches are seen to "grow" along with the gardens. At the same time, deepwater fish such as albacore and white

TABLE 1 Maho Village, Full-Time Residents, 1976

Ages	0–9	11–20	21–30	31–40	41–50	51–60	61–70	71–80	Total
Males	35	30	13	9	9	6	0	2	104
Females	33	32	9	11	5	5	2	1	98
Total	68	62	22	20	14	11	2	3	202

TABLE 2 Sabarl Dialect Group Population

Year	Sabarl	Nigahau	Panawina**	Total
1944–45[a]	207	—*	65***	321
1965[b]	326	99	104	529
1970[b]	354	117	148	619
1971–72[c]	365	124	152	641
1975[d]	370	156	179	705
1976[b]	380	158	187	725

Sources: [a]Australia Patrol Report 5, F. I. Middleton File: Misima, 18.1, Pre-war box 491; [b]census; [c]Patrol Report East Calvados, R. C. Mumme File: Misima "Tagula Patrol Report"; [d]Village Record East Calvados, John Bartlett File: Misima Patrol Reports.
   *Still being settled by Sabarl Island residents.
   **Split Sabarl/Nimowa.
   ***"Plus 49 in Gigila," a mainland prison.

TABLE 3 Other Saisai Populations

Year	Nimowa	Bwailahine (Panatinani)	Wanim (Grass)	Dadahai	Total
1944–45[a]	—	124	—	—	124
1965[b]	43	92	159	23	317
1970[b]	68	113	185	26	392
1971–72[b]	73	110	190	24	397
1973–74[c]	77	111	190	31	409
1975[d]	82	115	200	33	431
1976[b]	80	129	205	31	445

Sources: [a]Australia Patrol Report 5, F. I. Middleton File: Misima, 18.1, Pre-war box 491; [b]census; [c]Patrol Report East Calvados, R. C. Mumme File: Misima "Tagula Patrol Report"; [d]Village Record East Calvados, John Bartlett File: Misima Patrol Reports.

trevally begin schooling near the reefs, so that the season is associated with abundance, surplus, and favorable winds that encourage interisland voyages in connection with political trading and feasting.

But then comes the long northeasterly season (*suwai*) following the doldrums (*makasiu*) of November, and this time is more terrible by contrast: a period of scarcity and threatening weather when staple foods and access to them are limited. A nutritionally adequate diet can be derived from nuts, fruits, grubs, and shellfish,[21] but for the starches that are locally regarded as the staff of life, people must turn to sago and gleanings from the gardens of years past. Furthermore, the north-westerly winds are chill and high, and currents are strong. As a consequence deepwater fishing drops off; likewise interisland visiting, except in very bad years to request subsistence food or water from family and friends in other places. Since subsistence sailing is considered a "shameful" activity (I return to this in chap. 7), people will go to extremes to avoid it—for example, eating only coconut for days at a time. Unless they are desperate, they will tend instead to use the time to generate money for buying supplementary foods (such as rice) or to put toward school fees and taxes.

Yet in a region targeted by national programs for health and nutritional improvement, Sabarl people stand out as models of robustness and general good health (though falsiparum malaria has recently begun taking its toll here as elsewhere in Papua New Guinea). This good health is especially remarkable given the frequent food and water shortages and the reality that for several weeks out of every year children may go without any cultivated food because parents are trapped in the fields by stormy weather. In other words, Sabarl enjoy good health overall, despite the precarious existence that most people confront regularly and that lies at the root of Sabarl cultural identity and the cultural response to mortality.

Maho schoolteachers estimate that most children go two or three days without proper food every two months during the lean season. They present this as a major cause of spotty attendance: the children stay home rather than shame their parents before peers and teachers. Even aunts and uncles may be unaware of their situation, since by school age children are fully conscious of the shame of asking for food. Indeed, much as in rites of passage in other cultures, children must demonstrate that they can cook for themselves and avoid asking for help with meals before their parents allow them to enter school.

Meanwhile, it is the perception of the children themselves that they go hungry far more often: an average of two days every two to three weeks during the lean season. At such times children eat mostly coconut meat, grubs if they can find them, unripe mangoes or breadfruit if they have access, and shellfish if they have enough enterprise.

Sabarl tend to credit their prevailing state of good health to near-daily portions of *protin*, particularly fish and shellfish, and the enriching soup produced by cooking greens. Seafood and soup are thought to promote "blood circulation"—the sine qua non of good health. People also mention the superior vigilance of Sabarl watchdog journeyers-in-spirit, who guard against sorcery and witchcraft. These are subjects we return to shortly.

The Sabarl health profile stands in sharp contrast to that on Tagula, where there are many and complex culturally based dietary restrictions on persons in the early stages of development or in fragile states of health (Lepowsky 1984). For example, pregnant Sabarl women can eat virtually anything except foods that image obstructions to birth.[22] They are also encouraged to eat large quantities of shellfish (*kiwakiwa*) together with greens, sago or yams, and the less greasy varieties of fish.

Restrictions continue in other forms after giving birth, until the child begins to crawl. In general, fish is avoided only until postnatal bleeding has stopped entirely: the concern is that the watery coolness of fish blood might be transferred to the mother's blood, causing her to hemorrhage. Very sweet or "greasy" things are also avoided, since they are thought to generate heat in mother's milk that can blister the baby's mouth. Thus nursing mothers avoid much-loved pork fat, as well as sugarcane, pineapple, ripe mango and sweet varieties of banana, green coconut juice, and above all coconut meat. They also abstain from eating fish with red skins or red spots such as rock cod (*huyas*), for fear of giving the baby rashes and sores.

Ideally children stay at the breast for some three years, although the time may be shorter if the child loses interest or another baby comes along.[23] Infants are given garden food supplements to mother's milk after three or four weeks. They are not allowed fish or shellfish as long as they themselves are still dangerously cool-blooded (until they can crawl—that is, exhibit unfishlike behavior). Rice, which in children is thought to cause worms, is prohibited until this time also. Once the baby is crawling, "clear-blooded" (odorless, greaseless) types of fish are introduced, together with greens. No pork is given until the child is walking.

During all of this time efforts are made to keep children away from European foods, including the sweet trade-store cookies and lollipops they love and demand, which are nonetheless felt to be incompatible with islanders' blood and in no way contributive to "growing" (*-siu*) or "fattening" (*-tabwa*) Sabarl children. This thinking extends to adults. Partly because European foods are thought to originate in cool places, they tend to be regarded as inherently cool or even cold. Many people are revolted by fowl, with their cold, bloodless legs, commonly associated with cold bodies and death.

There was some debate on the matter of Europeans' internal systems. Most people I asked maintained that Europeans were different inside and out—that their blood had more white grease in it and that these substantive differences were indicated by an entirely different body odor. Still others took a formalist view, convinced that differences were only skin deep and that if Europeans ate and drank local foods and liquids they would change internally. Whatever their position, parents are pitted against willful children whose yearnings for "sweet kai" know only the limits of their parents' pocketbooks. Indeed, a good portion of the very small income of Sabarl adults goes to purchasing treats for their children against their own better judgment.

*

Food and feeding are intimately tied to "memory"—a "place/object of or for remembering." Growing a person (the process is likened to the worrying business of cultivating food in the garden) requires an investment of thought and effort of which that person's bodily presence is a living reminder—and also a corporeal sign that somewhere a debt of nurture is outstanding. Parents voice their expectations that someday their children will feed and care for them in return. By providing food steadily over time, one implants or "reconstitutes" (Munn 1986:61) oneself in the minds of others. As we shall see, such acts of growing a person are the roots of a more ambitious vision and more complex cultural feeding agenda that has as its object control of the memory of the dead. We turn to these more elaborate stories of giving in chapter 3.

INTERISLAND CONTACT

The social framework for interisland contact is a network of matriclans (*hun*) whose members are distributed throughout the Saisai region. When a person dies, representatives of his or her maternal, paternal, and affinal matriclans—a kind of "feeding triad"—come together for a series of feasts that honor the relationship they were part of. The feasts (*segaiya*) are held on the dead person's residential property, which becomes by means of them a site for remembering important transfers, distributions, and exchanges of valued things from the estate—of acknowledging the relationships those things helped to create and stand for.

With the exception of some events sponsored by the Catholic church, no other occasion gives Sabarl people such a profound experience of interisland community. This experience of clanship cuts across allegiances based on "place" (*paga*), and it is contrapuntal to what is locally expressed as the "power of place to draw" (*paga iyomwe pahavina*) both people and wealth back home to the lands of their ancestors.

Organizers rely on close kin and trading partners for the surplus food and object wealth that they need to sponsor and contribute appropriately to mortuary feasts. Borrowing and lending these social necessities creates relationship histories that establish the trustworthiness and political reach of individuals. But such relationships are perceived as fragile—as one young man explained it, like valuable beads tied together by a string that breaks easily. Exchange partners are easy to lose; partnerships are forever reassessed, repaired, replaced. Rewriting vital "paths" (*hiyela*) of relationship is a key objective of *segaiya*.

On these occasions, the work of "finishing the memory" (of decomposing the material domain of the dead) is initiated by the paternal matriclan and directed by maternal matriclan hosts. Their work is successful to the extent that they elicit subordinate behavior from junior affines and leave an impression of dominance on off-island guests. Dominance of parental clans is, in other words, the social premise but not the assured outcome of mortuary events. Indeed, though in theory the most valuable property (namely, land) descends through the matriclan by order of birth, *segaiya*'s "hidden agenda" is the opportunity it writes into "custom" for juniors, as well as paternal clanspeople, to challenge such ascendancy. Mortuary feasts are the primary occasions for pulling off significant coups with regard to descent.

"RETENTIVE MEMORIES": A NOTE ON EUROPEAN CONTACT

The Louisiade is a large chain of islands stretching in an easterly direction from the south point of New Guinea. Each island is encircled by a reef which frequently also stretches from one island to another, thus enclosing small seas in which there are very good anchorages where there are breaks in the reef to form an entrance. In the coral seas you must be aware that there exists this peculiarity with the reefs of that formation that outside of them to seaward no soundings can be procured at many hundred fathoms depth, so that a ship cannot anchor unless she can get to landward side of the reef into these small areas which I have mentioned. (Huxley 1935:366)

These are the words of T. H. Huxley, a scientist on board H. M. S. *Rattlesnake*, whose captain, Owen Stanley, would lend his name to Sabarl Island in 1849. The account indicates some of the navigational difficulties that figured in the history of contact between people of the Calvados Chain and European "strangers." Because they came from the direction of the mythical Dimdim reefs to the east, they were called *dimdims* then as today. (Europeans often have trouble with this, as the locals well know.)

Preceding Owen Stanley in the Louisiades were a number of European expeditions, headed by Torres, Bougainville, D'Entrecasteaux, Coutance, and D'Urville (Stanley followed D'Urville's excellent charts). However, it was Stanley's crew who first made ethnographic observations of Louisiade life during disappointingly brief encounters:

> Truly our voyage might have been one of discovery . . . but in a very different sense. For the Frenchmen, although they cruised along these shores and surveyed them for the purposes of navigation, never landed and were therefore wholly ignorant of their productions, etc. In this department might we with proper claim have been considered discoverers; but this was denied us. (Huxley 1935:366)

It was not until the 1870s that more regular relations were established in the eastern Calvados and on Tagula by Australian pearlers, planters, and bêche-de-mer traders out of Queensland. They were joined in the 1880s by labor recruiters to the Queensland sugar fields.

The stories that Sabarl retain from the period are invariably violent. A Sabarl girl is abducted, marries Captain Cook, and lives with him in England (or in other versions, Germany). "All the men" of Panatinani are taken as slaves to Kukitown (Cooktown, in Queensland) and never return. The Sabarl assist Panatinani warriors in murdering a cheating trader, and soldiers in ships come with guns and try to kill all the men of the islands.

There is little question that some of the traders were, in the words of one British officer, "of evil repute." Recorded incidents of native violence include most famously the massacre of the captain and crew of the *Emily*, a ketch out of Queensland, following the captain's failure to deliver promised rifles to a Panatinani leader. The massacre was duly followed by a violent punitive expedition where women and children were taken captive, villages burned, gardens wasted, and many men seriously wounded. One man, the putative killer of the *Emily*'s captain, was shot and his head handed over to the expedition leader in a basket by a trader hired as a guide by the British navy.[24]

The deaths at sea of a shipload of returning Cooktown laborers in July 1886 led at last to the recommendation by government officers that no new trading stations be established, for fear of violent repercussions "according to native custom." Yet considerable damage had been done in the meantime—though how considerable would not be appreciated by the rear admiral investigating the effects of the punitive expedition, who remarked:

The natives have retentive memories when they have suffered an injury [and] it appears to me unreasonable to sup-
pose we suddenly can change the manners, and customs,
and habits of natives; and though death falls to the lot of
some of our enterprising traders and at the hands of natives . . .

[However,] so soon as past offenses are got over and forgotten I think there are glimpses of a brighter future, and
that at no distant day. . . . The wretched ill-forced small ves-
sels, in instances with but one white man on board, that
cruise without molestation from the natives, alone tends to
show that the native hand is not raised as a principle against
every white man that comes under their power; on the con-
trary, by far the majority confidently cruise, and I am in great
hopes that as in other islands, patience and firmness will at
an early date, win the natives to, at all events, a considerable
extent our way. (Letter to the special commissioner, 24 December 1886; British New Guinea Annual Report 1886a)

What the officer seemingly failed to realize was that local people
would neither forgive nor forget the loss of their autonomy. On Sabarl
this theme was somewhat submerged in the gold rush period of the
late 1880s and 1890s. During this time European activity was concentrated around the gold deposits of Tagula, where relations between locals and *dimdims* apparently were good (see Nelson 1979 for an excellent brief history of the period).

However, the "retentive memories" would be refreshed in the
early 1940s, as cargo cult activity emanating from Misima led to the
murders of a European planter on Motorina and a native government
official on Panatinani by Calvados Chain warriors, the Sabarl among
them. And so another punitive expedition arrived in Saisai waters. As
Sabarl survivors tell it, there followed not only the shedding of innocent blood, but also the removal of a great many able-bodied men to
far-away prisons and forced labor camps. The only census figures available for this very critical period in Saisai history were produced in 1944
and read:

Panatinani	124
Sabarl	207
Panawina	65 (plus 49 in Gigila)

The "49 in Gigila," a mainland prison, probably represents a frac-
tion of the men detained from all of the eastern Calvados Chain islands. The assistant district officer writes in April 1943: "I am of the

opinion that the whole of the Calvados Chain and the Deboyne Islands are now quiet—in fact most of the male population of the Chain area are now in gaol awaiting trial" (Australia Patrol Report 1943).

I discovered the names of only thirteen Sabarl prisoners, five of whom died in detention. But whatever the actual numbers, the event was traumatic.[25] Even enemies to the west fled "up" the Chain, seeking refuge in Sabarl's labyrinthine caves and sinkholes. At Hebenahine village on Sabarl, a woman was shot in the back and killed by a soldier as she fled—a fact every young Sabarl child knows well.

The expedition soldiers also destroyed Sabarl canoes. It was a full year before civilians, transported temporarily to Panawina for organizational purposes, ventured to return to their homes to begin rebuilding their houses, transport, and lives. Although Sabarl women were capable navigators before this time, trading regularly with partners on other islands, afterward it was "the most important thing" to get back to the gardens, sago, and fresh water on other islands. Some told me they feared that the men would never return, and in fact one polygynous leader, the convicted organizer of the raid on Panatinani, took a detour of a score of years to travel the Milne Bay archipelagoes on a government vessel, picking up trading partners on Muyuw and Misima before returning home as Sabarl's first government representative.

It was shortly thereafter that the Catholic mission established a school on Nimowa, and people today recall that their parents wasted no time complying with the government's "request" that all boys be sent there for formal education. Despite the disruption, people were quick to see the positive side of pacification, which the government did accomplish. Traditionally, Misima and Panaeati had joined with the "lower" islands and the Engineer Group in raiding the "upper" islands and Tagula, which in turn raided each other—primarily for valuables—Yele being viewed as an ally to both Tagula and the Chain. Tensions along these lines are still felt today to an uncertain extent, and they surface periodically in accusations of sorcery and suspicions of European favoritism. Yet far more important in the Saisai view was the consequent florescence of interisland trade, not to mention the new world of wealth that a relationship with the mission and the magic of English had suddenly made accessible. People also mention their interest in the exotic "customs" of neighbors they had previously fought—in particular the new knowledge of alien magic they fantasized gaining.

Modern educational profiles reflect this readiness to reframe the trauma of contact. For example, in Sabarl's Maho village, over half the

TABLE 4 Educational Profile, Maho Village

	Total	6–10	11–17	18–25	26–30	31–40	>40
				Age			
				Males			
None	32	6	4	1	1	5	15
Preparatory, form							
1	3	3					
2	3		1	1	1		
3	20	6	2	7		4	1
4	7			5	1	1	
5	17		12	4	1		
6	2		1	1			
Vocational (formal and infor- mal)*	17						
Teaching experi- ence	3						
				Females			
None	32	12		1	1	5	13
Preparatory, form							
1	3	3					
2	6	1	2	2	1		
3	9	3	3	1		2	
4	7			3	2	2	
5	23		12	7	2	2	
6	7			3	3	1	
Vocational (formal and infor- mal)*	5						
Teaching experi- ence	1						

*Vocational students currently away in training: 17.

men and women aged 31 to 40 in 1976 had at least three years of formal education, with the characteristic Catholic emphasis on English.

One Sabarl leader made almost 50 percent of his political trading contacts during schooldays at Nimowa while his father was still in prison for cargo cult activity. Marriages across the boundaries of traditional enmity went from none before pacification to thirty-one within ten years afterward, all of them traceable to school relationships.

It is true in general that the influence of church and state is less pervasive as one moves farther west along the Chain. Yet it has been my experience that even those Saisai residents who are closest to the mission and government centers may harbor deep resentment and dis- trust toward Europeans. One small indicator of this came in 1976, when a rumor was started on Kuanak that I was a spy, sent to map the secret passages and caves of the Sabarl interior for a European army. Although those who knew me found this extremely funny, one of my friends nonetheless made a special expedition to put the record straight.

The local government headquarters are on Tagula, across the channel from the mission station at Nimowa. It is the site of a highly undependable airstrip and houses various government officers whom the Sabarl rarely see in their waters. The Sabarl view of the government is dim compared with their view of the mission. This situation could conceivably change if visits from government representatives were more frequent than the yearly census calls, if water tanks were in- stalled or repaired in this frequently drought-plagued region,[26] if aid posts were stocked and staffed, if freezers were installed and main- tained on key islands so that catches of fish and other seafood could be stored there for sale,[27] and if boats for collecting and purchasing catches could be counted on to show up when promised. As it stands, access to money and services is severely restricted for Sabarl especially, who live beyond the practical range of Nimowa- and Tagula-based pro- grams, as well as those based near the New Guinea mainland. Also, a crippling and antiquated head tax, on average 33 percent of the average Sabarl man's income and 50 percent of a Sabarl woman's,[28] has been a continuing source of anger to local residents.

More directly useful than government schemes is the mission- operated trade store at Nimowa, which is used fairly regularly as a source of twist tobacco, rice, tinned meat, tea, sugar, guitar strings, cloth, European clothing, fishhooks and line, sailcloth, and other lux- uries. The mission also organizes copra production and commercial fishing and shelling operations; it is currently competitive (as it was not in 1976) with the European-owned business at Nivani, near Mi- sima, and much more conveniently located.

SABARL ISLAND SETTLEMENT

Soter describes himself as the "historian" of Sabarl, by which he means the keeper of "true stories" about the movement of land and reefs between persons and, more fundamentally, between lineages.

One rainy afternoon I asked him to tell me how Sabarl had come to be settled. Now, it must be said that Soter is not a patient man. His style of mind is quick and nonlinear. If he begins to be bored he abbreviates shamelessly, and his enthusiasm for explanation is usually short-lived. However, on this occasion he seemed genuinely eager to tell me the story of Sabarl "from the inside," and it interested me that he wanted to do it "properly" by literally walking me from one end of Maho village to the other. This meant that we walked from east to west ("up" to "down") in the general direction of settlement, moving through the cramped residential sections or "hamlets" (*yawan*) that make up the village like clusters of beads strung along the shore. Because the hamlets were not in fact settled in sequence, and because a continuous chronology existed only within the hamlets themselves as the land descended through fathers and mothers' brothers to the current residents, our walk took us in and out of time, among the markers of modern and ancient events. In other words, the present structure of the village permitted the experience of a jumble of times brought forward to the present of the story we were walking.

This "presenting" was evident in Soter's reading of the boundary markers that divided the quarters, which he used as "memory stations" of the story of settlement. At one time all *yawan* "boundaries" (*luvi*) were marked by large, gnarled nut trees. Some had been replaced by markers that were more short-lived, such as coconut palms or bushes, or by nothing at all. However, in these spaces and substitute forms, Soter saw the once-present tree and the events that surrounded its removal or replacement.

In short, what was no longer on the spot carried the meaning of what now was, and many of these critical boundaries had only the longevity of Soter's own memory and the memories of those corroborating his story. I would come to recognize that for Sabarl remembrance worked this way, through latent images and "active absences."

*

From Soter's story and those of others I have restrung the beads of Sabarl settlement history to make a Western-style linear chronology. Of course, I have sacrificed Soter's spiraling associative leaps, his backtracking, corrections, and the like. But it was Soter's idea—how he wanted the story of settlement (and not his own personal mnemonic process) represented. What follows is thus a redaction of his walk with me on an otherwise uneventful afternoon.

A note: in 1976 there were three villages on Sabarl Island: Maho, Hebenahine, and Tandeyai. All three are on the southern coast, facing refreshing southeasterly winds and the garden islands of Hemenaha and Panatinani. On the northern side was the hamlet of Hetotoi, under construction, and the Maho school for primary-grade children. The

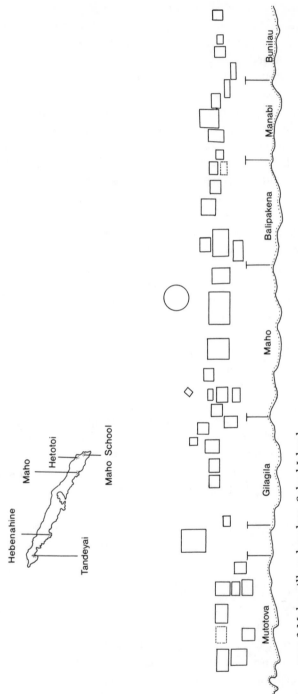

MAP 3 Maho village hamlets, Sabarl Island.

three matriclans that settled the island—Maho, Manilobu, and Guau—were still the only clans represented in the population.

The name Sabarl is taken from the Misima word *sabasabarl*, "rocky place." Although the name has stuck, the island's "true" name, which is rarely heard, is Gui or the Source. Claim was first laid to Sabarl land when Misima voyagers from the village of Ewena (then called Piliuyo) departed their homeland in the wake of a dispute and crossed the high seas, landing at Hetotoi cove on the north shore of the island. This journey would have called for extraordinary bravery. Even today some middle-aged Misimans recall being told that the legendary islands to the south were inhabited by cannibal giants. The Misimans claimed the cove for the Guau clan before moving on.

They were followed by the first settlers, Maho clan Misimans who arrived via Kimuta and built on the spot in Maho village that bears the name of their legendary leader, Manabi. Manabi claimed for his clan "all of the island's coves," apart from Hetotoi, by planting coconut trees. The land was gradually sold off as settlers of other clans arrived.

What Manabi saw in this "rocky place" were basically two natural resources. First, the atoll's tortuous caves and passages, its sinkholes, sharp coral precipices and paths formed a natural fortress against enemy raiders. Sabarl was in fact so secure that houses could be built on the beaches rather than in the steamy interior. In Manabi's day, dwellings were bow-shaped structures set high on hardwood posts. The larger ones housed polygynous families and the accumulated wealth of the entire settlement. Though scaled down after pacification, they would not be replaced by the box-style houses one sees today until the 1960s.[29]

A second attraction was the rich fishing grounds off Sabarl's reefs. Indeed, the second lot of settlers was a canoeload of Manilobu clanspeople from Utian (Brooker Island), who arranged with Manabi to use the Balinatuna area as a camp for smoking fish and later settled there. The same lure attracted Guau clan settlers from Panatinani to what is now Bunilau. It is likely that this Guau group had ancestral ties to Misima, since they brought with them an active exchange network in which painted enemy skulls were offered to Misimans for valuable mats, yams, stone axblades, large wooden platters, and canoes. Meanwhile, the eastern section of what is now the large quarter of Maho was being settled by a Maho clan group from Panatinani, though they would eventually leave to make gardens in the richer soils of Panabarli.

As yet these were times of a gardenless existence for Sabarl—

times just on the fringes of living memory, marked by fierce intergroup conflict. The fierceness of Sabarl warriors was by now becoming legend, as was the fleetness of the small Sabarl-built canoes. Indeed, Sabarl acquired rights to the primary garden island of Hemenaha as a reward for supporting the highland Panabusuna against their coastal enemies. Before this victory in the middle to late nineteenth century, Sabarl relied for food on fishing, gathering wild yams from the bush (which were, however, reserved for children), and raiding Panatinani for freshly processed sago.

Gilagila quarter was the next to be settled, by Maho clanspeople from Piron who would later found the new village of Hebenahine a few coves away, closer to the richest fishing grounds. They were joined in the enterprise by some of the Guau who had meanwhile settled Busunanata. A splinter group would soon afterward settle Tandeyai.

Another Guau group settled the western section of Maho quarter. This quarter once bordered a ridge of bush that extended into the sea, cutting Maho off from the neighboring quarter of Gilagila and dividing the cove into two hamlets, whose men often fought over women. The bush boundary was cleared about the time Boanuwa was settled by Manilobu clanspeople from Hebwaun on Panatinani (they would shortly move again to Hebenahine).

A group of victorious Maho clan highlanders from Panabusuna next arrived at the easternmost part of the village and called it Mutotova. Facing food shortages for the first time, the Mutotova women were the first to capitalize on surpluses of Sabarl fish and high-quality Sabarl lime, trading with their partners and relatives at Tokunu on Panatinani, Panabusuna, and Hesesai during times of shortage and journeying by canoe into waters where fighting men could not always safely go.

Last to be settled were the western parts of Boanuwa and eastern Mutotova, by Manilobu descendants of the first Utian migrants. The place is marked by the spot where Yele sailors who were allies of Saisai people used their powerful magic to make a great flood recede late in the last century. Their wooden anchor pole remains, high up from the current tideline and overgrown by a coconut tree alongside the houses.

The migration of the former owners of western Maho quarter to the village of Nigahau at the tip of Panatinani completes in modern times the list of places whose inhabitants speak the Sabarl dialect and identify themselves by their Sabarl roots. But the pattern of convergence and divergence continues. Most recently people have been moving away from overcrowded Maho village and have begun to build at

Hetotoi on the northern coast. Some also live for the better part of the year near gardens on Panatinani.

As told by Soter, this kind of settlement history is very different from that of societies (such as the Trobriands, for example) where ancestral origins can be traced to sacred spots in the local landscape. Sabarl was a brave new world, its original settlers migrants and entrepreneurs encountering stories of mythical predecessors piecemeal from their neighbors or else importing them. As a result, as I mentioned earlier, Sabarl are not quite at home in the mythical past, and they often referred me to Panatinani or Misima for fuller versions of stories they felt they knew only incompletely.

Yet the "marks" of the past are everywhere around them, in unusual patterns in the land or sea or cosmos—not the least unusual being Sabarl Island itself. Mythical tales of island settlement thus have a kind of abstract reality to Sabarl. Ancient stories may have little use value in claiming title to land or status, but they do have enormous interest value.

I have heard only one narrative account of Saisai settlement. It is tied to the story of island creation, the Story of the Bird and the Serpent I introduced earlier (see Appendix). The story continues: after the bird has killed the serpent and the parts of its body have become the islands of the sea, the eagle returns to his home on Tagula. There he learns from smaller messenger birds that a giant octopus living on Yele (Rossel Island) wishes to fight this proud bird that killed the snake. The bird takes up the challenge, but when he goes to fight he fails to see the arms beneath the sea, anchoring the octopus. The bird is pulled under the water and drowns, and his feathers float westward "down" the Chain and wash up on the beaches of all the islands. From each feather there springs a small white bird (*bwanebwane*, thought of as the juvenile version of the eagle or *manak*). These small birds converge on the great bird's mother, claiming to be her offspring. But in her grief she chases them away by pouring whatever she is cooking on top of them, staining their feathers in patches. Finally the mother bird dies of sorrow.

Throughout Melanesia, birds are totemic emblems of clanship. In Saisai, specific birds represent specific clans, "linked" to other animals, fish, and plants in ways that people no longer remember. In the story of the eagle and the octopus, what might be interpreted as the drift of settlement down the Chain, the marking of different clan groups (as the faces of the dead are painted with clan designs so that spirits in the afterworld will recognize them), and the estrangement from the motherland seem to indicate a far more ancient migratory pattern than Sabarl have knowledge of. No people I spoke with knew any stories about their clans or their totems, and most could name only three or four of their totemic emblems.

Yet other stories on the theme of the divergence of persons and resources are commonly heard. They address a prevalent Saisai preoccupation with the control of persons, objects, and things that, it is feared, tend toward randomness, moving out of range of one's influence and forever separating from their sources. Thus, for example, people tell how the best yams "flew" to Duau (Normanby) with a young man and his mother, leaving a hardworking sibling to grow the inferior yams that people have today. Or one hears how a stone ax blade was thrown into a fire on Misima, where it "exploded" and scattered small blades around the archipelago.

Clanship's function of contravening the dispersal of valued resources emerges in different contexts as a salient concern of Sabarl people, and its importance as a countervalue to dispersal, redistribution, ramification, extension, and so on, is a major theme of the pages that follow. It is clanship that transformed the "bones of the serpent" into parcels of land with histories, and as we shall see, it is the concept of the matriclan that orients loyalties to "place" as a "root concept" of Sabarl collective identity.

STRUCTURING VILLAGE SPACE

We have seen that Maho village is a kind of geoclan magnet, drawing Sabarl memories back to the Source of themselves as a people. As I mentioned earlier, Sabarl speak of this phenomenon as the "power of place/custom to draw" people and things—to gather, center, or focus diverse histories in "one homeplace" (*habana hotie*) that likewise functions as a launching point of new histories and future diversity.

The focal point of convergent and divergent actions is the domestic house—a virtual icon of the concept of Source. As the core of Sabarl life, the domestic family, is referred to as *bi hotiega,* the people beneath "one roof," the roof and walls, the "main parts" of a house, are made of materials from the coconut and sago palms—sources of the foods of survival and the minimal contributions of affines to mortuary feasting. Thus the affines who build and repair domestic houses are constructing the "memory" of a secure society—a society with a future.

The contemporary Sabarl house (*yuma*) is basically a rectangle set on wooden pilings (*pwopwou*) about five feet high. Its walls are the stems of sago palms (*lukluk*), split and lashed with vines. Its gable roof is coconut-leaf thatch (*bi*) sloping from a central ridgepole (*puho*) on a sapling framework. Ironwood (*bwalal*) slats are used for the floor, nowadays nailed to the frame rather than lashed. There are four doorways (*gana*); a front door facing the sea and one in each of the other walls. These are usually covered by crudely woven screens hinged at the top, which can be tied to the floor to discourage dogs and intruders or to show that the owner is away. A veranda (*baranda*) off the side or back door serves as a casual storage and gathering place for the family, and passersby often pause there to chat. Verandas may also bridge the separate houses of an extended family. Although partitions and rooms are currently popular, most houses have single-room interiors (*dauye*) supported by four interior posts (*kokola*), with a three-stone hearth (*paiwok*) in a sandbox in the center and a smoking rack (*helakelake*) above it.

These simple structures add something profound to residential land in that they give it an interior, private dimension as well as defining the limits of personal domains. The dark, cool interior of the house is the domain of feminine activity and influence, connoting order, restraint, and routine. Children are taught to behave tamely indoors to "show respect" for the hearth where women regularly cook and, since residence is ideally virilocal, for the relics of their father's maternal ancestors stored in the eves. The same respect is extended to the graves of the ancestors, which were traditionally beneath the house. By government order they are now at the rear of the property between the village and the bush. Children often forget and run over them, which is easy to do since these detached grave sites are neither permanently marked nor bounded.

A new bride has a very fragile claim to control of the interior space of her husband's house, where her husband's senior kin and the ancestors buried on his residential property are continual reminders of her subordination. However, a woman's influence builds up over the years in a process likened to the way rising smoke from the cooking fires coats the walls and ceiling, protecting the house against vermin. The services she renders in cooking for the household represent her contributions, which include providing her senior affines with children who will work for them. Yet on the negative side of the same symbolic image, smoke turns the house black and "dirty" (*bikina*), sullying its pristine, though superficial masculinity and compromising a woman's autonomy within a matrilineal system.

The shady underside of the house where women gather to talk and tend their children is feminine also—a "parlor" swept and tidied in the fresh morning hours. This space is associated with "cool" (*tuitui*) talk and cool thinking as against, it is said, the masculine excitable, "hotted-up" (*gnongon*) exterior realm of political battle, physical work in the sun, and (formerly) armed combat. In a sense, the shade beneath it is the house turned inside out. And keeping in mind that affinal graves were once situated there also, a woman's moments of public leisure are a kind of symbolic equation of rest to death (adding undertones to the adage that a women must never be still in the presence of her affines).

Bright, hot exterior space, and all that is public, including the shell of the house—the public profile of domesticity—has contrastingly masculine connotations. The areas behind and in front of the house are regarded as the personalized public space of its (ideally) male owner. For the most part the space behind is reserved for preparing foods for public consumption (e.g., during feasts). The space on the beach in front is where visitors arriving by sea are formally received and also where village meetings and prayer services are held, convened by men. Canoes, which men contribute as wealth to a marriage, are parked on the wet sand.

Nonresidential areas and structures in the village are also significant, but in another sense, for these tend to be artifacts (or in some cases dinosaurs) of "progress" in the European mode. In 1976 the two most imposing man-made structures in Maho were the Catholic church, built from hardwoods on a ridge of high ground, and the massive concrete ruin of a water tank in Maho hamlet, looming without a catchment over the graves. There was also a trade store, sometimes stocked for a few days at feast times, a smokehouse used for bêche-de-mer by a few enterprising young men, a copra shed in perennial progress (somewhat mysterious, since coconuts are not at all plentiful), and the shallow beginnings of a deep-pit latrine in the stony earth behind my house (begun not at my request). By 1986 a strong wind had seriously damaged the church (services were being held on the beach), the tank had become a mucky breeding ground for mosquitoes, the copra shed had vanished, and there was no trace of a latrine. In short, "development" in any sense of the word has not been a Sabarl priority. Maho school was no closer to being finished in 1986 than ten years earlier, although twin water tanks were in place and a new, small but dependable store opened at regular hours and tended to be stocked for slightly longer periods.

*

The voices of modernity and the hegemonic images of contact in the distant past as today have challenged the foundations of the "islander" ethos and of Sabarl cultural identity. However, this contesting reality is not always dissonant, nor are Sabarl strangers to the process of interpreting change and making decisions that may include—predominantly do include—reversing the direction of "progress" as formerly construed, or turning around or adjusting to failures in practice of former or current ideologies. The time I saw the people of Maho most angry, indeed, dangerously angry, was when they perceived themselves to be "sitting like prawns"—looking passively upward—while a local government authority laid down an unfair program of taxation and demanded an inappropriate amount of their time for community tidying up, refusing either to hear or to see the unique problems of living in a place that is "only bones." Ultimately, the response was to "forget him": his dictates fell right out of Sabarl history. In this case, then, inaction spoke louder than words or wordlessness. Indeed, a cultural predisposition to "forget" coercive authority and independently put new ideas to the test of practice provides a telling background for the pages that follow.

Part One

The Person:
Basic Distinctions

The events of my birth . . . and finally of my death are not accomplished in me or for me. The affective weight of my life *as a whole* does not exist for me. Only the Other is in possession of the values of the being of a given person.

Mikhail Bakhtin

One

The Physical Person

It surprised me to learn that to many Sabarl people the "most important" Sabarl narratives were "stories for children"[1] about the first human ancestor, Katutubwai (the name breaks down to "our ancestor's image"). "In the beginning," Katutubwai dies and gestates endlessly in the womb of Enak, the Creator, who has a penis but no vagina. Finally Enak uses his penis to create a way out for Katutubwai, and the child is delivered to the world: the first mortal human being, but also the first eater of human flesh—a monster with a huge mouth and ears and long hair and nails who makes a home in a cave in the bush and preys on playing children.

The reason, I was told, that the Katutubwai narratives are important is that they tell the story of death, and we shall find that their themes and imagery are prominent in *segaiya* performances. But what concerns us here are the striking images this mythical scene conveys of the primordial person in utero and the story of first birth—the birth of violence. For they give us glimpses of the "roots" of Sabarl personhood, conceived as a process that models the distinctions between constructive and destructive tendencies in human thought and behavior.

In original time, the time of (self) containment, the time before the opening, the time of cessation and growth in closed cycles, the time of peaceful androgyny and nonproductivity (in our terms, the time before "texts"), a separation occurs and otherness is born: a *consequential distinction* between generations, between sexual functions, between human beings and their sources. But, the effect of this birth, beyond separation, is interaction. A human, *because interactive*, being is born, with the promise (horrible and hopeful) inherent in human intercourse. In other words, the original scenario, taken as a precondition or pretext for understanding the human story, depicts a time before differences mattered, not before differences. If any one thing is embodied in the image of the child-monster Katutubwai, it is the specter of the ambivalently valued Other that haunts the texts of human life—texts taken as interactional or "dialogical" constructs, where the Other is historically an aspect of one's own self.

This ambivalent valuation of otherness is expressed most strikingly in Sabarl gender imagery. Indeed gender, as a categorical distinction, is taken as a vehicle of the expression and constitution of the other across virtually every domain of social discourse, representing variations on the problems of separation, divergence, and the dislocation of origins that reverberate throughout Sabarl culture.

Sabarl beliefs about conception, gestation, and birth retell the story of the first person, but with a constructive twist. As we consider this story, it becomes apparent that the vital, violent, initiating, dislocated element personified as Katutubwai is specifically masculine (this is also made explicit in the narratives in the Appendix). And as we shall see, this masculine element is itself a distilled image of the masculine inflection in Sabarl society. Special challenges to the practice of matrilineality on Sabarl inhere in the social work of turning this element to constructive purpose.

Tuwa (the Body)
PROCREATION

Western educational programs have done little to alter Sabarl notions of conception and fetal development. The widespread view is that new human beings are conceived when "white blood" (father's blood) commingles with "red blood" (mother's blood) in the heat of sexual intercourse. The bloods rise in a "gelatinous" mass (*guguloluina*) to the woman's breasts, darkening her nipples and brightening her face ("transforming" her—*didgana*). The mass then descends into the "womb" (*tini*), where the bloods separate into white and red body parts. After a time the parts "fall into place" (*habana hotie*) as a fetus.

The skeleton is the first part to form, providing a frame or "support" (*labe*) for the red flesh and organs. Fat or "grease" is added last, some say by subsequent acts of intercourse, supplementing or "completing" (*gaba*) the fetal body. The grease additive, which thickens the watery, "fishlike" infant blood, strengthens the bones, and generates heat, is thus the first gift of nurture the child will receive: an intentional, unsolicited "pure gift."

Given their categorical views on body composition (one subject on which there was broad consensus), Sabarl ideas about the brain (*pwatomina*) bear mentioning here as a study in anomaly. For one thing, the subject tended to generate debate. At issue was the fact that the brain is "greasy" and white like paternal fat but is cool, with creases "like the moon's markings" (recall that the moon is associated with women). Thus the brain is an image of gender conflated, a self-contradictory artifact, unlike androgyny and unlike any other thing people could think of. Unwilling to regard it as the product of a merging of bloods, most people saw the brain as somehow uniquely the new individual's. Its meaning for Sabarl as a sign of raw individuality as well as the locus of "mind" (*nuwo*) and free will, independent of gender, is worth noting. One woman told me that without a brain the child could not "decide" when to be born.

"CONFUSING" BLOODS

It is important to note that sexual intercourse is not linked automatically to conception. For example, I knew that several young women had had several lovers since puberty without becoming pregnant, and I was curious to learn how people would explain this. Did these women practice contraception? (When I asked in 1976 no Western varieties were available in this Catholic region, although by 1986 one couple used condoms smuggled in from Misima.) Not quite certain how to proceed in this delicate matter, I very quietly brought it up with Anastasia, the young mother who was helping me with housework—who leaned out of the house and shouted to her friends that Debi needed to know how babies were made. This drew a small crowd of female consultants and passing incredulous males.

It emerged from this session that a form of contraception was practiced by a few women who had learned from their mothers which "leaves" (*layawa*) to brew into contraceptive tea. But more fundamentally, conception was thought unlikely to occur if a woman was sleeping with more than one man, "confusing" or "mixing up" their bloods. This "rubbish" (*galawin*) could not produce a baby. Similarly, intercourse after conception with anyone but the baby's biological father could pollute the fetus and cause it to abort.

It is considered unwise for a boy and girl to have regular intercourse before their own growth is completed and their own bones have "hardened," since the baby can drain their growing bodies. One young man's tubercular death while his wife was still pregnant was explained in these terms: his white blood was still forming into bones and fat when he gave it away to make the child. A pregnant girl who was anemic was a source of concern because she still had the "blood of a fish": not yet thick enough for her to survive childbirth.

There are also among Sabarl traces of conception beliefs not linked to human intercourse. These beliefs seem never to have been elaborate, and observing them amounted to little more than avoiding ocean baths while menstruating, since women could somehow become pregnant in the sea.[2] Currently such a belief would serve no particular social or cultural purpose. There are, for example, no ranked lineages to be perpetuated by the return of ancestors in the form of babies (as in the Trobriands, through belief in the recycling of maternal blood) and no ancient identifying link to territorial ancestors to be manifested (as with Australian Aboriginal societies). What is interesting is rather the attention that the notion of parthenogenesis focuses on sociological as opposed to biological paternity among Sabarl, for whom the recognition of paternal contributions to the person is vitally important in cultural practice, especially on commemorative occasions (see Battaglia 1985).

HINONA

Apart from the artifacts of blood, there is one further element people speak of as an essential part of the living body—indeed, it emerges as the essence of life itself. This element is *hinona*, described as the "contents" of the person and a "force" or "vital substance" that "lives inside the body and makes it breathe." *Hinona* is something like energy in store: a discrete resource, independent of the body yet coursing through it. It is likened to hidden nourishment: "a fish in the hole," "a yam in the earth," and "coconut flesh" are all "like *hinona*." In the negative, *tan hinona* indicates emptiness or fruitlessness: "my garden nothing its contents" (*no baguya tan hinona*); or "his talk nothing its contents" (*wana lihu tan hinona*)—that is, "empty talk," or "meaningless talk"; or "he worked fruitlessly" (*ikaiwa tan hinona*). The connection of *hinona* with "fruit" is critical, since fruit is an artifact of the "essence" of whatever bears it: a sign, for example, of the "inner nature" of the tree. There are overtones of this when people speak of "the body's fruit/contents" (*tuwana hinona*) in reference to genitalia. When someone is sorcerized or bewitched, it is *hinona* that is eaten away by spirits—the physical future of the person.

SUPPORT AND COMPLEMENTARITY

Bones and grease represent respectively the "dry" and "greasy," "cool" and "hot" components of the human body. Throughout life, achieving and maintaining good health through nutrition is seen as a process of keeping these elements in balance. As I will discuss in more detail shortly, people regulate their consumption of intrinsically cool/dry and hot/greasy foods and liquids classified as "complements" of one another in the interest of internal body balance, at least to some degree. And underlying the human growth and health scheme are the principles of support and complementarity.

Labe or "supports" are just that: items that set one another up, one item structuring or positioning an analogous one without essentially changing it. Supports are equally valued in this function. The handle of a ceremonial ax is a valued support for the blade; one bundle of sago supports another as they hang in balance over a storage pole "like a husband and wife"; at exchange feasts, pigs provided by affines support the yams from the matriclan. In other words, *labe* works as a concept to obviate or in local terms "cover" (*yabo*) contradictions by stressing a common function or objective.

Gaba or "complementary" relationships are also viewed and talked about as supportive. However, they stress what Lévi-Strauss would call the oppositional aspect of paired elements and the process of completing, or bringing to potential, one of the pair through the other. Thus fat complements the bones and flesh of the fetus, completing the physical person. A man is said to complement a woman through marriage. This "exploitation of contradictions" (Wagner 1975:52) sets up dynamic tensions that "cover up" or obviate their static relationship as supports so that paired complementary items are neither in balance nor ever unequal *in any fixed sense*.

Standing back, we can see how the bloods of conception follow a course from conglomeration (in which state they complete a cycle from the womb to the breasts and back again), to partition and formation into blood artifacts (body parts), to a new state of integration—the child that is neither its father's nor its mother's blood alone, but a composite of masculine and feminine substances transformed. The fetus as a construct is thus an instantiation of a larger process of convergence and divergence—corporeal proof of the separate contributions to generation of a cross-sex couple.

Blood and Circulation

It is a Sabarl perception that human life is most fragile when the "blood" (*maliba*) is thinnest and coolest and when the belly, where blood is stored, is smallest. Infants and the elderly share this condition, and fundamentally the story of physical development is one of change from a fishlike condition of little and very watery blood to full-blooded viscosity in maturity, then back again as the blood dries up in old age.

The signs of little blood are seen in thin hair (blood feeds hair "as an underground stream feeds roots"), in the absence of teeth (fed similarly), and in the absence of an organized mind: in short, in the absence of things linked to "blood circulation" (*maliba ipatalei*).

Circulation is widely associated with fertility and generativity. Properly circulating blood is said to be especially "bright" (to have generous amounts of white grease but not so much that the blood is overly rich) as opposed to "dark" (*tege*) like the sluggish blood of pigs, which a polluting and disproportionately greasy diet have made over thick. Good circulation makes the body quick and "light" (*tuwaleli*) and ready for anything, as opposed to "heavy" and tired. It "brightens and transforms" (*didigana*) the skin and gives it an attractive "gloss" or "glow" (*wayaeya*). This is the condition of persons most likely to extend themselves not only physically but also socially. Persons of reproductive age especially enjoy putting on the glow of health cosmetically by applying coconut cream and scented oil to their skin and hair. By wearing on the outside the artificial signs of inner physical strength (see Strathern 1979)—as it were, exuding a healthy surplus of grease—they convert their skins into visual statements of social potential, addressing persons they wish to attract (and control) in love or in trade, or else simply (by way of others' approval) addressing themselves. One adolescent told me: "I oil my skin. My friends see me and know I am happy."

Although certain foods are thought to increase circulation, the tendency is for the blood to "slow" in later years. The addition of children to one's life begins the slowing process by draining parents of their brightness. This tendency is especially marked in women, who lose fluids in childbirth and breast-feeding. Also, I was told by the father in a large family that "worrying all the time about children" causes the brain to leak into the hair, turning it white.

CHILDBIRTH

Sabarl show a great deal of respect for their children as idiosyncratic agents of free will. To begin with, babies themselves decide the time of their birth, causing the contractions that help them along when they open their eyes to see the way out. Women who cry out in pain during childbirth are warned that they could "frighten the baby into staying inside," and those who recline and "sleep" through any part of the delivery are told they are extending their labor. I have witnessed entirely silent births and entirely vertical ones. Most women in labor either sit or squat, gripping the wall supports of the house as chains of seated women form behind them to hold them up. Neither men nor children are barred from birth scenes, and young husbands especially will sometimes hold their wives throughout their ordeal.

When the baby is born there tends to be general pandemonium as women rush everywhere looking for something appropriate for cutting the umbilical cord. The ideal tool in traditional terms is a sliver of sago palm from the wall of the house, which is said to be "warm" and gentle on the baby. However, the wood often proves maddeningly blunt, and women will resort to knives in spite of the metallic coldness they fear transferring to the child.

As soon as the cord is cut and the baby is pressed to its mother's breast to "teach it to suck," it is whisked away to be washed in salt water, rinsed in warm fresh water, and rocked gently as numerous fingers warmed over the fire press heat into all of its openings. It is easy to see why hospitals without bedside fires are not attractive birthing places, and only recently have Sabarl women gone willingly to the Nimowa aid station. Most prefer to stay at home.

After the delivery of the placenta (*bwanina*), as helpers are washing the blood from the floor and preparing to burn the birthing skirt beneath the house, the mother will make her way to the sea and wade waist deep into the surf to "stop the blood from flowing" and to wash, before returning to rinse her skin and drink hot water "to make the milk flow."

Meanwhile, the afterbirth itself is placed in a personal basket and taken by an unmarried woman of the mother's clan to the edge of the reef when the tide is low. She leaves the basket and its contents there for fish to eat, and it is thought that sharks, stingrays, and other "dangerous fish" in particular are attracted to the smell and subsequently reek of it when caught and cooked. This gift of the "first skin" is an essential sacrifice. Without it the child would have no right later in life to take fish from the sea.

As recently as twenty years ago, a new mother would remain in seclusion with her child for several months to a year following the birth. She would leave the house only to relieve herself, and then under heavy concealment of palm-leaf skirts and capes, with a large, newly woven utility basket covering her head and shoulders like an oversized helmet. It is said these measures were taken "to protect her" against the evil magic of other women who had seen her child and were jealous. But on another level, they also made the new mother a mnemonic sign of the related work of women as mothers and as mourners, since new widows dress and behave in much the same way immediately following the death of their husbands—that is, at the time of the birth of a new ancestor. The concealment, which allows women to move in a continuing darkness across all kinds of spatial and temporal boundaries, recalls the womb as it foreshadows the grave.

People today still recall with lively interest how the new mother-child unit would make its debut in the village. Their faces painted identically, their bodies shining with oil, with flowers in their hair and armbands, aromatic leaves, shell ornaments, and newly made clothes, they would be conducted by the woman's husband and accompanied by her mother from house to house, distributing food for a villagewide feast.

RITUALS OF CHILD GROWTH

There is a time just before dawn when the rays from the sun appear like spokes of radiating firesticks above the horizon, moving outward and slowly vanishing. Sabarl call this time *budobudo wali lakana siyaiyo*, "the sorcerers' apprentices withdraw their spears." It is an image of spirits extinguishing a bonfire by withdrawing the wood at the conclusion of a nighttime meeting.

Every day at this time also, nursing mothers awaken, build a fire and boil a kettle or a pot of fresh water, then descend the ladders of their houses, walking toward the sea. On top of their heads like domed caps they wear coconut-shell bowls *(kom)*. Slowly they advance into the water until they stand waist deep. Then they express their milk in arcing streams several times into the sea. Bending, they take a swallow of water from the ocean's surface, then dive to the bottom of the lagoon, gripping a rock as an anchor and drinking in several mouthfuls of seawater, "like a fish." Surfacing, they throw the shell bowl mouth-down onto the water, creating a deep, booming clap that reverberates throughout the village and off the cliffsides. The ritual is then repeated, with the mothers drinking more salt water from the shell bowl between throws, to "open the baby's mouth" *(memai hawana tagapwi)* and "make its voice strong." Afterward, the mothers return to their houses and drink several cupfuls of steaming hot water to flush or "clear" the salt from their bodies, using what remains to rinse off their skin. The rinse also bleaches their faces and bodies, leaving them "bright" and fresh.

The ritual I have just described is called, simply, *soga imun*, or "salt water drinking." Every Sabarl nursing mother performs it religiously, whatever the weather, until her child is walking, and sometimes longer. As one of two rituals to promote infant development it is said to be the reason Sabarl children are fatter and healthier than the Tagula: the mothers' milk is purified and "thickened" (enriched) by the ritual; the voices of their children are "opened" like the "mouths" at the ends of coconuts for drinking milk (coconuts are likened to "the heads of ancestors"). Like fish themselves, mothers nurture their still fishlike infants.

In addition, babies are bathed each day in warm fresh water in a ritual of strengthening the skeleton. This practice is called *hebini* for the strong "spine" of *laewa* tree leaves (Myrtaceae: *Eugenia*), and it is performed from the time infants crawl until they are walking. Women collect several *laewa* leaves each morning on the way to fetch water or firewood. Upon returning, they float the leaves in a basin of warm, clear water where later they bathe the child, pressing the leaves firmly along the backbone and limbs.

Women also take over the work of fattening children during breast-feeding. Their milk is a product of paternal blood, but also of the saltwater rituals, where the purging, heat-generating properties of salt add more grease (more body) to the milk.

The *hebini* and *soga imun* rituals continue postnatally the prenatal fabrication of bone and fat that the "father's blood" began. Since this function is later symbolically reassumed by a representative of the paternal clan, the early child-growth rituals can be interpreted as the mother's tending temporarily to paternal nurture—an effort that society "remembers" (publicly acknowledges and rewards) should her husband die before her.

Food and Physical Constitution

Sabarl maintain that the body functions "properly" only when in a state of internal balance. Achieving this state is mainly a matter of balancing the intake of certain types of foods and liquids that are viewed as compatible with (assimilable by) bodily substances. We considered these substances in the context of conception and gestation: the body is composed of elements that are red and white, dry and greasy, cool and hot. Solid foods and liquids are classified similarly, and decisions about what and when to eat or drink are guided by that classification to a large degree.

As opposed to "inedible" things (*nabnabat*), all edibles are categorized as innately "dry-lean" (*kevekeve*) or "greasy-sweet" (*posa*) (shortened here to "dry" and "greasy"). Dry foods are intrinsically "cool," whereas greasy foods are "hot" and are thought to increase body temperature. Certain foods that are emblematic of these properties and symbolically represent them in ritual and on ceremonial occasions are referred to as the "real foods" (*hanhan suwot*) of the Sabarl people: foods of the ancestors. As homologues of the elementary substances and orderings of the human body, "real foods" invoke powerful associations with the origins of human productivity and reproductivity and hold a central place in cultural practice as objects of "memory" that unite persons with those origins in a very concrete way. Sabarl separate food, then literally ingest and internalize the distinctions, putting substances to use as complementarities in a circumscribing bodily system.

All other foods in the Sabarl diet, including those introduced by Europeans (*maigololo*, "foreign food"), are fitted into this basic schema and used or rejected accordingly. For example, sweet potatoes (*puteti*) are classified as dry and treated as yams; likewise white or "red" (brown) rice, which is becoming a ceremonial staple; flour, which is dry and may be used like sago; tinned fish or meat (*protin*) used like greasy-sweet fresh fish and pork; and so forth. Although on important occasions there are still no substitutes for the "real foods," the scale of a feast can be increased by adding the appropriate store-bought ones.

Beyond maintaining internal balance, certain foods are thought to actually "generate" (*ginoi*) blood and to increase blood circulation, and when possible they are eaten every day. These include fish and shellfish, as well as wild greens (*kalolo* or Malvaceae: *Abelmoschus*, and *pwasuwa* or Gnetaceae: *Gnetum gnemon*)—foods that transform the cooking water into a rich, white, brightening "broth" (*sui*) that is easily absorbed by the blood. Indeed, the positive effects are carried less in the seafood and greens than in the soup, which brightens and transforms sluggish blood. Beyond enhancing the Sabarl diet, these foods contribute to Sabarl identity as the stuff that generates the special robustness of the population, as well as the sexual energy to which the large number of children on Sabarl Island is generally attributed.

Even more essential to good health than broth is water, which in

TABLE 5 Greasy-Sweet and Dry-Lean Foods

Greasy-Sweet (*Posa*)		Dry-Lean (*Kevekeve*)	
Raw (*Holena*)	Cooked (*Mola*)	Raw	Cooked
Pork (*seseyan*)	Pork (*seseyan*)	Yams (*laha*)	Boiled yams (*punlau*)
Fish (*yalogi*)	Fish (*yalogi*)		
	Sago-coconut pudding		Baked sago cake
Coconut (*niu*)	(*moni*)	Sago (*kabole*)	(*bwebwai*)

the order of the "real foods" is classified as intrinsically either "cool" or "hot." I mentioned earlier a Sabarl narrative that tells how the sun (masculine) and the moon (feminine) once traveled together across the sky and "swam" together across the waters of the earth in perennial company. Observing that nothing on the earth could grow if they continued in this way, the moon suggested they separate and "swim separately," the sun in the sea at one time of the day and the moon in fresh water at another. In this way the moon separated fresh water from salty, also cool from hot, night from day, dark from light, and in general, feminine from masculine domains of productive space and time.

Sabarl in fact distinguish three types of water: "cool," "fresh" water (*bwai*), "slightly salty" water (*yeluyelu*), and "seawater" (*soga*), which is classified as "hot." Water has a particularly direct effect on internal body "temperature" (*luvi*), although salt water can also thicken the blood and quicken circulation.

Only *yeluyelu*, water that is partly salty, is found on Sabarl Island, where it collects in sinkholes affected by the tides. It is used for cooking but should not be drunk as fresh water, even in emergencies, although this has been known to happen. It is also used for bathing and for washing clothes. Pools for bathing and washing are separate from those used for cooking water. *Yeluyelu* is a concrete sign for Sabarl of the reunion of opposites separated in original time, and it is regarded as a resource that, properly used, is especially effective in promoting physical and mental balance.

MAKING FOOD MORE LIKE PEOPLE

Particularly when feeding visitors, it is important that food be prepared and arranged according to "custom" (*paga*)—that is, in a style that represents Sabarl favorably and makes the occasion of eating a memorable one. Cooking food properly is said to "show respect for the food": for traditional nurture relations, for the social relationships constructed and honored at present in the giving and accepting of it, for the future that the memory of the food *as an impression* can promote. Demonstrating care in preparing and displaying food is in this sense as much a gift as giving it away: an unsolicited act of potentially great persuasive force.[3] The food in turn is "strengthened" by this attention to tradition by being made "more like people"—that is, more the model of the memorably nurturant self one projects through giving.

There are several ways of making food "more like people." One is to warm it up, either by applying heat in cooking or by adding heat-generating "grease." A second way is to reinforce or "complete" the food with food "complements": pairing it with food in the opposite category to increase its positive effect on the body or displaying and giving it away with object valuables, completing it as people are completed socially by valuable things. A third way is to "support" the food, either with other kinds of food or literally, with a wrapper or container.

Cooking

Food that is "cooked" acquires "value" and becomes absorbable (the terms are the same: *mola-*) within the body, and accordingly, cooking methods are chosen in reference to the "dry" or "greasy" nature of the food itself. I was told, for example, that baking yams would render them too dry, which is why on Sabarl they are always boiled and why grease-generating greens and coconut cream are added on special occasions. Even pork is boiled to preserve its greasiness and to create a rich, blood-compatible soup. The exception is sago. In everyday use, sago is usually mixed with coconut shavings and grilled into pancakes that are eaten either alone or with a greasy complement. On ceremonial occasions it is baked into large, flat cakes in stone ovens (*humu*), sometimes with coconut mixed in, to create the ideal dry-food complement for pork and fish. Since food with coconut will spoil overnight, cakes made without coconut are preferred when the food is to be taken away by off-island guests. In other words, alone among cooked foods, dry-cooked sago retains the highly valued quality of storability that raw foods share. It is also the most filling of the dry foods, and for this reason is the sine qua non of feeding large numbers of people.

Sago is also an exception to the rule that dry foods remain in the dry category even after grease has been added. The case in point is sago-coconut pudding (*moni*), where coconut cream is added to a sago and water base, overwhelming or "covering" (*yabo*), I was told, the dryness of the sago. The coconut also transforms the pudding from a "dry" red food to a "greasy" white one.

This brings us (somewhat circuitously) to some interesting observations about cooking and gender. To begin with, foods that remain classificatorily dry in the cooking are prepared by women (unless men or boys are away on a fishing or sago-making trip and are cooking for themselves in camp). Greasy foods are prepared by men. Thus, although dry and greasy food potentiate one another within the body (as in forming the fetus), and although the base of subsistence foods and feasting is sago, produced ideally by men (as bones are within the body), the masculine "plus" of greasy foods is the object of attention and striving.

Gender may furthermore be seen in cooked food forms and imaged in food displays on ceremonial occasions. Thus, for example, sago
pancakes (*havaege*) and ceremonial cakes (*bwebwai*), both cooked by
women, have mottled surfaces that women say recall Dedeaulea, the
woman in the moon. The cakes in their red wooden serving platters
(*nohai*) are referred to as "the moon's shadow/reflection" (*wahiyena
kanukanunu-*): the moon with a red ring around it (a "menstruating
moon," which portends cyclonic winds). "Red" sago pudding, without
coconut, may be cooked by women, who stir it with anything available. But its transformation into a "white" greasy food is controlled by
men, who alone scrape and add the coconut, and who stir the pudding
only with ornately carved "red" wooden paddles (one man likened
the procedure to "fucking"). To eat *moni* prepared by a member of
one's father's clan is strictly forbidden; I was told it would be "like
draining your father's blood." In other words, the only people suitable
to ingest semen in this symbolic form are members of another clan.
No such restrictions apply to other cooked foods. The central place
of sago-coconut pudding in *segaiya* is, as we shall see, a statement
about the special importance of paternal gifts of nurture in social regeneration.

Yams are "like people" in other ways. First, they are spoken of
colloquially as "the children of the garden." Also, they come in red or
white and short or long and are labeled feminine and masculine accordingly. Yams are displayed at mortuary feasts either cooked (as *punlau*), in smoke-blackened pots that are likened to a widow's charcoaled
mourning skin, or else raw (as *laha*), within a blackened basket (*yogowa bibikina*) with the same metaphoric association. Seed yams are
on the same occasion wrapped in fresh banana leaves that form a tear-
drop shape and set in a pot (*suluwalata*), in which form they are said
to be the image of a pregnant woman's glowing skin and swelling
breasts and belly.

Sabarl are quite explicit about relative food value. Greasy foods
are not improved by being dried in the cooking. Although it is best to
eat greasy foods with dry food "complements"—for example, fish with
rice or pork with sago cakes—in fact most people feel they are running
to dry most of the time (a trend also in aging) and can use the extra
grease in their systems. But although symbolic clues about gender
asymmetries and the subjective valuation of masculine substance are
evident at a glance in the handling of "real foods," this is not the whole
story of nurture—the strands of which we pick up again in chapter 3.

Androgyny and Supplementation

Marilyn Strathern (1987a) has proposed an indigenous theory of production for Melanesian gift-based societies, to the effect that"relations between opposites produce an object (such as a child) which in being neither of them is also their relationship objectified and thus both of them. The product appears as an addition to their identity."

Sabarl conception and gestation beliefs reiterate this theory of productivity as a "model of and for" the forming of relations through things that are "like people." However, the child in this model is only half of the "relationship objectified." The other half is the *self-sufficient* mother. Empowered to substitute other natural substances for semen and to render them masculine (and therefore compatible with the masculine components of the body), the mother is for a time in her and her child's developmental cycle herself an androgynous figure: symbolically (but not merely symbolically), she is both parents. Symbolically (and not only symbolically), she is the Creator. In short, the mother takes her earliest social identity as a mature woman from her child; her child elicits her "bothness" in gender terms. Thus, as her child is strengthened in utero by fat, she is strengthened socially by the masculine substances (the *hebini* leaves and salt water) she employs in her own cultural tool kit. What makes this appropriation so interesting is the act of agency it represents. The new mother is the agent of her own and her child's creation. In other words, relations between opposites have produced another, objectified relationship, the matrilineage masculinized.

But human androgyny has one important characteristic that must be taken into consideration here. This characteristic is partibility. As Sabarl construe it, the androgynous product must always be able to be undone, to be deconstructed, and that product returned to a categorically gendered condition.

KATUTUBWAI AND THE GIRL WHO DRESSED AS A BOY

One of the most interesting Katutubwai stories opens as islanders are fleeing their village, terrorized by Katutubwai, who here takes the form of a giant pig. One young woman is left on the beach when no one will find room for her in a canoe. As the fleet pulls away, the woman enters the water, steps into the mouth of a large clam shell, and there gives birth to a baby girl. She raises the child on fresh and salty water. The child grows up and decides to hunt and kill Katutubwai. She dresses in a boy's pubic leaf and takes up a spear. In her pursuit of the giant, she tricks death a number of times. For example, at one point she throws a pot of hot soup into Katutubwai's mouth and accidentally falls in with it, but she escapes through his anus. Finally she spears and kills the pig. She cuts off the testicles and throws them away (normally male feast givers eat the testicles), then roasts and eats the pork. Afterward, she goes to Katutubwai's house and destroys it, returning to her mother with all the food and valuables stored there. She then constructs a miniature canoe from parts of the giant's body and sends it as a message to those who fled that the giant is truly dead. The villagers return, and she greets them from the door of the house she shares with her mother, dressed magnificently as a young man. However, her maternal uncle is not fooled. He tells her to go inside and to change into women's clothes. She does this, and she cooks for the returning people of the village. But afterward she announces to her uncle that she and her mother can get along well without them and that they should leave. The villagers decide instead to stay.

I chose this particular Katutubwai tale for three reasons. First, it is a story not of social construction, but of social reconstruction—that is, where destructive separations (e.g., of an individual from her social relations and therefore from humanity, of a woman from her feminine work and identity) have positive consequences for society. The story, in other words, shows how deconstruction is integral to construction and furthermore motivates it: Katutubwai exists as the violent precondition of the achievement of a reformed, cooperative social environment; he is the monster (death) who provides the ultimate thing to overcome—the reason to reinvent. To the extent that Sabarl recognize in Katutubwai their own ancestral past (and their own past selves), the story is a reminder of the social value of killing that aspect of themselves. Second, the story delineates Sabarl notions of androgyny and supplementation, showing that behavior has effects at the level of substance. Third, it shows that Katutubwai (the masculine principle individuated, terminal, and unqualified) makes history, whereas the girl heroine (the supplemented matrilineage) corrects it—converting negatively valued consumption into a positively valued feast.

Thus what emerges very clearly is the theme of matrilineal self-sufficiency (the birth in the clamshell) and the culturally mediated, ultimately *reversible* androgyny that serves it (the heroine's appropriation of the weapons and the dress of males in her campaign of triumph over death), juxtaposed with the counterproductive force and irreversibly fatal outcome of unmediated masculine aggression.[4]

The happy ending is a return to domestic order and a kind of standoff between the forces of convention (the uncle) and invention (the heroine) (see Wagner 1975), manifested here as the driving forces of a "strong," resourceful, matrilineality. Finally, we see that whereas the memorial artifact of this mortal combat is a miniature object (the canoe fashioned from the stuff of death, what death has been reduced to), that object is also the vehicle of interisland contact and communication. Conversely, the product of convergence and of friendly relations is food (the feast the girl prepares for the village), although it is food that is used to remind the girl of her feminine duties and to define her domain of influence. In accepting her return to control over food and the accoutrements of domesticity, the heroine accepts cultural constraints on extending her grandiose masculine behavior beyond the crisis that inspired it.[5]

*

Dislocation is the "first problem" of Sabarl cultural history. Petrified "marks" of Enak's canoe, cooking implements, genitalia, and so forth, scattered in stone around the Louisiade archipelago are mnemonic signs, like the tales of Katutubwai, of the separation of created objects from their sources: images of diversion and dissemination.

Solutions to this problem are cast in terms of either convergence and reintegration (a new androgyny) or the turning of divergent forces to positive use (as supplements). We find the first solution in the figure of the human fetus, who in opposition to Katutubwai is indeed created in the image of Enak, the self-contained androgyne. Yet at the same time the formation of the fetus in utero is a story of fluctuation and progressive change. Beyond a mere duplicate or reproduction, and again in opposition to Katutubwai as a representation of consumption (a force of subtraction), the child represents a new addition to human society. The child's status as a social increment or supplement is distilled in the culturally ascribed properties of "grease."

Each human child obviates by its existence the effect of the violent first birth of Katutubwai (and justifies the violence of birth itself). He or she is the positive outcome of the separation of masculine and feminine functions: the maternal and paternal "relationship objectified." Beyond this, as a being in flux, the child also represents the *history* of relationship objectified.

The dynamics of supplementation reveal a great deal about Sabarl value production and what appears at first glance to be the "weighting" of masculine contributions to social production. On the one hand, as Derrida writes of it, "The supplement adds itself, it is a surplus, a plenitude enriching another plenitude, the fullest measure of presence" (1977:144–45). Yet on the other hand, "It adds only to replace. It intervenes or insinuates itself in-the-place-of; if it fills, it is as if one fills a void. If it represents and makes an image, it is by the anterior *default of a presence*. . . . its place is assigned in the structure by the *mark of an emptiness*"(emphasis in original).

The supplement—and particularly the masculine supplement—is in other words the mask of its own as of the other's (its complement's) deficiency: the sign of a mutual absence. As we shall see, it is ascribed by this logic the status of a mnemonic sign of relationship par excellence in the context of *segaiya*.

BODY DYNAMICS

Sabarl notions of the physical person produce a picture of the body as a map of the basic relationships and processes of Sabarl social life. The body can be "read" as a complex of schematic signs of fundamental life orders: a complex icon, "siting" (and citing) the dynamics and dialogic tensions of support and complementarity, feminine and masculine substance, construction and deconstruction (convergence and divergence), relational and individual identity. In this sense the body as a seemingly systemic whole is belied by the reality of flux and trajectory.

Once a child is born, people "work with" the body in flux as they do with the physical resources of their environment—not as a closed system, but rather as something mutable. They correct and supplement it inside and out. Painting the body on special occasions with lime paste and black paint, oiling it and adorning it with new clothes and decorations merely articulates the masking process. As important as it is to convey an impressive image and self-esteem, many people (although they do not put it in quite these terms) find it too obvious to spend much time "writing" (*luluwoli*) on the body what their cultural observances write into being every day.

Lindenbaum (1987) has noted that "Papua New Guineans live in a gender-inflected universe in which polarities of male and female articulate cosmic forces thought to be located in the human body," such that "indigenous theories of human reproduction contain within them an implicit recipe for social reproduction." This is dramatically true of societies such as Sabarl's, where "ingredients" from males and females, and the dynamics of balancing these within the corporeal as within the social body, articulate relations of "complementarity" (*gaba*) and "support" (*labe*) that contain the "bio-economic potential" that all persons share, regardless of gender (see also trathern 1981a).

This potential is distilled in the notion of *hinona* or "vital substance," which by its partibility from the domain of the body—its capacity for leaving a mortal vacancy—represents the possibilities for appropriating and recomposing the productive and reproductive "content" of life, against the fact of mortality.

Two

The Metaphysical Person

Sabarl have no generic term for "person," although the word *tolomo* may be used in certain contexts for "mankind," suggesting basic humanity (with a significant masculine inflection). In discussing the qualities that make someone not just physically but morally human—a being capable of discerning the rules of sociality—Sabarl (who tend to resort to simile when explaining such things) return repeatedly to examples of commonplace social interactions that demonstrate *nuwo-*, a capacity for ordered thought, or *nuwa-*, a capacity for feeling.

Nuwo-, "mind/cognition," is the root of *nuwotu*, "thought," understood as an act of organizing experience—of "focusing" or "assembling" distinct perceptions and ideas and gathering them together into "one homeplace" (*habana hotie*). I was told, "It is like we hear one story and another story and then [all at once] we recognize they are [parts of] the same story." In this sense, perceiving the separateness of things is a precondition of *nuwo-*, which entails drawing them into relationship *as if* for the first time: as if back to sources, though the result is inevitably a new story or new "text."

"Memory," as a "place/object of or for remembering," is metaphoric of this process of convergence, where the different "stories" are the different histories, intentions, perspectives, and so forth, of the persons whom the "memory" puts in mind of one another. Of course, it can be argued that the true source is the convergent mind and idiosyncratic history of the person who intuits a connection (in the case of "memory," for example, a common system of value the object or place represents) between the "stories." But here it is important to note that Sabarl represent and understand themselves as products of social relationship, where individuality serves the very limited and temporary purpose of calling attention to oneself in particular contexts for particular (usually political) purposes (see also Strathern's discussion,

1988:270–72). Acts of *nuwo-*, like acts of remembering, are in other words intersubjective in nature.[1] A capacity for *nuwo-* is essential to human "understanding" (*-lapu*). Those who distinguish themselves in this area are spoken of as "learned" or "knowledgeable" (*-siba*), and they tend to be prominent figures on occasions that call not only for organization but for foresight.

As the life of the mind invokes images of convergent thinking, divergent images predominate in the realm of "feeling" and "emotion" (*nuwa-*). In cultural practice, this is most apparent in the giving away of things "from the center/heart" of the person; giving "out of feeling" (*henunuwana*)—what Mauss (1954) talked about as "pure gifts." Part of being accounted a mature person is the ability to recognize social expectations about what and when to give, but the creative person learns also how to give outside the rules, as the heart dictates—to let go of calculated expectations of returns. Indeed, a "pure gift" or "offer" (*toto-*) is like giving the feeling part of "oneself" (*toto-*) to another person. If I offer to give somebody something and she or he responds by saying "*totom*"—"yourself" or "your offer"—the person is signaling an absence of obligation to reciprocate. If I announce "I forget it" (*abunbunen*) when I make a formal prestation in public, I am saying that this act of giving takes place outside the bounds of indebtedness; that the gift neither cancels nor creates a debt.

Such gifts are statements of trust and sentiment.[2] I will discuss this more fully in chapter 7, in relation to Sabarl attitudes toward shame and the nobility of offering. The point here is that giving of oneself emotionally generates many of the "unofficial texts" of social relationship: the perennial small gestures of "empathy" (*nuwalelei*), the shows of tolerance for and sensitivity to the moods and "soul searchings" (*nunuwatuk*) of others, the expressions of sincerity and gestures of politeness—all of which are taken as serious measures of the person as someone worth "remembering" (worth giving to in recognition of his or her ongoing value to self and others).

Social relationships are personalized by such softening gestures, which contribute quite unsystematically to a form of giving that is potentially the undoing of systems of descent and alliance, since it tends to foster exceptions to social rules according to a logic of emotional analogy.[3]

Emotional acts that have an impact on the social domain are the "challenging voice" to rational giving directed to maximizing gain. As we shall see, enactments of emotion are part of the definitive syndromes of giving and taking that are established deep beneath the flow of relating, at the very core of self-constitution.

THE OBSTRUCTED PERSON

For Sabarl, an openness to exchanges of feeling and thought is the precondition of meaningful social interaction. Threats to this condition are construed primarily as physical blockages: if the ears, eyes, mouth, or brain are "obstructed" or "closed" (*kaus*), social exchange is critically impaired. Obstructed persons are designated "*kowakowa*." The term denotes impaired capacity, but with connotations of foreignness or otherness—possibly in relation to the notion that blockages are for the most part introduced into the person's system by external agents. The perception of *kowakowa* persons as substantively but not inherently blocked leads people to hope they may be "cleared" at any time by cumulative effort and local magic substances and words. Thus, for example, a boy who was hearing impaired was classified as *kowakowa*, although he and his parents had devised an elaborate sign language and he participated fully in society, eventually marrying a hearing person. However, effort never ceased to unblock his ears. A man whose brain was damaged at birth was *kowakowa* also—not a "bad" or "rubbish" person (a nonproductive person), but merely blocked for a time, and once again he received regular magical attention.[4]

Sabarl develop a sense of self, and recognize their own self-worth as generative persons, to the extent that they are able to construct and reconstruct new channels of social relationship. The channeled person—one who is physically, intellectually, and emotionally "open" to engaging in the flow of relations—is a living sign for Sabarl of an absence of blockages and reflects health in society itself. As we shall see, this image of a concretely manifested openness guides the form of social action on commemorative occasions, where the process is one of reconstructing a "memory" of the dead as just such an ideally open being.

Projections

Beyond their physical bodies, living persons are thought to possess a "spirit" or "soul" (*yayalowa-*) and a "shadow/reflection" that is the projectible "image" (*kanukanunu-*) of the spirit.[5] In general, little is heard of *yayalowa-* outside Catholic discourse. However, *kanukanunu-* is of vital concern to Sabarl, for, beyond external appearances, the spirit image manifests the partible inner "self" of the person and the "substantial being" of all animate-category things.

There are those who claim extraordinary control over their spirit images, sending them at will on journeys in and out of their bodies. Depending partly, it is said, on the magic spell used for the purpose, partly on the sender's disposition and intent, these detached shadows or reflections function either as benign "seers" (*hebakunyolyol*) who spy on events in the invisible world on behalf of anxious villagers at home or else as deadly cannibal "sendings" (*waunak*) with power to bring about illness and death.

"Beliefs" (*goru*)[6] about the negative potential of supernatural agents are by far the most deeply rooted and resilient of any in Sabarl culture. In discussing them, people turn to images of consumption.

"Without *Segaiya* There Would Be No Death"

The fact of human mortality is in large part attributed to the sociality of *waunak*, who serve human flesh in place of pork at invisible *segaiya* in the spirit world. Because even *waunak* have trading partners to whom they are indebted for loans of "pork" on past occasions, there will always be death in repayment of their loans; new occasions for spirits to indebt other spirits, forming or reaffirming nefarious debt-based partnerships. I was told once, "Without *segaiya* there would be no death." Death is ex post facto evidence that sorcery and witchcraft work as they are thought to, and *segaiya* is the "writing on the wall" that portends more death. Debt and death—"negative signs" of social and physical personhood, respectively—are linked inextricably in Sabarl thought as original contexts or preconditions of social exchange.

A Story of Consumption

In September 1976, Kiukiu, baptized Vincent in August 1953, died at home on Panabarli. He had been ill for quite some time. Yet as usual in the case of a major landholder, there was much speculation about the cause of his illness. This talk had begun when Vincent fell acutely ill during a feast at the Catholic mission two weeks before. Privately, people were saying that Vincent's spirit image had already been destroyed and his "vital substance" (*hinona*) depleted or "eaten" at this time; that he was "already dead."

Vincent was old and frail. The official verdict from local "healers" (*tosawal*) and learned spiritual "experts" (*saksak*) was that he had died of pneumonia (*wagatubu*, or "ancestral canoe"). In view of Vincent's history of illness and the repeated failure of indigenous methods to cure him (he refused outside treatment or hospital care), the illness was regarded as an innate weakness in his physical makeup—as someone explained, "like something wrong in the soil when God made Adam and Eve." Several postmortem divinations supported this interpretation. Nonetheless, it was assumed that "*waunak* business" had played some part in the final failure of Vincent's system. Possibly he was the victim of "envy" (*huge*) and spite in connection with his exceptionally fertile gardens, possibly it was some mistake of his own in calculating when to repay the loan of a valuable or a pig. These were more or less conventional explanations of mortal decline: loss of physical energy and loss of a spiritual identity, linked to some interpersonal problem.

Sabarl identify four main types of *waunak*, all of them beings who literally feed off these mortal weaknesses. There are *waunak* who reside in the natural environment (floating reefs, sinkholes and the like) or in natural phenomena (such as waterspouts); those who live in human refuse (such as rubbish heaps); the *waunak* who come from overseas; and last and most important, human *waunak*—spirits of the threatening "others" in one's life (commonly a rival leader in another village or hamlet, a resident of another island, another generation, the other sex).

Only the human *waunak*—transactors of human "pig"—are sources of abiding concern.[7] They reap the reward of their murderous plotting on the night of their victim's burial. Drawn to the spot by the "stench" (*buwonga*) of death, the *waunak* converge on the grave site and there begin to dance—drumless, it is said, and heavy footed, jarring the dead body upward through the earth and then spiriting it away to wherever their feast is being held.

Physical signs that such feasts have occurred are presented to people in the visible world as the fatty *muho* (the ambergris of killer whales) that *waunak* discard when butchering human "pig." *Muho* is harvested by ritual adepts, usually village leaders, who distribute it to all female heads of households in the village. Women take shavings of *muho* to the gardens and burn them there in rites for "fattening" growing yams. In other words, the artifact of paternal substance that is most powerfully emblematic of supplementation and increase in the living person is likewise the refuse of malevolent consumption—the stuff of recycled violence.

This point is important in that it indicates a critical distinction within the Sabarl system of reproduction: namely, between decay—the random, uncontrolled falling apart and dispersal of valued substances, things, people, and thoughts that occurs naturally or as a result of neglect—and deconstruction or decomposition—the guided dissemination, separation, and release of people, things, and so on, that requires human agency and entails a plan or objective. Whereas the former process works against social reconstruction, the latter is integral to it: a "countertext" of sociocultural generativity. And whereas the former process is a negative value for Sabarl—and in reference to the subject at hand, an analogue of forgetfulness and accidental memory loss—the latter is positively valued, an analogue of deliberate "forgetting" that enables reconstruction, new relations, and the building of new "memories." I will discuss the symbolic implications of *muho* more fully in chapter 5. The point here is that beliefs about *muho* reveal the ambivalence surrounding the figure of the *waunak* as an agent of death whose actions have the positive consequence of separating and releasing a valuable resource for use in a new productive context.

Only male *waunak* leaders (*saksak*) are thought to have the authority to convene invisible meetings where murders are plotted and the details of spirit feasts discussed. So too, it is these spirit leaders who are "seen" by the sendings of vigilant persons that spy on the proceedings—typically, rising young men in local politics or clan or religious leaders, who report back to their villages the names of the men of high profile in the spirit world.

VIGILANCE AND MEMORIZABILITY

Virtually any adult can put himself or herself forward as a seer, a person with the power to "fly in spirit" into unseen realms, acting the role of investigative reporter. If someone has died or is gravely ill, the rest of the worried community will find reassurance in the vigilance of seers, whose "flights" are, however, completely solo and unwitnessed. This means that their credibility as seers is judged on the basis of their public flight reports alone.

A typical report goes something like this one, delivered to the assembled villagers of Maho by an established expert in 1976. The expert, Luke, was also the senior Guau clan leader. He was responding to several cases of pneumonia in the village, including that of his sister's daughter's infant child Salote, who nearly died.

> This illness. Do you know about this illness? Mothers, fathers, children, do you know? How is this illness going around this place? The canoe of this illness, children play and it comes around. That baby, Salote, was nearly taken. The canoe was red [here the color of danger, bloodshed, sorcery]. They came for me, the *waunak* inside, but found her there instead. They came for me or maybe for Bani or Council [two other village leaders]—maybe they know more about this. They tried to take her to Ailuwa [a faraway island], but I blocked their way. And little Salote came back

again. It is like the serpent that came before [a huge poison-
ous snake eel spotted in a cave near Hebenahine village]. Its
master sent it to Hebenahine. It wanted to come to Maho,
but I stopped it. Maybe Tandeyai has no *waunak* there now
[a reverse reference to the suspect, who was in fact living at
Tandeyai]. We planned a meeting when our place was in order [had no illness in it]. Just to set up watch against illness.
But then we forgot about it, and this happened behind our
backs. This sickness comes, and somebody comes on top of
it [someone is specifically responsible for it]. If no one came
on top of it, the illness could not be so strong. Our acquaint-
ances in other places always blame Sabarl. Those places
down by Brooker [the "lower" or western Chain islands]
blame us too [as practitioners of "*waunak* business"]. I
slept, and in my dream I saw one sick woman's image and
waunak taking her around. Yesterday she was breathing
well. If this sickness stays below the navel, it is fine. I can
cure it. But if it moves into the chest, I don't know about it.
I gave her medicine, but still she is ill. And now when I sleep
I no longer see her image. This illness should not be this
strong. Someone is on top of it. After today's meeting we'll
see if she improves. You must watch your gossip. One
woman went down to Hebenahine to buy things from Mr.
Ryan's boat [a trade-store boat from Misima]. I slept, and I
saw her inside the boat, her head underneath the tarpaulin,
sleeping. The boat was red. You cannot talk about your
friends who are buying things. Now she is sick. Today I am
blowing the shell trumpet [to convene a village meeting]. I
want everyone to come down and play drums and be happy
here [set up a watch to keep *waunak* away]. No one must
sleep in the house. My mother, my sisters, you must not
look dirty. Be clean, dress up. Put oil on your bodies. I will
stay and watch over you all. Before, I brought Salote's image
back. Maybe her ancestors were calling her; I don't know.
Maybe Bani knows.

Bani stood up at this point to report his own vision, building on
the basic scenario of the red canoe and embellishing it with the image
of another sick woman in a red coffin, carried by a plane with *waunak*
pilots that bursts into flame, but not before Bani has snatched up the
woman's image and returned it to safety.

And so the stories continued before an audience of the entire village, somber and attentive—each report repeating the vague, open-

ended format of the first one, established or aspiring village leaders taking up the cultural option of adding to or modifying the narrative discourse. Few if any of these flight reports are brilliant pieces of oratory (it is a frequent complaint of the audience that the speakers tend to ramble on, liking too much the sound of their own words or worse yet, losing distance on the occasion by talking about their own physical problems and anxieties), but together they create an affecting impression of vigilance. Sabarl people I knew who were not themselves players on this stage indicated that they found this (rhetoric of) vigilance very reassuring.

Significantly, suspect female *waunak* are never mentioned by name on these occasions. Whereas males retain their physical identities at spirit gatherings, female *waunak* are believed to disguise themselves in a type of "negative masking" by wiping their faces clear of distinguishing features. Females also tend to "fly" collectively in a hot blur, as meteorites or comets (*yoyova*), swarming or clustering at their destinations in overwhelming numbers—individually unrecognizable in the density and confusion.

This feature of *waunak* imagery reveals a theme of memory not yet touched upon, but one that receives considerable cultural elaboration on Sabarl—the theme of memorizability. Female *waunak*—convergent forces that are dangerously indistinct and effaced—are in some respects cultural images of "memory" subverted: metaphors of the threat to social order of all that is unmemorizable, ungraspable, elusive. By contrast, males are distinct and notably memorizable agents of destructive convergence: illicit organizers who instigate social disruption and personal loss, the images of the force of "memory" perverted.

The distinction is elaborated in the scenarios people paint of the *waunak* who are supremely feared. In stories of legendary *waunak*, the ultimate sorcerer is depicted as a *bibiloia*—a being who possesses all forms of malevolent knowledge but is known for dematerializing his own body and materializing it[8] long distances from home and for traveling at supernatural speeds. The *bibiloia* appears at his destination scorching hot and transformed by the journey from a human being into a monster with long, matted hair, talons, and flapping ears. The basket he carries (which is called a *paos* and has no equivalent in normal society) is extremely hot, like the sorcerer himself, and it is filled with the "hot" (magically powerful) things of a sorcerer's kit so that anyone reaching in would instantly die. A *bibiloia* does not join the *waunak* who dance on graves, nor does he participate in cannibal feasts. He transcends if not the *waunak* category, at least the human need to rationalize killing and death—indeed, like the ancestor Katutubwai, the *bibiloia* thrives on death.

The female counterpart of the *bibiloia* is the *waunak yoyova*, who flies in a pack as a comet or meteorite. As she shoots across the sky, fresh from a cannibal feast, she and the others are described as the image of a woman with a human skull under her arm. The image is an interesting (and powerful) one because the head of a pig is the part that in ordinary, visible *segaiya* is presented to the most honored guest. Accepting the head constitutes a pledge to return the same part at a future feast. In short, it is women who are seen as corporately bearing the symbolic standard—the "memory"—of a past and future death.

On the level of politics, the function of women in this regard obscures their own identities, and thus their own futures as distinguished political actors. That a woman can never publicly be accused of eating human "pig" (can at the most stand up and implicate herself) dissipates the interactive tensions—the potential for dialogic interaction—that inhere in accusations. This severely restricts her range of negative kudos and therefore the political capital that a reputation for sorcery can generate. The practical utility to her of knowing (or being thought to know) "*waunak* business" is limited by male rhetoric. She can never be challenged by a male spirit leader to match wits and the strength of her support in the village or clan in the political arena where sorcery accusations articulate power struggles.

THE REPRODUCTION OF CULTURAL KNOWLEDGE

Memorizability is a problem for Sabarl largely in connection with the reproduction of cultural knowledge as social power and of social power as gender linked. It follows that distinctions we note between different modes of power (power that is merged and indistinct versus power that is salient and distinct), are reproduced as gender-linked models for transmitting cultural knowledge.

People come by knowledge of spirit sending in one of two ways. Either they work at acquiring certain magic spells and procedures, usually by laboring for relatives who possess them, or else they receive their knowledge in the womb through their mothers' blood. The difference this produces is basically between what we might term sorcery and witchcraft, and as in so many other cultures in and beyond Melanesia, the former is associated with males and the latter with females.[9]

THE SWALLOWED ONES

Persons who inherit their knowledge of spirit sending through their mothers' blood are thought to have a very different life history from normal human beings, since for them social personhood begins in the womb. These are the "twice born" or "swallowed" ones (*tinon*), women (for the most part) who are thought to have experienced a spiritual birth before their physical one. It is said that a pregnant female *waunak* transmits her spiritual knowledge (and sometimes also a proclivity to cannibalism) to her baby as she eats human "pig." Afterward she gives birth to the child in its spirit form, and together they fly to the realm of Suweni, the ruler of *waunak*, where the child is formally presented as a future liege. The baby, now a member of *waunak* society, is then swallowed by its mother, who later gives birth in the usual way. This second birth is the one the village sees. The child, marked by a tendency to appear mentally elsewhere much of the time, is born fully capable of anything.

ACQUIRED KNOWLEDGE

In the realm of acquired knowledge, magic "spells" (*kukulu*) and instruction in the use of "magic substances" (*ngengaiya*) are commonly sought by young men from their fathers or maternal uncles. Most enter into an apprenticeship for the purpose, either working for their chosen adept or paying him outright. A case in point is James, a clan leader of Maho village, who told me he worked for an uncle on Panatinani for five years (roughly from age eighteen to twenty-three) in return for his uncle's book of magic spells and tutorials in "sleeping with leaves" (flying in spirit). He then stayed for three months with another uncle at Dadahai, paying him with an ax blade, and after that with his father's brother at Hesesai, where he learned more magic for flying. In this instance he showed his gratitude with the gift of a pig. Still another uncle at Hebenahine taught him protective magic, until finally, at the age of thirty-six, he learned sorcery from a distant uncle on Misima in exchange for three months of hard work in his gardens and sago groves.

James had begun his apprenticeship with a ritual for flushing the body of any impurities that could block his inner "sight." This ritual, which he referred to simply as "salt water drinking" (*soga imun*) began at nightfall (*gogou*) with James drinking salt water from the Sabarl tide pools on an empty stomach, together with gingerroot charmed by his teacher. Afterward he slept alone on his mat until just before dawn, awakening as the sun's rays appeared. He proceeded to drink hot fresh water and then the heated juice of a young coconut (*bwaku*) before going into the bush to defecate. Following the purge, he fasted throughout the day. James claims that no magic words accompanied this procedure, which "opened the way" for more specialized instruction. He went on to learn more about "sleeping with leaves" as well as how to steal spirit images.[10] He also learned protective magic, which he considered essential life insurance for any person known to know sorcery, and along the way, something of the healer's art.

James represented his specialty to me as "sleeping with leaves" (though others feared him as a sorcerer), indicating that he wished to be thought of (and portrayed in my book) less as an aggressor than as a vigilant defender of Sabarl Island.[11] Knowledge of "sleeping with leaves" and command of the language of spiritual vigilance are, however, prerequisites for full participation in the aggressively competitive arena of magical-political rhetoric.

*

No amount of magical knowledge can shield a person entirely from the invisible spears of malevolent thought, but it is possible to reverse their effects. Classically, this is accomplished by persons with knowledge of healing, who "recite backward" the words that were used against the victim originally. The words are spoken while the healer is chewing "hot" ginger (since ill people are thought to be moving dangerously toward coldness and death). Then the ginger is sprayed from the mouth in a fine mist over the person, his or her personal effects, and the interior of the house. In short, the healer coats the "personal domain"[12] of the victim with magic, *as if from the inside.* That is, insofar as the interior of the house, like the interior of the person, is an arrangement of the artifacts of primary operations of productive life (domestic accoutrements, food in storage, sleeping mats, caches of valuable objects and the like) and the acts (sexual and nurturant) that constitute the "contents" and "stories" of intimate life, the healer's intervention works like internal medicine for the person as a self-other (not merely as a corporeal individual). When subsequently he sucks the "spear"—the foreign embodiment of evil thoughts—out of the body and physically produces it (e.g., as a bit of sassafras root, a match, a bullet, or the like) and then destroys it in front of the victim, the healer's concentration on the object is literally an abstraction: a reduction of the problem to a physical one.

Three spirit spears were removed from Vincent's body by different experts. However, the third expert, a favorite nephew, confided to me that he was "only acting" when he removed the spear—that Vincent was "already dead." The experts agreed afterward that Vincent's spirit image had been stolen and destroyed by a *waunak* long before the spiritual surgeries. His body, they said, was only "going through the motions" of living.

Since Vincent was a leader in the community, throughout this period spirit senders were flying to determine who was responsible for his illness, what had happened to the *kanukanunu*-(spirit image), and which words were used to guide the spirit spear or spears that eventually "hit" him. Their reports were various: his *kanukanunu*- was found "in a sinkhole," "in deep water," "in Kalipoiya's basket," whereas in private people were murmuring that it had been "burned" or otherwise "lost for good." Because Vincent had close kin in other villages, a number of public meetings were held throughout the Saisai islands, and vigils were kept around his house to ward off evil spirits. Throughout the night, young people in his village sang and danced *gitar* (popular string band music), sometimes joined by older men and women playing traditional music, singing, and dancing. Had he recovered, Vincent would have shown his appreciation by hosting a feast for those who had demonstrated their concern. But he grew weaker.

At the point when it became obvious that Vincent was "already dead," attempts to save his life were replaced by magic words to postpone his death until all of his children had arrived from other islands. Had Vincent named his assassin while in this state of liminal existence, his accusation would have been dismissed as the ravings of a man whose "head was already finished." In fact, he died silently and quickly—too quickly for the last rites of either church or "custom." The latter are administered when experts decide it is no longer possible to keep the body alive, with the purpose of "allowing the body to die by setting the spirit [*yalowane*] free." With words that evoke the "clarity" (*waiyaiya numo*, "foreign clarity") of the early morning damp "as in cold places in the world," a spiritual expert pours fresh water over the dying person's head. The water, being "cold like a spirit person [*baloma*]," carries the spirit away toward its final metamorphosis. The coldness travels upward from the fingertips and toes, marking the spirit's passage out of the body. Then, with his last breath, his *yayalowa* departs for the afterworld.

At this moment the spirit is said to reunite with the spirit image that was separated from it by illness.

Afterworld

Growing in the center of the spirit village of Haniewa, beneath the gardens of Hemenaha Island, is a *kunika* tree (Combretaceae: *Termi-*

nalia) with a branch for every clan in the world and a leaf for every living person. When somebody dies one leaf falls, signaling spirits of his or her clan to expect a new arrival in the village and to prepare a welcoming feast.

It is extremely important that a person's body be respectfully interred, since journeys to the afterworld begin the morning after a burial. Sabarl "custom" dictates that the dead be laid to "sleep" with feet pointing toward the rising sun, so that when the spirit awakes at dawn it "sees the sun" and follows its path to the spirit village. The spirit's only companion on its journey is a spirit guide (*toseseyok*, "one who ventures out"). The guide is the spirit of a living person specially trained for the work, which is usually taken up by aged political leaders (male or female) as a kind of retirement position. The guide walks behind the spirit "to look after it," as on ordinary occasions noted persons are followed by juniors who "watch their backs." Then, when the spirit reaches a "fork" (*noaveveiwo*) in the path, it turns to the guide and confides the one true cause of death.

At the fork of the path is a hibiscus bush (*kalas*). Some say the bush blossoms in many colors, others say the blossoms are red. However, if they are closed, it is a sign that the spirit "has blood on it"—that the person has been active in "*waunak* business" and must take the path away from eternal life and toward annihilation. This journey is made alone, and people tell different stories about the fate that awaits evil spirits at the end of it. In one story, the spirit plunges into an enormous hole that is the mouth of the original monster, Katutubwai. Another tells how sorcerers and witches dwell with *waunak* colleagues north of Sabarl, in a patch of black stone outcroppings called Hailuwa. There they await certain destruction by the vengeful spirits of their victims. Cannibal spirits retain their rotting spirit forms and the putrid smell of their own dead bodies for as long as they exist. And such spirits are never at peace—can never relax their guard.

If the blossoms of the hibiscus on the path of the sun are open, a spirit may proceed in the direction of eternal life. Depending on whether the death was properly mourned and acknowledged according to "custom"—whether, that is, it was a "good" or "bad" death in Sabarl terms[13]—the spirit goes on to become some form of afterlife being and a cultural image of one of the different fates of a human "memory."

The Un-remembered

The spirits of persons whose deaths have been properly acknowledged with a funeral and shows of grief will travel to the spirit village (Haniewa is the usual spot for Maho villagers), where their former, mortal images are replaced by the eternally "shining" form of a *baloma*. *Baloma* are undifferentiated spirits of the matriclan—the idealized products of deliberate cultural acts of "forgetting." Meanwhile, persons whose bodies are for some reason not interred—victims, for example, of accidental deaths or suicide where the body cannot be recovered, or of war and (in former times it was feared) cannibalism, where the body is butchered, mutilated, or discarded, are transformed instead into *piwapiwa:* "wild" spirits who float through the bush of Panatinani as dismembered body parts. In contrast to the lovely *baloma*—the constructed illusions of wholly beautiful beings leading wholly unconflicted social lives—*piwapiwa* project the fearful specter of, among other things, forgetfulness: the arbitrarily disconnected and scattered parts of the imperfect memory of a person.

Both *baloma* and *piwapiwa* are said to lose entirely their memories of the living: I was told, their minds ("foreheads") are "erased" (*maleleka*) of thoughts of the living, and their hearts "forget" them. In the case of *baloma*, "forgetting" is achieved in a process that sets them free from painful memories of personal attachments and responsibilities in their former life.

The (historical) and personal forgetting of *baloma* is represented as a story of progressive replacement of a living human "image" that is all too temporary by one that is stable and forever perfect. It is a story that begins on the path to the afterworld, where the spirit is walking with its guide and protector until it reaches a stream of cold, swift-flowing water. As the spirit pauses at the edge of the channel, hesitant to take the plunge into another world and time, the guide gives it a gentle shove, and it topples in. The spirit swims the channel, and as it emerges on the opposite bank, a *baloma* of its own clan drops a golden coconut on its head. The impact dislodges the spirit image—the image of the putrifying corpse that is the person's "old skin" (previous identity). This skin sloughs off into the channel and is eaten by "dangerous fish"—sharks, rays, snake eels, and the like—that absorb the stench of the image, as they do with the person's "first" placental skin and the victims they have killed or "eaten" as embodiments of *waunak*. What emerges from the cold water is thus a blank human spirit—the person as space. However, that it is not yet completely purified of its recent humanity (not yet forgettable) is signified by a clinging odor of putrefaction.

Its clan mates lead the spirit directly to a two-story smokehouse (described nowadays as a "spirit hospital"), where it is looked after for a period corresponding to the length of the fatal illness. The spirit climbs the ladder to the upper story and lies down on a newly made sleeping mat. Meanwhile, in the room below, an elderly clanswoman tends an eternal fire. As the spirit sleeps, formless, exposed, and vulnerable, smoke from the fire slowly roasts it back to strength. Noxious odors are smoked out completely, and a new and idealized form, that of the *baloma*, is slowly baked on.

When the *baloma* is fully formed, it arises to be dressed and decorated for the feast of its rebirth. Its new skin, a model of health, shines "like the moon," which is always full over Haniewa. It wears flowers and aromatic herbs that are eternally fresh and face paint that never smudges; its body and hair have a permanent coconut oil sheen. Amid the admiring comments of fellow *baloma*, it descends for the welcoming feast in its honor. At the feast there is food in indescribable abundance but no fish, since there is danger of mistakenly eating its own skin (and *baloma* are not, of course, cannibals).

Baloma, which never die and which have legitimately severed ties with ("forgotten") the living, exist in blissful abdication of their former indebtedness or any other form of responsibility to them. Stories about their antics when they do return for a visit depict them as irresponsible pranksters, disrupting social relationships and making trouble like naughty (but powerful) children. For example, two cousins go fishing. A *baloma* disguises itself as one of them and tells the other that he will look after the fish they have caught while the cousin goes back out to the reef. Instead, the *baloma* eats them. When the real cousin returns and asks for his share, there is confusion and bad words between them until they happen to look over and see the *baloma*, transparent, with the fish visible in its stomach. In another very popular story, a *baloma* disguises itself as a beautiful girl who appears at night to two young men, causing trouble between them until they catch on that she is only an illusion.

Baloma, in short, are powerful but insubstantial beings: the image of that which is seemingly attractive and only apparently ideal. They represent in life all that remains as detailed memories fade of the social contracts that make individuals concrete but problematic presences in the lives of others. Their lovely qualities are discernible to the extent that they remain in their place—unindividuated and domestic projections of the enduring matriclan.

Piwapiwa, spirits of the uninterred victims of violent death, likewise are said to have no memory of the living. However, unlike *baloma*, they lead an unintegrated, untamed existence in the bush. They "have no leader, and no language"—no sociality. Also, they die and are afterward regrown from seeds of blood into new *piwapiwa*. Since their life spans are shorter than most living persons' and they copulate indiscriminately and at a furious rate, the *piwapiwa* population is said to be enormous. It is men who encounter them most often, in the bush while out hunting wild pigs. *Piwapiwa* show the violent breakup of the relational person.

Baloma ("memory" idealized, liberated from the ongoing concerns of human beings) and *piwapiwa* ("memory" unmoored, undisciplined, in disarray) figure in everyday Sabarl discourse as more or less useless (juvenile or scattered) figures—of little value to adult persons involved in the reciprocal and reproductive strategies that structure social life. These strategies require a capacity to "remember" others (as expressed in ongoing giving that denotes the location of the other in the mind and heart of the donor) and to be remembered by them (to persuade others to give). For this, people tend to turn to an "ancestor," or *tubu*. A named ancestor stands in contrast to both the *baloma* and the *piwapiwa* as a being still tied to the living through material objects and remains, names, commemorative songs and tales, and other "marks" of "memory."

In Sabarl thinking, the *tubu* population is an omnipresent audience to the efforts of the living to inscribe their own impressions on society through "custom"—in which success requires ancestral support. It is the *tubu* who is turned to for blessings and guidance in fishing, who is invoked to "watch over" the garden, whose grave the bravest men approach for help in finding wealth. Any spells that accompany the magical potions for influencing a trading partner are addressed to a *tubu* personally. A *tubu* may even materialize ax blades during a mortuary feast, as we shall see. A *tubu*, in short, is "present *in absentia*" (Todorov 1981:13): "a place/object of or for remembering" *displaced*. Once the physical body is removed as a polluting obstacle to the orderly flow of everyday life by mortuary observances, the result is a new, though invisibly present, source of power over one's own future.

Overview

We have seen how the physical person is created as a "memory" through a process that involves, on the one hand, separation and the observance of distinctions (for example, between sexual substances and gender-linked body parts) and on the other, convergence, reconstitution, and the reorganization of distinct elements (for example, of body parts into relations of support and complementarity). However, this created object "of or for remembering" is not memorable in itself. Memorability—the quality of being worth remembering—requires a social history: it exists to the extent that others invest in its production through acts of giving and receiving that create the person as a self-other. It also occurs to the extent that one extends oneself to others—making an impression on them as distinct from (though not exclusive of) the impression made by those one represents (especially parents) in extension, as a social supplement. In short, memorability is always intersubjective.

However, the quality of being memorable is positively valued only insofar as it is perceived to be life extending (in time and in space). The quintessential Sabarl example is the *tubu*, the "absent presence" that personifies the hope of constructing from death a new social history for the dead and a new future of empowerment for the living. The *waunak* is the negatively valued counterpart of ancestors in this regard—a force of the subversion or perversion of the "memory" of others. A representation of death-within-life (as the *tubu* is life-within-death), the *waunak* is motivated by a greed for space and time that constricts the time and space—the "memory" potential—of others. The most concrete expression of this greed is the image of the *waunak* feeding upon *hinona:* the invisible "vital substance" and generative future of others. Of course the greed for space and time of those who defy its constraints, for example, by walking or flying great distances at unnatural speeds, is the average islander's nightmare. But it is also the ambitious person's dream of limitless mobility and influence.

Stepping back, then, we can observe in the relation of the physical to the metaphysical aspects of the person the cultural countervalues of the centered and expansionist self. Each of these opposing forces, centripetal and centrifugal, contains an element of its opposite, which it is the concern of social persons to control and "turn" (*havile*) in the proper direction; to bend back on course. Thus within the "thinking," coherent, organized person are the forces of will, autonomy, and individual initiative, and a tendency to give and take emotionally (partitioning the material domain of self or others). These countervalues are dynamically related as text and intertext: as the notion of the matriclan is to patrilineality; as support is to complementarity; as the children in the tales of Katutubwai are to the monster.

Part Two

Relational Personhood

Everywhere the pressure of remembrance.

Don DeLillo

Three

Giving and Indebtedness

The day I first arrived on Sabarl I received a most extraordinary greeting. We had anchored the small mission outboard on the north side of the island and crossed on foot at a narrow point, descending into Maho by a back path. We were spotted first by the elderly women who perched in the sun behind their houses, and they flocked to meet us. From a distance they seemed very fragile, but also aggressive. Suddenly the smallest and most ancient one seized my arm and began to suck at my breast. She was repeating over and over some urgent phrase; her small eyes were terribly intense. I was embarrassed and also—How could I explain it to myself?—ashamed. All these venerable women who had so much to teach me, behaving as insistent supplicants. Later I learned that what they were saying was *"Tinau, tinau, apayebo"*: "My mother, my mother, give me a smoke" and, in the language of gestures, "Tobacco is my mother's milk."

Verbal requests for pieces of black twist tobacco[1] became more subtle the longer I stayed in Maho, and eventually they vanished altogether into amusing nonverbals. A man who had become my "uncle" twirled a black-tipped feather as I passed him on the beach. His eyes twinkled mischievously when suddenly I realized he was asking for a bit of black tobacco. A younger "sister," searching around in the tangled nest of fiber at the bottom of her basket, smiled slyly when she saw I understood she was asking for tobacco to hide there from her friends. I was always tucking tobacco away near doorways and cracks in the house so that people who helped me could later return and retrieve it when friends were no longer watching. If I left the village to visit other places, women I knew would sit beneath my house, singing little tobacco songs that called for pieces to fall through the floorboards. Gradually people stopped asking for tobacco and simply waited for it to be offered. Beyond saving themselves the "shame" (*mwalina*) of asking, they spared me the possible shame of having to admit my supplies had run out.

It was not so much the size as the constancy of the flow of small gifts that eventually earned me at least superficial kin relations among the people I was living and working with. Once the flow was established, I noticed a growing interest in claiming me as a member of someone's father's or mother's matriclan. People compared, for example, the lines of my palms with theirs and interpreted them as they saw fit: left hand for the father's clan, right hand for the mother's. They were seeking some mark, some physical evidence, of my membership in a universal social order patterned on the Sabarl one. But no one would have cared to recognize my place in such an order had I not consistently demonstrated the capacity to give and to receive appropriately.

Selfhood is expressed and constituted by acts of what Sabarl gloss as "feeding" or "nurture" (*pahan*). Nurture, which encompasses the giving of comestibles and of culturally valued objects, carries deep significance and a broad range of social consequences. Beyond an investment in the physical and social growth and strength of others (and thereby in the donor's own self), the "memory" manifested as the gift coordinates the different life "stories" and perspectives of donor and recipient, as well as creating a new point of orientation from which to develop their future relationship. In other words the gift, as a "memory," embodies concretely the objective distance inherent in the subjective experience of relationship. It is in this sense an icon of reflexive self-formation, deriving much of its power from its status as a homologue of the knowledge one gains of one's self by standing apart from one's self—collapsing the distinction of self and other.

Sabarl project themselves onto what they give away, and they are seen by others in their gifts as an absent presence. Thus giving, as an act of displacement, has the potential to create (or inscribe) an impression of the donor in the mind of the recipient (see also Munn 1986). Indeed, much giving is motivated by the hope that one will be "remembered" by those to whom one has given things in the past when support is needed for some future project.

But by the same token, giving creates a "debt" (*vaga-*)—the perception/experience of an absence of an object—that is no less a "memory" than its physical counterpart. Indeed, as a "memory" removed—the artifact of displacement—it is the image of the gift's intrinsically temporal dimension: an emblem of the extension of the relationship into the future. Social life on Sabarl to a large extent revolves around gestures of projective nurture, conceived as acts of remembrance.

Within the matriclan, nurture is an expectation expressed in the recognition of shared substance (especially maternal blood). In acting out blood bonds by nurturing according to the cultural rules, a person's self is inscribed within clan limits. Outside the matriclan, gifts of nurture build a bridge to an other, defining the self, as it were, by contrast. But either way, relations are constructed, in the sense that they are subject to being judged by the cultural signs of persons' capacity to "remember" their rights and obligations vis-à-vis other individuals and to seek out or extend themselves to others through giving.

It was inconceivable to my Sabarl friends that I should be returning home one day to a place without clans, and they pitied me for it. The "matriclan"—*hun*—is for Sabarl synonymous with security: an unconditional assurance of belonging and the structuring element in civilized exchanges with others. It is the concept of clanship as a corporate ideal that along with "place," draws people together on mortuary occasions and creates an affecting image of common purpose out of disparate personal and social histories.

Giving from the Heart

Yet matriclanship is also the source of a fundamental ambivalence, particularly in a society such as Sabarl's where children usually grow up in the father's house. Sabarl children expect to be nurtured by senior women of their clan, especially in the form of food. From senior clan males, and mothers' brothers in particular, they expect "direction" and a chance to earn the respect that can lead eventually to inheriting landed resources. One is loyal first to maternal kin who have fulfilled these primary-care expectations.

However, children have strong affective ties to their fathers, from whom gifts of nurture are never expected and who in turn will hope for, but never expect, support from them. As nonclansmen, their fathers will discipline them only as a last resort (e.g., if their mother has failed completely and if no maternal uncle is available to do it). Anything a father or his "line" (*labu*) gives to his children will be viewed as a gift of pure generosity—a gift "from the heart" or "out of feeling" (*henunuwana*)—that children feel morally obliged to acknowledge. In this way fathers can win their children's loyalty away from mothers' brothers—that is, by initiating nurture out of love rather than out of duty.

The father-child relationship undergoes a twist in the course of the developmental cycle, as male children (especially) begin to "turn" the direction of giving back toward their fathers through "loans with interest" or *powon* (cf. the Trobriand system discussed by Weiner 1986 as *pokola*). They do this with the help of their mothers—on one level, to establish a claim on postmortem inheritance, but on another, to express their "otherness" to their fathers as nonclanspersons. For example, Desalle lends his mother an ax blade to *powon* to her husband and her husband's siblings (Desalle's father, father's sister, etc.) on his behalf, knowing that they need support in purchasing a canoe. He makes it clear when he gives the axblade that this constitutes a bid for his father's residence land, which his father's siblings and their children might otherwise inherit through the clan when his father dies.

Because *powon* is different from expressing gratitude for nurture—even morally in conflict with it, since *powon* contains an element of overt self-interest—the relationship takes on ambivalence. Acknowledging paternal nurture is at least as important as any gesture for personal gain; moreover, it is vulgar to act as if the two are related.

However, there is no instituted path available to children for expressing gratitude to their fathers directly. Instead they must turn to their fathers' sisters' children, that is, to the very cousins who are competitors for their fathers' property. This ambivalent giving in the name of gratitude is expressed in the form of a ritualized feeding relationship between cross-cousins (*nubaiu*), who call each other within this relationship "my father" (*tamau*) or "my child" (*natu*). A "father" is a father's sister's child; a "child" a mother's brother's child. The relationship, which is arranged by their parents when the cousins are very young, is meant to continue until one or the other dies.

The exchanges between cousin "fathers" and "children" consist of gifts of "young coconut" (*bwaku*), also called "bones" (*titiwa*), and countergifts called "swimming" (*lobulobu*) or more simply *segaiya*.

Whenever the "child" is seriously ill, his cousin "father" will present him with green coconut and other foods "to make him buoyant and healthy again," as well as sago pudding and stone axblades "to make him strong." The soft green coconut flesh is said to represent bones that are not yet hard, not fully developed: the skeletal core of the child that is formed at conception by semen and the dry (*kevekeve*) part of the body—the part that physically endures after death. Sago pudding is symbolic of the semen itself. In addition, stone axblades "add grease" to the foods; they figuratively add another product of semen, on the model of paternal contributions to a child in the womb. In other words, ax blades are the object concretizations of productive masculine energies (see Battaglia 1983b).[2] Indeed, all gifts to "make children strong" when they are ill are products of masculine effort—whether this effort is exerted by males or females.

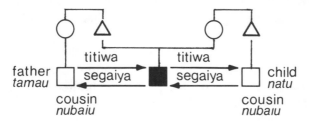

FIGURE 1 *Titiwa-segaiya* exchange relationships.

Thus, on one level a gift of "bones" is a statement of paternal responsibility for the development of children, as well as a bid for whatever material appreciation that concern might inspire. But it is also a pledge that the ritual "father" will act as a custodian of the bones—the physical remains of the "child"—by digging the grave and preparing the corpse when the "child" dies: the relationship is in fact a pact between the "child" and his or her undertaker. If the "child" recovers and is "well enough to swim again" (to find food on its own), appreciation is expressed by presenting the countergifts known as "swimming" or *segaiya*.

Segaiya prestations of a recovered "child" to his or her "father" typically take the form of "future food," such as puppies (for those who eat dog), young fruit or palm trees, and the like. In addition, the "child" may host an "informal feast" (*sulili*) for the "father," featuring a baked sago cake and gifts of domestic wealth such as mats, pots, baskets, or skirts. More than expressing thanks, these gestures convey a promise from the child that the "father's" concern, as well as his or her services as undertaker, will be rewarded in the future at a feast that honors the paternal clan.

"Bones," then, refer to the artifacts of paternal nurture—the beginning and end of the physical person and the endowments from paternal kin. As a masculine, dry component of the body, they also represent resistance to decay, relative at least to the flesh of the body produced by the mother's blood. Prestations of *segaiya*, meanwhile, prefigure the occasion when bones are transformed into sago pudding—that is, are symbolically turned back into semen, and in this form reclaimed by the paternal clan.[3]

Thus the interactions of cousin "fathers" and "children" not only extend the rudiments of exchange beyond the natal home, but mark the beginning and end of a person's public life, the incipience and closure of paternal nurture. They are, concretely, what paternal commitment amounts to in the way of survival insurance for the individual and for the paternal line. We can also see that the *titiwa-segaiya* exchanges involve, on the one hand, reciprocity—the linear exchange of things of equivalent value as initiated by the "father"—and eventually a cyclical process of replacement or reclamation. Reciprocal exchanges of coconut for "future food" occur during "children's" lifetimes. Reclamation or replacement occurs at their death, when sago pudding and wealth fulfill their promises.

It is interesting that this transactional arrangement is modeled as if "children" die before their "fathers"—a logical requirement of the fact that conception can be, as it were, put in reverse (cf. Mosko 1985). The father is conceptually both junior and senior to the child, and the beginning and the end of a child's life. This scenario recalls the stories of Katutubwai, where the children devoured by the giant somehow manage to escape from its body. The rebirth of the "child" is predicted in the relations that recall the myth.[4]

Giving to Show Respect

I mentioned earlier that it is common for siblings of either sex to act interchangeably the role of "father." Likewise, "children" of either sex are given the same ritual treatment at death. Yet formalized giving between persons who are actually separated by generation is significantly less gender blind—a reflection of the fact that the problem being addressed has to do with the different future (the different consequences) of "memory" for males and for females.

Like ritualized giving from cousin "fathers" to their "children," the giving of time and things to respected senior kin involves junior persons in a process that amounts to investing in their future selves. They do this by means of *powon*—by lending labor and valuables to senior males (and to their mothers' brothers and fathers especially) with the expectation of receiving in return more than they have given. This expectation may be casual and generalized or it may be calculated and explicit, depending not so much on the "social distance" between the parties as on the degree of faith each party has that nothing and no one will intervene to derail the return on the loan.

Consider the case of Desalle and his uncle. There is potentially among Sabarl a special bond between mothers' brothers and sisters' children, particularly the male children who will ideally inherit the mother's brother's place in the social order. A nephew is called by his mother's brother "my first" (*nogama*) and calls his mother's brother either "my uncle" (*noheiu*) or, to reflect his special regard for the uncle as a source of security, "my man" (*notau*): the "last person" he would ask for anything he needed because an uncle feels obligated to give it. During his uncle's lifetime, a nephew works to gain his uncle's respect by laboring in the uncle's gardens and sago groves, and by giving material support to his social projects in the form of *powon*.

When his uncle dies, the nephew represents his interests and his clan at the mortuary feast, in effect standing in for his uncle at his funeral. The nephew's reward is public recognition of his new senior standing within the lineage. Thus, by showing respect for his mother's brother and in time lending him valuables to use in exchange, a nephew is investing indirectly in himself.

In Desalle's case, a younger uncle asked him to *powon* one ax blade, so he could exchange it with his brother's widow during *segaiya*. Because the request was explicitly to *powon*, Desalle could expect a return with considerable interest (say, five ax blades) sometime during the younger uncle's lifetime. If, however, Desalle was short an ax blade and unable to wait for the repayment, he could ask the young uncle to return his *powon*—although by shortening the "life" of the interval he would be forfeiting the interest (the "supplement" to their relationship.) If it happened that the uncle died before repaying the *powon*, the debt would fall to his children (i.e., a cousin "child" of Desalle's), who would have to pay even more interest than their father would have. They would do this out of respect for Desalle as their father's "memory."

Although *powon* is not always a loan from juniors to seniors (for example, a cousin "father" may *powon* wealth to his "child," as we observe in chap. 6), it always refers back to a respect-based asymmetrical relationship—in this case (somewhat obliquely) the respect of the cousin "father" for his "child's" actual father as a senior clan male.

Placing *powon* in the context of the gifts of "bones" between cousin "fathers" and "children," we see that since the "bones" given to a "child" in the form of ax blades may ultimately be used by him to *powon* his own father and mother's brother for different types of essential resources they control, "father-child" giving in effect initiates a process that results in the descent of all the valued things a child inherits from male relatives during his or her lifetime. Interestingly, the process is characterized as an extension of what the father builds in the womb, not merely as a contrivance. This "naturalized" paternal continuity is built on the structure of cross-cousin symmetry, yet it works through the dynamic asymmetry of uncles and heirs, fathers and children to separate the father and the uncle in the man: that is, to allow some things to descend to a man's own children and some to the clan heirs.

The seeming paradox is that cousin "fathers" are simultaneously "children" vis-à-vis other cross-cousins. The titles used during mortuary feasts reiterate the point. As I have already noted, ritual "fathers" are called "feast eater" (*tohan segaiya*) at the feasts for their "children," whom they call "my sago pudding" (*no moni*). Nonetheless, the "father" in a person "dies for good" at the death of his or her "child." There comes a time in the series of feasts when the "father" is recompensed and the partnership is dissolved, when he or she is reduced to a "child" to be one day "eaten" by his or her own cousin "father," as in myth the first mortal ancestor "dies for good" and the children who were fed upon continue to live. In short, the father (by contrast with the mother's brother) has existence only through the child.

It is important to note that "father-child" relations cannot be understood by looking at the death of a single person but must be seen as a movement back and forth between nurturing and consuming, "feeding" and "eating," through time and through the younger generation of persons who are laterally connected.

This said, I now turn to placing asymmetrical exchange relationships in context of the greater support system.

Giving to Support

For Sabarl, all matriclans are created equal. Then, at marriage, things change. One clanic group becomes indebted to another for the gift of a wife (in recognition, that is, of the absence they have created), and it falls to the groom to express this indebtedness by giving "bridewealth" (*wisebua*) to the bride's mother. The acceptance of *wisebua* constitutes a contract that members of the two groups will "offer" (*toto-*) one another labor and material support whenever it is needed. In other words, it is a mutual aid contract to protect inmarried groups against the "shame" of having to "request" (*-wanun*) support. "Collective affinal support" is called *muli*, and it is represented by food and object wealth supplied by the members of one group to those of another in the name of affinal force. The arrangement is such that relations based on mutual respect and complementarity are built up over time and "written" into history whenever one group hosts a *segaiya* and is supported by the other. Because neither side requests the support, neither side is even temporarily denigrated by accepting it, or elevated in the giving.

In addition to *muli*, a marriage contract pledges "individual" support (*labe*) by the junior affines of one side to the seniors of the other. A junior person in this position is called *tovelam* by the seniors and is expected to offer everyday labor and material support, as I will shortly discuss in more detail. Unlike giving collectively, *tovelam* support derives from a condition of "shame" that is inherent in persons indebted to nonclan seniors for the vital gift of *muli:* the "memory" of the force of senior affines. Marriage contracts define a key tenet of Sabarl culture—the value of sacrificing autonomy for the collective good.

On one level, then, we can see how the death of one spouse or the other would freeze the give and take and throw one matriclan group into the superior position of kin vis-à-vis affines. If the husband dies first, which is the cultural expectation, the wife givers return to relative parity with the wife takers. However, they do not relinquish their former status easily.

The widow is expected in this situation to return her *wisebua* to her husband's kin as an "appeasement offering" or *solu*, particularly if she plans to remarry. This gift is an important component of the "final *muli*" from her group. It is also a formal plea for release from *tovelam* status (and *tovelam* shame) and from the social and economic "direction" of her husband's senior kin. The widows of men who have given *wisebua* repeatedly and lavishly during their lifetimes often remain unmarried as a result. The only economically sensible alternative is to choose a junior man from their husband's matriline, when and if they remarry, since all other suitors must compensate her husband's group with a very large prestation of wealth "for stealing their widow." Supposedly since ancestral times, this "deathtime" (*segabgabula*) payment for stealing the widow has been set at thirty ax blades, two tusked pigs (*sok*), and one shell necklace (*bak*). The amount is very discouraging for the "wrong" suitor, who faces, in addition to *segabgabula*, an obligation to provide *wisebua* to his new wife's maternal kin.

Should a wife die before her husband, her kin "look after" (*matahasik*) the widower, making certain that he "remembers" them. He will still have to pay *segabgabula* if he wishes to remarry, unless he chooses a woman within his wife's matriline, and additional *wisebua* to his new wife's kin. In short, there is a penalty at every turn for upsetting the wife giver/wife taker relationship. Men can effectively mortgage their futures as influential persons by tying up their wealth in this way; women who refuse an appropriate partner can remain unmarried for the rest of their days. It is possible for a man to take the edge off the asymmetry only by lavishly outgiving the opposition and by enlisting the support of his children. In a sense, *muli* given as support in *segaiya*, and the equivalence it expresses and establishes over time, can be viewed as an iconic image of the leveling a man undertakes to achieve within his lifetime: his hope for overcoming his individual shame.

As much as any kind of interclan tension, it is "support"—*labe* and *muli*—that is put on display during a *segaiya*. This support is expressed through food and object wealth, the concretizations of individual and collective labor. It is the subject worth looking at in greater depth.

Objects and Projection

For Sabarl, social security and social worth are largely determined by the "power to draw" (*iyomwe pahavina*) supporters for social projects and to "direct" them effectively. This political relationship is modeled in the control of senior persons over junior affines, and it is extended to controlling the public projects of persons who live within one's hamlet and the actions of trading partners with whom one constructs a debt-based relationship involving the exchange of wealth.

In the pursuit of this elusive power and its fullest extension, it is not enough to possess (i.e., to internalize) culturally valued personal attributes: a compelling intellect (*senapu*), acquired knowledge (*siba*), physical attractiveness (*dodohabina*), and a way with words (*lihulihu iposa*) are among the most often mentioned. In addition, one must externalize and project personal attributes and abilities. The cultural vehicles of this process are the valued things that function as "memories" of "custom" itself. On Sabarl, these things fall into two broad categories: portable wealth (*bigebige*) and landed wealth (*kelakela*).

Portable Wealth

Included in the category of portable wealth are significant foods and valuable objects. Such things are social persons' detachable, concretely projectable selves (see Battaglia 1985)—what others can consensually experience of them without knowing or even meeting them. They are also the social person's projective defense against feelings of worthlessness, within a system where the real power lies in ramifying, dispersing, and deploying supporters and wealth, but without losing control over them. From this perspective, giving wealth away is all about rewarding those who dare to expose themselves—to reveal their internalized attributes and, I shall argue, even their corporeal ones—as they invest their power to draw in things that represent them in space and time.

FOOD WEALTH

As I mentioned earlier, Sabarl have a special regard for foods that were the "choice" or "real foods" (*hanhan suwot*) of their ancestors—foods that are featured in *segaiya*. To review the basic categories briefly, real foods are divided into dry-lean (*kevekeve*) and greasy-sweet (*posa*). Yams and sago are the archetypally dry-lean foods; pork, fish, and coconut are the archetypally greasy-sweet ones. Within the dry food category, yams and sago represent respectively the feminine and masculine forms of food wealth, just as flesh and bones are regarded as the fundamentally dry feminine and masculine substances of the human body. Dry foods are said to be "complemented" or "completed" (*gaba*) by the greasy foods associated with masculine activities, as fat in the body is supplied within the womb by men. Pigs represent such foods as wealth.

Beyond forming the "base" of a feast (the means of feeding large numbers of people), yams (*laha*) and sago (*kabole*) are formally exchanged and distributed as wealth. The economic value of yams in this context is calculated in baskets, whereas sago is wrapped up in chunks and bundled into countable pairs.

Like sago, pigs (*seseyan*) are valued individually. But unlike either of the dry wealth foods, pigs are "path" (*hiyela*) wealth, sought out and exchanged for other pigs or for object wealth by partners whose connection is the "path" of reciprocity and debt. Alternatively, pigs may be "purchased" (*pamola*) as commodities. Pigs are distinguished as "domestic" (*bohiyeba*) and "wild" (*bekik*), although only domestic pigs are considered appropriate for exchanges between partners. They are sized as "tusked" (*sok*), standard (*seseyan*), and "juvenile" (*natu-natu*—"too small to be carried on a pole").[5]

The gift of a pig as part of *muli* (affinal support) on commemorative occasions creates a "debt" (*vaga-*) that must be canceled on a future occasion—similarly with gifts of "pork pieces" (*bunima*). Pigs are the quintessentially masculine expressions of affinity. They literally "grease" interisland political trade between partners, who are traditionally members of each other's fathers' matriclans. Since husbands and wives ideally have their fathers' matriclans in common (this actually happens about one-third of the time), pig exchanges model the articulation of two clan groups and the coordinated efforts of junior and senior males.

We have seen how in the tales of Katutubwai the monster himself may take the form of a pig that meets its end at the hands of trickster children. Contemporary junior affines inherit the problem of this original termination—the termination of the aggressive patrilineal principle. It is their challenge to restore the pig during *segaiya*.

Overall, the dry-lean foods are spoken of as "support" for the pigs, and conversely, what the affines supply in general as "support" for the kin's sponsorship.

OBJECT WEALTH

Object wealth, when it appears on the scene of *segaiya*, upstages food wealth entirely. Basically, there are two types of object wealth. One includes relatively permanent things that, like pigs, are counted and exchanged individually. These permanent, unit-value objects are called *gogomwau*. They consist most importantly of canoes (*waga*), "green-stone" ax blades (*tobwatobwa*), chama shell necklaces (*bak*), and beaded spatulas used for eating lime powder (these limesticks are called *gobaela* in the form of ceremonial wooden objects, *hiyenga* in utilitarian turtle shell), as well as clay pots (*huye*), pieces of gold-lip shell (*daperli*), black-lip shell spoons (*kepu*), wooden sago pudding stirrers (*hepovine*), wooden platters (*nohai*), and money (*mwani*). Store-bought cooking and eating utensils are sometimes counted as *gogomwau*, and I will explain why shortly. Basically, *gogomwau* are the object counterparts of pigs in that they represent the masculine mode of production.

A second variety of object wealth includes the relatively ephemeral things economically valued and exchanged in bulk. Such things are called *palo*: "things too numerous to count," mixed up together and measured in "piles." The primary *palo* items are coconut-leaf skirts (*vali*) and pandanus mats (*lam*) and baskets (fancy personal baskets called *tiltil* and larger utility baskets called *yogowa*), as well as cloth and store-bought clothing. All these items must be new, never worn or used, in order to be counted as *palo* (cf. Weiner 1976 on Trobriand "women's wealth"). They are displayed in women's exchanges as jumbled piles representing the undistinguished products of many women's labor.

Palo is spoken of as "support" for the *gogomwau*, as (according to the Sabarl) women support men, clan groups support individuals, and yams support pigs. Quickly amassed in "one place" and just as quickly dispersed, like the children of the matriclan, like the yams of matriclan gardens, it represents in effect female substance and the natural yield in feminine labor objectified. That is, it is feminine strength reproduced as a cultural icon of collective strength—moreover, strength that is easily collected and redistributed on short notice.

The counterpart of *palo* in the marriage context is the red shell necklace, which is emblematic of bridewealth (*wisebua*). Shell necklaces are forever being taken apart and restrung into shorter "chokers" (called *samwakupwa*) for children and youths, then recombined into long "lines" or "sides" for use on ceremonial occasions. The *bak* is procured by senior women through their daughters and reinvested in their sons when bridewealth is needed, or in land purchases. However, women do not manufacture shell necklaces (which are for the most part the handiwork of Yele or Tagula males) and are therefore only comanagers of them.

Wealth, Power, Gender

Sabarl emphasize a distinctive division of labor wherein women "help" men to produce or procure "masculine" (*moluwani*) things and men "help" women with "feminine" (*yoyova*) things. They refer to this arrangement as working *sabsabarl*—that is, working across the grain of cultural models elsewhere in the region in order to survive in a "hard" place.

However, what emerges when we look at food and object wealth together is a cultural predisposition to label as "masculine" the production and procurement of things that are more durable and individually valued (unit-value objects, pigs, and sago) and as "feminine" production and procurement of things that are more ephemeral and collectively valued (yams and bulk wealth). The former are furthermore always displayed in contexts of exchange as discrete items and manipulated in one-on-one exchange transactions, whereas the latter are placed in piles representing a group's contributions, where the group represents the matriclan in interclan exchanges. It is interesting that certain things that are marginal in this regard—for example, relatively permanent things that are given unit value but are easily divisible (money, store-bought domestic utensils, shell necklaces, sago)—are most prone to control by women and to a *sabsabarl* mode of production.

Sabarl tend to emphasize not the gender-linked nature of domains of production and exchange, but rather gender-specific *modes of imaging* strength—control over convergence, control over divergence—in wealth form. Permanent, unit-value things are said to "draw" people. However, it is difficult to collect such things and people in one place: they are inherently scatter prone, and it is men who typically are expected to chase after and control them. Ephemeral, collective wealth has no such magnetic quality. In the context of *segaiya*, what is inscribed through the patterned control of these two types of wealth, both of which possess as a positive quality ease of assembly and disassembly, is the value of reconstructing "memory." To trace the movement of wealth is to trace the dynamics of cultural mnemonics.

If wealth is the vehicle and evidence of one's "image viability" in the realm of exchange, "land" (*kelakela*) is the means by which one's place on the social landscape is "anchored" to a material historicity. This is the subject we turn to now.

Four

Gardens and Sago Groves

An interview with a six-year-old girl:

> Q: Do you like going to the gardens?
> A: Oh, yes! We plant bananas and potatoes and taro and pumpkins. Our parents plant yams.
> Q: And do you help make sago?
> A: We help with sago. Cut out the pith with an ax. Boys and girls, men and women. Mostly we go with our mother and father, also our uncle. Our bodies really pain, so we don't sing. And we do not sing in the garden. We respect the yams. [There] we put on a new grass skirt.
> Q: Why?
> A: Because the yams like to see our bodies looking nice and smelling nice.
> Q: And if you don't wash?
> A: The yams shrivel.
> Q: Do you like gardens or sago work best?
> A: The gardens!

A Word about Gardens and Sago Groves

Until very recently, cultivable land was not perceived to be in short supply in the Saisai islands. For Sabarl, the gardens and sago groves of Hemenaha have been yielding adequately since late last century, supplemented by the ample resources of Panatinani. In 1976 Hemenaha gardens were lying fallow an average of five years. Although this is considerably less than the ten years agriculturalists recommend, Sabarl gardeners had not then begun to plant in inferior "red soil" before the richer "black soil" had reappeared—this being the indigenous sign of soil depletion. However, by 1986 the fallow period had shrunk to three or four years, the soil at planting was predominantly red, and there was widespread consternation.[1]

Partly the problem was and remains one of population expansion. Ten years earlier, an especially farsighted Sabarl leader named Stefan had already announced that ancestral spirits were moving to Panatinani because of overcrowding in Haniewa—the main spirit village on Hemenaha. This meant that spirits would be locally available to watch over Panatinani subsistence activities.

Meanwhile, Stefan had himself acquired a supplementary garden on Panatinani, in spite of the discomfort and risks of swarms of mosquitoes, crocodile-infested swamps, large herds of wild pigs, and roving spirits of the unburied dead. Two couples from Maho village were already gardening on Panatinani's north side when he made the move. By 1986 the number of gardening couples had grown to thirteen, four of them with residences built out over the sea on spindly piers, beyond the mosquitoes, four with substantial houses in the bush. All the persons involved continued to maintain permanent residences in Maho village and returned there during the months between planting and harvesting. Only one-third continued to garden at Hemenaha.

Panatinani landowners were meanwhile becoming anxious about the trends they perceived on Hemenaha and announced that they were raising the price of land they once sold outright to Sabarl for the price of a modest secular feast (*sulihi*) to something close to the cost of a new canoe. At a meeting of the Panatinani clans in 1981, it was established that the people of Kuanak, some of the Panabarli, and a worrying trickle of newcomers from Utian (Brooker Island) farther "down" the Chain would henceforth be required to pay clan owners from K5 to K10 per sago palm—the demand for sago having increased as gardens shrank. Sabarl were given special dispensation owing to their "hard" *sabsabarl* existence; also because of a history of intermarriage with the Panatinani. Nonetheless, tempers ran hot at the time, and Sabarl I spoke with had no sense that their problems with the Panatinani had been resolved in any permanent way.

However, the balding hills of Hemenaha had another cause besides overuse of the soil. I was walking one day with a young married man named Peter along a path to his family gardens. The path wound through the vast Hemenaha fields of useless kunai grass, in and out of scorched patches of earth that looked from a distance like the shadows of clouds on the pale landscape. We had just been discussing the barrenness of the terrain, so much less arable than ten years before, and I had been ranting about the "custom" of burning the kunai and preventing the return of secondary growth. Peter was nodding solemnly in agreement—when suddenly he pointed to a blackened patch we were just approaching and announced with evident pride: "My father burned that." Needless to say, I stopped short and, embarrassed, quietly asked him to tell me his father's story.

It seemed that on his way to the garden one day, Peter's father had noticed that lying in the path were two pieces of grass, knotted loosely together. Instantly he knew by this sign that a sorcerer had gone ahead of him, working malevolent magic on those coming after. He therefore lost no time setting fire to the grass on either side of the path, purging the area of evil forces, then patiently waited for the ground to cool and continued on his way. Because of his quick eye, he had saved himself and innocent others also.

This is not the place to discuss the workings of sorcery beliefs on the peace of mind and daily routines of Sabarl people, but certainly in regard to gardening they figure strongly. Away from their villages, Sabarl feel very vulnerable to attacks by enemy spirits. Particularly in their gardens, they fear that others, especially clanmates jealous of the size or quality of their yields (or hoping to acquire the seed), will try to bring harm to them or their loved ones.

How much the fear of sorcery accounts for the generally modest size of Sabarl gardens can only be surmised. It is true that most people make no more than one small garden in ordinary years, although surplus gardens may be planted when owners are planning to host a feast of some kind. It is women who ultimately decide whether to plant surplus gardens, since it is they who control the household's food supply and make decisions about the distribution of food for feasts.

Sabarl islanders make only two types of garden. One is the "large" family garden (*baguya keinana*), the other the "early garden" (*kabu*), usually worked by individuals. A typical large garden might measure 140 by 40 meters and contain some fifteen to twenty baskets of seed yams, with an expected yield of double that number, barring some disaster.[2] Individual gardens are roughly a quarter the size of family gardens, with room for about five baskets of seed yams. Both gardens are worked with bush knives, axes, and digging sticks with or without metal tips.

The types of garden foods regarded as traditional or "real" include yams (*laha*), sugarcane (*tuwa*), betel nut (*lasi*), and tobacco (*laewa*); also arrowroot (*bebaewa* or *Canna edulis*), described as the "first food" of the Sabarl migrants, although today it is peripheral and used mainly for feeding pigs. Only yams (*Dioscorea alata* and *D. esculenta*) are objects of serious efforts to influence the quantity and quality of yield, either by the use of magic words and substances or by attention to technical matters. The space between the yam mounds, usually 60–80 centimeters, is adequate for their development, but overall there is little finesse on the technical side in Sabarl gardening. For example, the vines are left to crawl along the ground, as opposed to being trained upward along poles where the leaves can gather the sun more efficiently. Nor do Sabarl cull inferior tubers or do any very fastidious weeding. People will say that the surest way to keep a garden healthy is to keep it "clear" (*wayaeya*) and "straight" (*lumwalu*), not allowing it to become "jumbled" (*lemwlemwa*) or "polluted" (*galawin*) and overrun by weeds and foul-smelling people and animals. But in fact Sabarl gardens are typically a mess, especially by comparison with, for example, the well-known Trobriand gardens, managed by men whose political identities and efficacy depend so much on them (see Malinowski 1935). My Trobriand assistant, Silipolakapulapola Digim'rina, was shocked in 1986 by his first sight of Sabarl yam vines crawling all over the ground (he was told, "to keep the weeding down") and by what can only be described as a very relaxed gardening aesthetic.

In addition to the "real foods," most gardens contain large proportions of "foreign foods" (*maigololu*). The most important food in this category is sweet potato (*Ipomoea batatas*), sometimes planted separately in plots of flat land called *bwaonu*. In addition there are prickly yams (some seven varieties of *Dioscorea esculenta*), tapioca (*Manihot esculentus*), pumpkin (*Cucurbita moschata*), bananas (some nineteen varieties), pineapple, papaw (*Carica papaya*), tania (*Xanthosoma sagittifolium*), winged beans (*Psophocarpus tetragonolobus*), tomato (*Lycopersicon esculentum*), and taro (four varieties of *Colocasia esculenta* and *Alocasia macrorrhiza*). The fast-growing foreign foods are the main component of the individual early gardens, planted after the yams to feed the workers while they clear and plant the main gardens. Early gardens may also be used as nurseries, supplying seed for the main fields, and in some cases they are the only type of garden a person will plant in a year.

Although in the abstract gardens are described as conforming to an orderly, centralized aesthetic pattern with banana trees in the center of grids created by sugarcane-lined boundary sticks (*biyoyo*), the reality is usually quite different. First, the gridwork of sticks is found for the most part only in large gardens, to indicate boundaries between "plots" (*gungun*). Otherwise there are only perimeter sticks, and plantings are scattered everywhere between the mounds.

In very few cases will a large garden yield enough produce to feed a household beyond October, and while I was staying on Sabarl in 1986

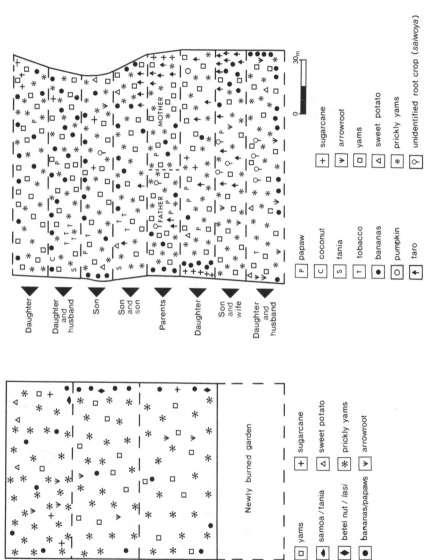

FIGURE 2 "Early" and "large" gardens (survey and map by Silipokapulapola).

and pigs were ravaging the gardens in unusually large numbers, the food was expected to finish by September. Afterward, people turned to store-bought supplementary foods and, of course, to sago. For Sabarl, the value of sago over yams is basically reliability of supply.

So dense are the sago groves and so spiky, the palms are generally not counted individually. The larger groves (*hotn*) tend to be owned and worked by clan groups, while smaller stands (*yawou*) are owned by individuals or sibling sets. Five varieties of sago (*Metroxylon* spp.) are recognized locally and valued according to how "concentrated" (*maha*) they are. Productivity is gauged by the number of bundled pairs of sago chunks the process of leaching the palm of starch will yield. By local estimate, five people typically plan on producing fifty pairs (*bosangat*) of sago in a week, though one variety yields only half that amount and another closer to seventy.

Unlike garden cultivation, Sabarl use no magic words for increasing the yield of the sago palms without increasing labor. Since the dirty, strenuous work of sago making invites no envy, even the most ambitious producers are not subject to attacks by sorcerers or witches on this account.

The Garden's Children

A garden is viewed as a sensuous field—its growing things critically aware of smells, sounds, and appearances. It is itself under constant scrutiny by ancestors who are sensitive to signs of neglect, which they interpret as disrespect for food and for them as the ultimate food providers. People think of their growing food as being "like children," and they see themselves in the role of parents who by giving nurture now will later be nurtured by their offspring. Their particular affection is for yams, the "children of the garden." The yams in turn are believed to recognize their family of gardeners and to shrivel if approached by unauthorized visitors.

Just as children in the womb are delicate and vulnerable to pollution and nutritional imbalances, so the yams must be kept free of pollution and properly cared for. In contrast to sago production, metaphysical procedures are considered essential to the "proliferation" (*parara*) and "fattening" (*tabwa*) of yams.[3]

Pollution

As relaxed as they are about garden tidiness, most Sabarl are very conscientious in matters of pollution, particularly with regard to foul odors (*bwalena ignak*). Of primary practical concern during the bush pig crisis in 1986 was that bad smells might attract pigs. However, odor also affects the sensitive yams directly. People avoid eating turtle or clam meat for several days before entering the garden, since the smell is considered "too strong" (*gaisi*) for the growing yams. They also abstain from sexual intercourse for one to four nights before going to the garden, believing that no amount of bathing would wash away the scent—pleasant and sometimes provocative to adults, but too "strong" for the "children" of the garden. Women stay away from the garden while menstruating and for about a week afterward because of the odor; new mothers until their blood stops flowing; midwives for several days after exposure to the strong-smelling afterbirth; widows and widowers until they have performed a saltwater ritual to cleanse them of the "stench" (*buwonga*) of death. Nor will people go directly from sago making to the gardens, for fear of tracking the reeking sago residue (*mus*) into the garden and polluting the food.

Odors that are less offensive, for example, the "sour" smell of sago or flying fox, are classified as *mwakaskas*, and it is wise for them to be kept out of range of the growing food, though in themselves they are polluting only to a very new garden. Small children's odors (vomit, defecation, etc.) are not considered "bad smells."

It is also primarily owing to smell that "new" clothes are worn in the garden. For example, a woman will put on an old skirt for the wet journey to Hemenaha, then change into a fresh skirt near the shore. Yams record appearances, so that a bright new skirt is a sign that she has bothered to dress up for them. Men and women generally apply a bit of casual face paint from the black mangrove mud and dress their hair with aromatic garlands for garden work.

Finally, joking, rude talk, and even singing are judged disrespectful. Singing is said to attract certain birds with humanlike "voices," for example, the *hatakena* (sulphur-crested cockatoo) and *kulihi* (brown-collared bush turkey), which dig below ground for their food as human beings do. Also, singing indicates that a person's whole mind is not on the yams, for garden magic is "the yams' song" and no other.

The *Muho* Solution

By far the most potent substance used in gardening rituals is *muho*. As I mentioned earlier, *muho* is ambergris, a waxy substance believed to be the fat of human bodies, and from time to time it washes up on the shores of Sabarl Island. Belief in the magical efficacy of *muho* remains widespread (even among those who have substituted nonindigenous substances for it).

Typically, senior clan leaders will claim the chunks of *muho* that drift onto their clan's land anywhere on the island and bring it to the village for distribution. (However, I witnessed a case where *muho* was plucked from the sea by an up-and-coming leader who saw his name etched into it.) Discoveries of *muho* are public knowledge, and once claimed it must be divided between all clan elders, who in turn give shavings to any household head (especially female) who requests it. Should anyone other than the rightful managers attempt to organize the distribution, he or she would be risking immediate attack by *waunak*. There are those who swear to having seen a block of *muho* bleed when cut by the wrong person.

Sabarl gardeners use *muho* either with or without accompanying spells, but they will seek out a clansperson (male or female) who knows the magic words before making do without them. The ritual takes place in the garden a few weeks before harvest. I was told that in the classic version, where all the correct ingredients are used, shavings of *muho* are mixed with coconut oil and the bones of white trevally (*habewa*), then placed in a coconut husk, set alight, and carried round the garden perimeter "in the direction of the sun." While the mixture is burning, magic words are "sung" to the yams and charmed ginger is sprayed over the earth, "closing" the garden until the food is ready to be harvested (about one month later). Afterward the husk is laid in the center of the garden and left to burn itself out.

The extraordinary thing about the *muho* ritual is how explicitly it articulates the logic of recycling masculine energy through the agents of death back into human growth cycles.[4] Basically, the object of the *muho* ritual is to transfer "grease" to garden food. In other words, yams are being treated like fetuses fattened by "father's blood" within the womb. The effects of the grease are carried on the pungent odor of the *muho* mixture, "guided" into the yams by the magic words. It is said that *muho* from one chunk should never be mixed with shavings from another—that is, from a "different person"—or the mixture will become "mixed up" and "polluted" (*galawin*) and the "children" of the garden will shrivel. As we have seen, a similar notion exists in connection with pregnancy beliefs, where mixing the semen of different men obstructs conception and endangers fetal development.

We have also seen that *muho* is described as body fat. Its waxy whiteness embodies the glow of health, heat, and strength *in surplus* and reflects the extra measure of survival within the human body. Likewise, the large white trevally that school abundantly at the start of the harvest season have strong associations for Sabarl of all of these things, which the bones of the fish represent in concentrate. Indeed, the *muho* mixture is explicitly said to make the yams "bright and fat like *habewa* fish." But the *habewa* ingredient is, in addition, a "memory" for Sabarl of a tale of domestication's triumph over the wild harvests from the sea, and over wild (antisocial) behavior more generally. Until recently, this tale was performed as a ritual celebration of the new year, about the time that the constellation Gamayawi (the Pleiades) appeared in the eastern sky. Although nowadays it is rarely seen,[5] the story is fresh in the minds of young and old, and is fondly retold.

On a night early in the harvest season, the men and boys leave the village to go fishing together for *habewa*. They take along with them a traditional fiber net (*puwot*) with spells woven into the strands. When a school of *habewa* fish is spotted, the men and boys cast and ring the net in the usual way and attempt to close it over the catch. If the fish escape, the young men shout abuse at the older ones and sometimes even dare to strike them—actions normally so unthinkable that young people blush to speak of them. If they are successful, the older men whoop excitedly and "pat their bald spots," taking credit for the catch that could have succeeded only with the help of their experience, magic, and special knowledge of ancestral ways. They return to the beach near the fishing grounds to count and divide the catch. Then, still as it were "backstage" of the ritual action, they dress "to look wild," smearing black and white war paint on their faces and tucking pieces of bush plants into their hair and clothing. When the women see them again it is as a fleet returning to the village with the booty of war.

The women have meanwhile prepared and cooked large quantities of garden food, which they carry in wooden dishes on their heads as they dance out sedately to greet the wild "warriors." However, one man has sneaked on foot across the island well ahead of the others and joins the women on the beach, dancing threateningly with a spear in his hand. This figure is the "jealous husband," out to murder the man who has slept with his wife. At one point he is joined by the women, who stop dancing and begin flinging food at the men in the canoe. Shouting wildly, the men fight back by throwing fish at the women. At this point the jealous husband throws his spear at the men in the lead canoe. However, the spear is caught in midair and the "lover," whooping with the others, jumps out and begins to wade toward shore. He is met halfway by one of the women, who stuffs a whole cooked yam into his mouth, gagging him and symbolically taming him. Afterward the catch is brought ashore and everyone celebrates the start of a harmonious new year.

The bones of the *muho* mixture—the "dry" base of "support" (*labe*) for the human body and an artifact of male nurture—recall the *habewa* scenario and the "hot" (wild) masculine behavior transformed by the mediating efforts of women (their weapon is the "dry" food of the garden) into its "dry," stable counterpart ("bones"), a metaphor of enduring productivity. The final ingredient of the *muho* mixture is the coconut oil candle, which releases the other ingredients to impregnate the garden. Coconut oil, as we have seen, is the classic greasy additive to "dry" foods, with the transforming power to render food dishes "masculine."

Thus we can see that what the *muho* solution amounts to is, first, an inventory of the archetypally "greasy" foods—fish, coconut, and (human) pig. Conjoined with yams, the effect is to unite nurture from sea, village, and garden. Collapsing distinctions between realms of nurture—bringing them all to "one place"—the *muho* ritual constitutes a "memory" of the original creative condition: this world before Enak created distinctions. The ritual is restorative of time before death. Yet to gain access to the creative potential of this "first time" condition, Sabarl "work back" from the present time of distinctions by achieving separations of critical substances from contexts in which they cohere in the present.

In addition, the *muho* ritual conveys an important transfer. For in the form of the *muho* solution, paternal substance (semen, bones, and fat) is routed from the masculine domain of (wild) deep-sea space through the masculine domain of (domestic) residential space that is the site of both graves and houses, to its final resting place in the maternal realm of the garden. It is a journey of metaphoric fertilization-cum-secondary burial.

Stories of Garden and Sago Land Acquisition

The growing shortage of garden land has lately focused Sabarl on acquiring gardens and sago groves (in their view) to an unprecedented degree. Yet even without these pressures, people have traditionally tended to expand their holdings beyond the family garden once they begin to have families of their own. The pattern is clear in the local model of land tenure.

A typical Sabarl garden (*baguya*) is subdivided between the garden's owner and his or her clan heirs. If the owner is a woman, her heirs are her children; if a man, his sister's children. The process of division is a gradual one: children work their way into larger and larger plots as their parents' portions shrink. Because garden land is commonly (and ideally) owned by sibling units, cousins from different clans may find themselves working side by side in adjacent garden sections or plots owned by a parent. However, only clan heirs will have permanent rights to the land they have worked. It is easy to see that over time the lots might become very small and that individuals might be motivated to purchase or otherwise acquire rights to garden land elsewhere or to buy out their cousins. Also, as I mentioned earlier, people look to supplement garden food by expanding their sago holdings. It is useful to consider some of the ways they manage to do so.

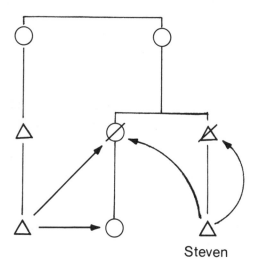

Steven

FIGURE 3 Land acquisition, story 1.

STORY ONE: *WEWEL*

Steven's father owned a lush piece of garden land on Hemenaha, with a river running through it. Lining the river were pockets of sago palms. His father was old and no longer able to work the land, which he had inherited from his mother. The land had been owned by her clan for as long as anyone could remember. Steven had worked it with his parents ever since he was a small boy, having at the age of six been given the use of a tiny plot for raising manioc and sweet potatoes. Over the years the plot grew as his father's portion shrank.

Meanwhile, Steven's father's sister's daughter (FZD) had been given an adjacent plot of the same property. Steven called this cousin "my father." It was she who nurtured him with gifts of food and valuables in his father's name when he was ill and who would inherit or "consume" at his death a sizable amount of wealth from his clan. Had Steven been allowed by ancestral law to marry her, they would have consolidated their portable and landed wealth within their lifetimes. As it was, he married a woman without much land of her own, and his cousin married a land-rich man from Mamanila and moved there with him. Steven saw it would be helpful to continue to use his father's land: his own mother had several older sisters, each with many children to feed, and there was little of their own clan land to go around. Thus, shortly after he was married, he presented his father with K10 and two ax blades as a first "use payment" for the land he knew and had worked for most of his life. The payment was called *wewel* ("fresh water"), and its meaning takes us deep into *sabsabarl* consciousness.

In its most limited sense, "water" payments are made to a clan other than one's own—though ideally one's father's—to secure vital access to the minimal survival resources of sago and fresh water. If his own matriclan were ever to fail him, Steven would be able to provide for his family from the safety net he had constructed with his father over a lifetime of "water" payments. Often, as in Steven's case, a *wewel* payment earns a person access not only to water and sago, but also to adjacent garden land. For Sabarl, "water" land inspires a special debt of gratitude to the paternal clan, which has no standing obligation to route its resources through those who are not clanspersons.

Steven commented that he would always remember his father for this kindness. Nonetheless, when his father died, Steven's use rights were automatically canceled. He renewed the contract through his father's younger sister, making new "water" payments to her. But he was unable to amass the wealth he needed to make a substantial gift of pigs and valuables to his father's clan at the commemorative feasts where claims to continued temporary or permanent use are traditionally made. Likewise when his father's sister died. With both of his one-to-one relationships defunct, his gifts of inter vivos wealth were easily overpowered by a more distant cousin (his FMZSS), who gave lavishly at both his father's and his father's sister's mortuary feasts. The outcome: Steven was allowed by the distant cousin to continue to use a small portion of his father's land, out of "respect" for the work he had put into the land and for his "water" payments over the years, but his children would have no use rights at all. Steven commented somewhat

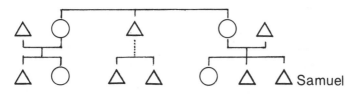

FIGURE 4 Land acquisition, story 2.

bitterly that the cousin should simply have married Steven's cross-cousin "father" long ago and saved himself the wealth. The land, meanwhile, was lost to his father's clan, Steven's father's sister's child having lost interest in it since moving to her husband's place at Tagula.

STORY TWO: EMOTIONS, AGE RANKING, AND DESCENT

Samuel and his two elder siblings lived at Nimowa village with their mother and father. Their mother had moved to Nimowa from Sabarl at the time of her marriage, leaving behind an older sister and brother. Samuel had developed close ties of affection and support with his mother's brother—closer and "more emotional," in fact, than those of his older sister's children in the same village. They were also closer than his uncle's own adopted sons, who had moved away to the mainland, married, and found work there in Alotau.

As the uncle grew old and too frail to work the large holdings of land he shared with his siblings, he began to hand over his land to Samuel, regardless of the "rule" favoring senior sisters' senior children. When his uncle died, Samuel planned to finalize the transfers by outgiving his senior cousins at their uncle's mortuary feast and taking control of all of his uncle's garden and sago lands. He doubted this would be a problem: they would feel a moral obligation, he said, to give him land out of gratitude for his years of attention to their uncle, "just as if he had been [their] uncle's child." Also, they were far more interested in securing their uncle's residential land, which they had no intention of allowing his wayward sons to win away from them. For this purpose they would want to reserve their traditional wealth for the "fight" with money the sons might wage from their work base in town.

Meanwhile, Samuel's older brothers and sisters were pleased, since through their younger brother they would have rights as siblings to use of the land. In short, Samuel was on his way to "feeding his *tubu*"—his matrilineal progeny—through his sensitivity and constancy.

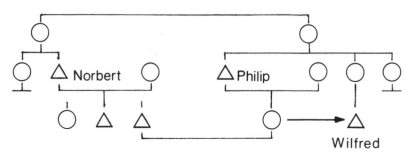

FIGURE 5 Land acquisition, story 3.

STORY THREE: PATRILINEALITY AND DESCENT

There were once two Maho clan cousin "brothers" named Norbert and Philip, who were very close friends and lived side by side in a Panabarli village. Between them the two men held a great deal of adjacent garden and residential land. Norbert had several children, but his sister was childless. Philip had a girl child. His sister's son Wilfred had no interest in the land, having received large parcels on another island from his mother's childless sister, whom he "looked after" there.

Wishing to consolidate their land "out of friendship," Philip arranged with Norbert for his daughter to marry Norbert's son. Together they would then acquire the land from Wilfred, the uninterested heir. The purchase would require a special "land transfer feast" or Tagalekeleke, rather than gifts of wealth at the deaths of Norbert and Philip, since the land would be moving outside their clans. Furthermore, because the mothers of Norbert and Philip had initially acquired the land from their Guau clan father, the Guau clan would have to be compensated equally. It is thus that the memory of past payments, but not of past ownership, dies with each generation. The land continued an erratic patrilineal descent, which Norbert's son hoped would carry on into the next generation, since "now there is pressure on land, it is better that men control it because a woman might not be strong enough and might lose it." Specifically, his concern was that a woman might move away to live at her husband's place and not be able to work the land and keep her claims alive.

STORY FOUR: *POWON* AND PURCHASING

Toby lent his maternal uncle a number of ax blades, which the uncle needed to "purchase" (*pamola*) a piece of garden land from a distant cousin "brother" on another island. The uncle had asked for the ax blades rather than waiting to see if Toby would produce them as an

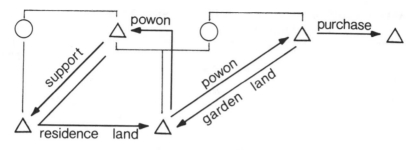

FIGURE 6 Land acquisition, story 4.

"offering" (*toto-*) of his support on the day of the purchase feast. Thus it was understood that his was a formal "loan with interest" (*powon*), to be repaid, if possible, during the uncle's lifetime.

Meanwhile, Toby was also asked to lend his mother ax blades with which to support his father in "helping" his father's sister's son purchase a canoe. Again this was *powon*, but Toby made it clear that his father need not rush to repay him: Toby had his sights set on his father's residential land. If his father died before repaying the loan, his father's sister's son would "remember" the loan that had benefited him and take responsibility as clan heir for repaying it. Furthermore, since Toby would have waited beyond his father's lifetime, a substantial amount of interest would have to be returned to him as well—two or three times the amount he would have received in vivo.

In fact, this is what occurred. Because *powon* was involved, it was incumbent on the heir to "repay the loan" (*powon lase*) very shortly after the death, "to wash his dirty hands of it" (*nimabikina*). The interest alone constituted a substantial reduction in the amount the heir would require to hand over the residential land. As a result, Toby was "strong" enough to persuade his FZS to give him possession of the property. Meanwhile, his uncle repaid his loan within a few months, adding as interest a small section of the garden that Toby's loan had helped him purchase.

*

From these stories, the guiding principles of land transfer emerge against the dual realities of a regional system and the idiosyncrasies of personal history.

In theory, land should descend through the matriclan, from senior to junior siblings. However, alternative mechanisms, culturally endorsed and prominent, ensure the option of use, purchase, and postmortem inheritance by junior clanspersons and by persons outside the

TABLE 6　Landholding Survey (Adjusted, 1986): Sago Groves and
Gardens, Maho Village

	Garden Land	Sago Groves
Females	23　(47%)	18　(44%)
Males	26　(53%)	23　(56%)
Total	49 (100%)	41 (100%)

Note: Households surveyed, 29 (78%); largest male and female landholders omitted.

TABLE 7　Maho Land Acquisition Survey, 1986

	Garden Land	Sago Groves
Acquired from father's side	38　(68%)	31　(72%)
Acquired from mother's side	13　(23%)	9　(21%)
Acquired from neither side	5　(9%)	3　(7%)
Total	56 (100%)	43 (100%)

clan who have affective ties to the original owner and a history of having supported the owner in the traditional forms of labor and wealth.

The central relationship in most interclan land transfers is that of a father and his children. Considering not the ideal scenario of descent but what actually happens, we see in fact that garden land and sago groves are acquired from the father's side significantly more often than from the mother's side.

The proving grounds of all claims to land, whether from within the clan or outside it, are the mortuary feasts for the most recent owners. Even a generous and consistent history of in vivo giving will not obviate the need to give lavishly "in the memory" of the dead. In part this is a veiled expression of the cultural value ascribed to sibling solidarity over individual contracts established when the owner was alive: ultimately, land descends to sibling units, and sibling coordination makes them potentially the readiest to amass the wealth required for large-scale mortuary giving. If the sibling unit is from within the matriclan, they will not have to face the work of reestablishing their land claim with each generation: other clans may petition them with wealth, but at least in recent history, there is little likelihood of their challenging holding rights. However, if the unit is, for example, the sons and daughters of a deceased male landowner, their progeny will face the eternal specter of challenges by their father's clan descendants, no matter what price they paid to win the land for themselves originally.

Although land quite regularly moves between clans, there is a feeling that garden seed in particular should stay within the clan, and if possible within the lineage. Typically, seniors will give some seed to clan juniors who help in the gardens (although seed does sometimes move between clans in this way also). In addition, seed may be purchased from outside the clan as a commodity—usually in exchange for sago or lime—though it remains a preference to buy from a clan member on another island.

This retentive attitude toward seed yams is an index of their value and meaning to Sabarl—and I will return to the matter later in discussing food as wealth more fully.

Working *Sabsabarl*

There is, in the tradition of small-scale societies everywhere in Melanesia, a tendency among Sabarl for part of the work of subsistence to fall to one sex or the other. For example, in gardening men tend to clear the land, burn off the secondary growth, and build the mounds and dig the holes for planting seeds; women, meanwhile, plant and harvest and do most of the weeding. The garden shelters (*nakanaka*) that are built just outside the perimeter of any sizable garden are the work of men.

Likewise in sago making: men cut down the sago palms, and women join them in stripping the bark and beating the pith. Women also fetch water for leaching the starch from the pith, which is done by both sexes. It is usually men alone who break the solidified sago into chunks and wrap them in leaf casings to form paired bundles.

The Sabarl habit of downplaying gender distinctions at the level of praxis—stressing complementarity and junior/senior asymmetries over gender-based ones—is misleading. For against the social "facts," men continue to praise "women who work like men" (*tabwa moluwani*) while disparaging "men who work like women" (*tabwa yova*). Thus women are encouraged to do the hard labor of men in the gardens and sago groves, to sail large canoes, develop trading partners on their own for finding valuables and pigs, organize feasts, and the like. This, both sexes will agree, is *sabsabarl:* working across traditional categories to increase the chances of surviving in a place that is "only stone." But for a man to spend too much time with infants or to cook in his house or go too often with his wife to make lime is judged somewhat disgraceful, and neither women nor men will respect him for it.

Nonetheless, dividing up the work of the gardens and sago groves is emphasized less among Sabarl than sharing the load. So it is that gardens and groves may be owned by either men or women but "call to mind" the couple who work together there. It is in fact more usual to come across mixed-clan teams of husbands, wives, and their junior affines and grown children making sago than to come across single-clan work teams. Similarly for garden work, which often falls to the nuclear family. If asked about the anomaly, people will simply, again, say "*sabsabarl*": a survival strategy. Indeed, in this region the only women to work sago at all are Sabarl.

We see now another dimension of the question posed in the first chapter: What is the created "object" of cross-sex marital relations? One answer, of course, is the children of the marriage. As an artifact of the Sabarl sociocultural process, including working *sabsabarl*, a child embodies the notion of the fluidity of work across gender categories that Sabarl couples historically stand for with respect to survival and that predicts a future for the Sabarl people. However, the mother's "bothness" as a mother plus a substitute father in growing the baby's body leads us to further conclusions. For it is this that validates, possibly even motivates, her efforts afterward to go beyond herself as a woman, to "work like a man": she does it for her child, identified with the child as the social product of masculine and feminine energies and modes of productive "work."[6] Her own brother is her logical extension in this regard.

In contrast to the routinized giving of mothers, extended in social space through mothers' brothers as directors of lineage land, the giving of his own substance and resources is for the father episodic and overtly linked to situations of mortal risk. As discussed in chapter 3, the first time his child falls seriously ill, a father will arrange for a sister's son or daughter to present the child with a young coconut (likened to young bones), in a gesture of "strengthening the bones" of his offspring. The relationship between the cousins will continue throughout the child's lifetime, and at his or her death this paternal cross-cousin (ideally) will be rewarded or "fed" for the care he or she has shown. Put in the context of land, substitute fathers in this way displace to the village what actual fathers accomplish in the sago groves with gifts of "water" land. Moving "fall-back" resources from the margins of domesticated space toward the center of cultural life, they bring public attention to focus on the father-child bond when giving "from the heart" is most apt to be forgotten.

The point here is that cross-sex relations between a man and his sister alone produce a very different kind of object. The new relationship is still about social survival, but survival through death (here equated with continuing dependency), not self-sufficiency. It is fitting that the cross-cousin unit, the "addition to the identity" of a man and his sister, should be, in a sense, a negative artifact: a relationship that stands for a vacancy—for the absent father and for paternity in a matrilineal society. Land-use patterns inscribe the distinction as one between the pitted path of dependency on fathers and the straightforward access to resources of the matriclan. *Sabsabarl* work patterns, which are viewed and experienced as a solution to an "islander" predicament, "cover" the distinction with a circumscribing cross-sex productivity.

Five

Support

The central place of married couples and their corps of junior affines in Sabarl thought and cultural practice creates a dialectical tension with clanship that lies at the core of social dynamics. We need to mark this relationship carefully as we turn to discuss the alliance process and its artifacts.

Edmund and Melissa are a young couple, recently married and living together in their own house on Edmund's father's land in Maho village. The story of their courtship and marriage is a typical one. The two grew up together in Maho (it is still preferred to marry within one's village), and after a period of "trying out" other partners from about age sixteen to eighteen, they settled down to form a steady domestic partnership. Both Edmund and Melissa describe these single days as a time of intrigue and pleasure, but also of considerable anxiety.

First there was the matter of attracting lovers. Edmund worked hard for his father and maternal uncle, hoping to gain possession of their magic spells for attracting girls (*helovanakau*, "looking for women": "You put the words in her betel nut, and while she's chewing she is suddenly aroused and thinks of you"). Melissa, meanwhile, worked for her mother, hoping to be given spells for "attracting single men" (*helobobola*). Perhaps needless say, the work they were doing for others in itself made them attractive to potential marriage partners and their families. For Edmund the pressures were greater. Not only did he need to keep a steady stream of "love gifts" (*buwa*) flowing in the form of betel nut, money, tobacco, and the like to the girl he had chosen, but he also had to show himself a hard and consistent worker to the ever-watchful village elders in order to be judged "suitable" for marriage. Edmund had been raised to believe that wives were scarce and difficult to win. As a young boy, he and his friends had fantasized about marrying well and joining mature society as men to be taken seriously. Melissa's parents meanwhile were eager to see their daughter married to the kind of man who would sooner rather than later provide her (and her lineage) with a canoe.

Canoes are the most valued wealth objects on Sabarl, in both utilitarian and prestige terms. They are also objects that women do not possess the skills to manufacture. The vital importance of canoes turns on the simple fact that the sea separates people from what they need in order to survive. People speak of *sabsabarl*, the hard way of atoll life, as the single most important motivation for seeking the security of marriage—of acquiring through alliance the surety of access to transport and food and water, as well as a labor force of supporting affines.

Once they had decided to marry, Melissa and Edmund sought the approval of their fathers, who consulted with their mothers. The following day Melissa sent word to Edmund that her parents had consented, and he began asking his relatives (parents, uncles, and older siblings especially) for "help" in assembling his "bridewealth basket" (*nabwa luluwoli*).

Typically, bridewealth takes the form of a utility basket (*yogowa*) filled with items representing the wealth procured or manufactured by the men and women of the groom's line: from the women, a good grass skirt or a length of store-bought cloth, one or two sleeping mats, a few enamel dishes and utensils, five to ten fancy personal baskets, and sometimes money (K2 normally, or about K20 if a woman is earning a regular wage); from the men, perhaps one stone ax blade, one or two store-bought shirts or pairs of trousers, and money (from K2 to K10 normally, or about K30 if wage earners are contributing). Last and most important, the basket should contain one or two long "sides" (about 1 meter) of a red shell necklace. This necklace, which is an emblem of bridewealth, is placed inside its own small personal basket (*tiltil*) and constitutes "earnest wealth" toward the day when the groom can supply his bride with a canoe.

On the day of the "betrothal" meeting (*kaukauwalolu*), Edmund and his kin went to the house of Melissa's parents and sat down in a group on the floor across from them. This was the occasion to discuss the marriage arrangements (where the new couple would be living, the bridewealth details, etc.) and to voice any objections to the alliance. Objections range from trivial observations about a boy's appearance to serious ones concerning his work behavior: "he has no garden," or "he never makes sago." Everyone will have been quite aware of these problems beforehand, so that mentioning them here serves only to "shame" him in front of his kin—and them by implying that the boy was not raised properly. In such a case they would all leave quietly, without rebuttal. But in Melissa's house the mood was serious yet pleasant as Edmund presented the basket of wealth to his bride, who in turn passed it along to her mother. Missing from it was the emblematic necklace, which Edmund had promised would follow—as it often does a year or so later, after any serious problems with domesticity have either been worked out or not.

A childless marriage where no bridewealth necklace has changed hands is easily dissolved; the bride simply returns to her natal home. If a necklace is involved the dissolution is more complicated, requiring discussions between the families and settlement decisions. On Sabarl Island in 1976, there had been only three such dissolutions within living memory, compared with seventeen that year alone on Nimowa in a population half the size. When I asked about the discrepancy, I was inevitably answered in a single word: *sabsabarl*. It was a matter of social security in such a "hard place." In fact, answers lie more deeply buried, as I will shortly explain.

Melissa's mother accepted the basket that night, and after the guests had left she distributed its contents. The "men's things" went to her brother to distribute to other uncles and nephews; she herself distributed the "women's things" to aunts, nieces, and Melissa's older siblings. The necklace she eventually received she would keep to manage as she chose, ideally reserving it to help a son in his attempts to marry or else using it in mortuary distributions—for example as a "peace offering" to the clan of her "child" cross-cousin at his death.

The necklace is significant symbolically, but not merely symbolically. On the one hand, its two "sides" can be seen to image the two matrilines brought together by this marriage (see Battaglia 1983a); its constituent beads represent the generations of countless women of the matrilines and the red mother's blood that constitutes the "flow" of societal continuity. It is also the hopeful image of the daughter's future role in that reproductive process, and the mother relinquishes control over it to her son-in-law with the acceptance of this concrete artificial substitute. Not surprisingly, mothers and daughters become very attached to these necklaces, and I have seen women openly weep when pressured to part with them. With the gift of a bridewealth necklace, a man claims the right to "direct" (*-logugui*)[1] the futures of children of that marriage—as it were, exchanging an artifact of cultural posterity for the real thing. Meanwhile the female recipients can only hope to use it to "reclaim" to the matrilineage such valued resources as land or canoes or the support of their sons' children.

For a few days following the betrothal, Edmund was forbidden to sleep with Melissa inside her house, as he had been doing secretly and "very, very quietly" for years. Instead, they met in the bush as he waited for Melissa to one day call him to her parents' house and, in daylight, invite him to eat with them. This act of "eating together," *hanpase*, is the marriage ritual proper. That night he stayed in the house with the parents' consent, talking with them until dawn—the parents joking about their plans to work him to death in the days and years to come when they "directed" him as a junior in-law, or *tovelam*. Meanwhile, having taken the days between betrothal and marriage to prepare a new sleeping mat, bedsheets, and pillow for their future years of "licit sex" (-*hanapean*, as opposed to "illicit sex," -*dubwale*), Melissa was herself preparing to leave her natal home for that of her husband.

The "Trick" of Tubu

The courtship and marriage of Edmund and Melissa was a model of Sabarl propriety in every respect save one: the marriage was incestuous.

Sabarl prohibit marriage between persons "within the body" of the matriclan (*hun*), as well as between cross-cousins (MBC or FZC—called *nubaiu*). In the latter case exceptions are made if a great deal of property, especially land, stands to be gained by the alliance. Ideally, however, it is the nonclan children of the cross-cousins who will marry and consolidate holdings.

Marriage to anyone in the relationship of *tubu* to oneself is likewise proscribed. The term is applied bilaterally to all relatives of the grandparents' and grandchildren's generations—the generational poles—although its meaning on Sabarl is primarily in terms of the "respect" owed to seniors and the "shyness" (*mwalina*) shown in their presence. As I will discuss shortly, this is so regardless of the fact that one calls *tubu* certain relations other than grandparents and grandchildren.

Tubu relations represent the threat of the clan distinctions' collapsing persons into an exclusionary relationship of identity. I was told: "A young *tubu* cannot call the old ones by their names, otherwise the old ones' teeth will fall out like babies' teeth." That is, forget the *tubu* honorific, and seniority collapses into dependency. But the covert message is that the middle generation—the parents of junior *tubu* and the children of senior ones—is dangerously prone to disappearing from the map of property inheritance, of being bypassed altogether owing to the strong security-based affective ties between polar *tubu*. Sabarl refer to this aspect of the *tubu* relationship in the saying that when you are drowning, your "elbow"—your *tubu* relative, who is "close to the body of the clan"—will always pull you out. Thus the mutual identity and solidarity of dependents is seen, paradoxically, to be their strength. Just as the strength of arms and legs is said to lie in the joints that allow them to extend and return to the body, the strength of those persons united at the turning points of descent allows them to turn properly inward toward the clan.

The fear is addressed very directly in the rule against marrying one particular *tubu:* the MMBC, who is the archetypal "elbow" (*nimana pokokona*). This was the prohibition that Edmund and Melissa violated—although, it must be said, with the encouragement of parents who knew he was in love with someone else, who knew of ancestral warnings that the children of this *tubu* union would be born with the tails of pigs, and who nonetheless saw how the "trick" (*tabwayalu*) of marrying a *tubu* would benefit Edmund and his line directly in material terms.

Understanding the "trick" is actually a simple matter of understanding that Melissa's mother had the special relationship to her MBC Edmund of ritual "father." We recall that this is a contractual relationship arranged by parents, wherein Melissa's mother would act as a symbolic father to her "child," giving gifts of nurture on behalf of her maternal uncle, the "child's" natural father. On one level such gifts would be "remembered" with wealth and feast foods as part of honoring the "child" after his or her death. But they were also an expression of her uncle's feelings toward his own children, to whom he should not give directly things that rightfully belong to his sister's children and clan heirs.

Thus, as "father" substitute to her cross-cousin "child," Melissa's mother diverted support away from her clan in a kind of in vivo matrilineal detour to a patrilineal destination, anticipating a postmortem return of the investment to herself and her clan. Consider, then, how the waiting time is canceled if Melissa's mother's cross-cousin "child" marries her own child. What she gives, she now gives to both at once. Such an arrangement concentrates support, preventing the dispersal of valued things within Melissa's mother's generation. It also unites the dependents in a self-serving lock of property within a three-generational triad of *tubu* relations. All *tubu* marriages are "too close to the body" in this sense, threatening to work as a hinge promoting the "turning" or directing of wealth back into the clan, and constricting the possibilities for interclan exchange and alliance.

In talking about the ingrown nature of incestuous marriages, Sabarl use the image of a tree that fails to sprout new buds. Indeed, it is the image of any "story" not properly told so that robust new stories spring from it. Growthlessness is a prominent concern of Sabarl islanders, living in their island world *sabsabarl*.[2]

*

Sabarl marriage rules work on the premise of a three-clan system. Ideally, people marry into clans that are neither their mother's nor their father's. The marriage of Melissa and Edmund circumvented this rule also, creating the ultimately self-contained system. I asked Melissa's parents whether they might not have "tricked" the system more easily by guiding Melissa toward a non-*tubu* marriage within her father's clan—that is, cheating without the danger of producing pig-tailed progeny. (Nearly 50 percent of Maho village marriages were of this type in 1976.) Their response was to draw my attention to perhaps the most critical element of Sabarl alliance, at least in everyday social terms, namely the "junior affine," or *tovelam*, work force that marriages create.

Tovelam

There is no way of overemphasizing the importance and the extent of the transformations wrought in the lives of Melissa and Edmund by their marriage. From this time on, instead of calling each other by their "true names" as they had done all of their lives, they would address one another as "my husband" (*mwaniyeu*) and "my wife" (*poniyeu*) or use each other's baptismal names—names with no deep meaning to them. Furthermore, any persons to whom they related as affines, whatever their former relationship, would be called by affinal terms rather than by any previous relational terms or personal names.

This meant that as well as being brought into relationships with people they knew only slightly, Melissa and Edmund also experienced a stressful and ambivalent transformation of relationships of long-standing intimacy and familiarity into more formal ones, with definite behavioral restrictions. They expected, they said, that for the rest of their lives they would feel uncomfortable with this new formality, and they spoke of using the formal terms with close friends almost ironically. In short, far from merely "bridging" relations between groups (as they are often depicted in anthropological literature), marriages reinforce distinctions and may actually introduce additional conceptual space between persons.

Meanwhile, to all senior affines they would now be known simply as *tovelam*—junior affine: part of an undifferentiated army of junior supporters drafted by marriage into lifetime duty. Of course, they themselves would be acquiring a *tovelam* force as their own junior siblings and children married. But this seemed at times small and distant consolation to the newlyweds as they began their married life and faced a lifetime of "direction" by affinal elders within what in former times resembled the relationship of slaves to their masters (and where the latter had power over life and death). Though this relationship is currently much more relaxed, nonetheless certain seniors do make onerous demands on their *totolamwau* (plural) for labor and material support. There is even a case where a woman's demands on her son-in-law drove him to divorce his wife and kept her other grown daughters unmarried and tied (with illegitimate children) to their natal home.

Basically, what is expected of *totolamwau* is that they make a "gift" or "offer" (*toto-*) of their services and material resources to senior affines, without being asked or ordered to. As I discuss in chapter 9, such actions convey the permanent "shyness/shame" of juniors vis-à-vis seniors more generally in Sabarl society. This "support" translates on an everyday basis as women cooking for their senior female affines, fetching water and firewood for them, tending their young children, bringing them garden food and helping them weed their own gardens, sweeping inside, under, and around the house, and generally anticipating their desires. At the end of each day, junior women bring a plate of cooked food to these women at their homes and have the plate returned with cooked food by young go-betweens in acknowledgment of their routine attentiveness—an exchange known as *talaot*. They also contribute women's "bulk wealth" on ceremonial occasions, in support of their senior female in-laws. Men, meanwhile, who do not usually live within their affines' space and are therefore somewhat freer of their scrutiny, help with the manufacture and routine maintenance of senior affines' canoes, sails, houses, and the like, as well as with sago making. They too offer material support in the form of valuables and pigs, especially when needed by in-laws for hosting mortuary feasts.

It intrigued Sabarl kinship enthusiasts that the terms for "same-sex affine (junior/senior)" differed depending on the sex of the persons involved. That is, Melissa called her husband's mother *yawaniu*, and

Edmund called his wife's father *halayau,* although, for example, both called their "opposite-sex affines (junior/senior)" *bwatau.* The same restrictions on behavior, the same rights and obligations precisely, obtained with either *yawaniu* or *halayau.* Juniors could, for example, "put a hand inside his or her basket," which is the Sabarl way of indicating that a relation is based to some degree on trust (although this is done only with *yawaniu* or *halayau* permission). They could also eat with their *halayau* or *yawaniu.* Neither of these behaviors would have been allowed with a junior or senior opposite-sex affine (*bwatau*).

One explanation for the different terminologies was ventured by a young man who observed that the "roots" of the terms could refer to the different roots of the support-based relationships: the women's in the *yawan* or "domestic quarter," where they are thrown together by virilocal residence, the men's in *hahalau,* "subsistence-related sailing."

If we accept that there may be an experiential component to the *halayau/yawaniu* relationship, then the immutability of behavior toward *bwatau*—opposite-sex affines (junior/senior)—stands out all the more. The archetypal *bwatau* relationship is between young married people and their spouse's opposite-sex parent, extending to their spouse's opposite-sex older siblings. More so than any other relative, a *bwatau* is avoided, deferred to, and otherwise "shown respect" (*hawa guguyonga*). Asking people to speak of *bwatau* relationships elicits an immediate response of "shame/shyness": giggles covered by a hand, downcast eyes, sometimes scratching the scalp and clearing the throat. For example, Melissa would never allow herself to be alone with her husband's father or older brother, and they would never eat together. If they meet unexpectedly on a path, she stoops and makes a gesture of shame in passing. In their presence she quickly covers any gaps in her skirt. In a group she always stoops (*kululu*), walking behind them or slightly bowed. Rising from a sitting position when they are present she stoops and backs away. And rather than walking across their property, she walks well into the surf or through the bush and around it, whenever they are in the house. With a *bwatau,* "you never put your hand inside his or her basket": you are never so intimate as to reach inside a *bwatau*'s personal space.

Interestingly, the only other relative whose basket is completely off limits is a "cross-cousin" or *nubaiu,* the person with whom there is an expectation that a "father-child" relationship will eventually be contracted (as in the case of Melissa's mother and her "child" Edmund, above). It seems, then, that in respecting and avoiding a *bwatau,* as with a *nubaiu*, a distinction or distance is being reinforced at the site of a socially dangerous convergence, the danger in both cases being the proneness to collapse of the asymmetrical ordering that a socially attractive, too-proximate nonclansperson represents. Together, *nubaiu* and *bwatau* stand for the principle of permanent contractual (as opposed to generationally or sexually based) asymmetry, which, as we shall see, occupies a central place in the Sabarl value system, and in the process of commemoration.

One last point needs to be stressed with reference to affinity. In time, Melissa and Edmund should enjoy reciprocity—receiving the kind of support from their *totolamwau* that they give to senior affines. But the ever-present burden of being *totolamwau* themselves, and the undefined and seemingly limitless expectations they imagine their seniors to have of them, dominates any experience of mutual respect or any balance in the scheme of things. You may be a *bwatau* or *halayau* or *yawaniu*, but as long as you are married and junior you are fundamentally aware of being a *tovelam*, and any mutuality that technically exists between you and your senior in-laws, any mutual respect that may develop, is eclipsed by the fact of it. This is true even for leaders of clans and villages.

The question, then, is what one gains by being a good *tovelam*. And the answer is, first, the promise of collective support from senior affines, especially when sponsoring a mortuary feast. Men in particular gain the right to continue to "direct" their own children, even if their wives should die; also, one gains the right to bury a wife and children on one's own land. A woman, meanwhile, works for the right to stay on with her children in her husband's house, as well as to take control of his canoe after he dies. It follows that if children move far away and out of one's sphere of control, or no longer need their parents' assets, the gains for working hard as a *tovelam* are reduced considerably and, as one woman told me, "your heart goes out of it."

The demands on *totolamwau* by senior affines are currently decreasing. Since 1976, "respect" for elders has noticeably diminished as Western forms of authority have become more prominent in the daily run of life at the village level. Increasingly, catechists, school and government committee men and women, and local council representatives carry the voice of the outer world's ideas and dictates to the village in almost daily meetings to coordinate community repairs on public structures, community church services and special events, community cleanups, community fishing and diving expeditions for money to pay an exorbitant head tax—all activities that cut into individuals' time and energy for *tovelam* work. Younger people, with their greater exposure to the world beyond the reach of the Saisai values, still remain too delicate to hurt the feelings of their elders. Quietly, however, young men and women wait in the wings for them to step down or passively fail to offer the help expected.

This is not to suggest that the process is inexorable. In 1986 people were beginning to ignore even the bellowed orders of the district officer-in-charge that community work be increased. It is *sabsabarl*, they said: we cannot take time away from the gardens and the sago for unimportant things. We must attend to our in-laws. But in this year also, there were six unmarried mothers in Maho village alone (up from two in 1976) who had chosen to "work for themselves" rather than "slave" for affines. They lived with parents, using their canoes or the canoes of clan relatives, making ambitious gardens to feed their children (with the exception of two women who had chosen the gardenless "life of a dog" and ate or went hungry according to the resources of their clan elders), but otherwise thinking of their old age not at all.

We are now in a position to appreciate why Melissa and Edmund were encouraged in their incestuous *tubu* marriage rather than marrying into each other's fathers' clans. First, if a *tovelam*'s senior affine (e.g., his wife's father) is a member of his own clan (e.g., his mother's brother) there will be no serious contradiction, since one's attitude toward an MB is exactly the same as toward one's WF or her MB: that is, one puts one's hand inside his basket only with his permission, and one is generally "directed" by him. This is exactly the position of cross-cousins who marry. However, the voluntary, contractual nature of the *tovelam* relationship is done away with: working for what is coming to one as a clan heir is considered very different from making an effort to honor nonclan seniors and in that way earn control over one's own children (in the case of men) or the right to live without shame on one's husband's land (in the case of women). In short, blood ties obviate or "cover" constructed ties with seniors. As we saw in chapter 3, this is exactly the opposite of what is truly valued in Sabarl society, where the effort one makes to give when there is no clan-based obligation to do so is honored over and over again: by the giving between fathers and children, between cross-cousin "fathers" and "children," between a *tovelam* and senior affines. Melissa and Edmund avoided this trap by staying within the three-clan model. Furthermore, by marrying across generations, they gained a generation of *tovelam* supporters—in effect trading off the known assets of Melissa's mother and mother's brother against the unknown quantity of support they

Hamlet leaders Luke and Margaret and two of their children talking on the veranda after the evening meal.

Anastasia at the hearth.

A collection of children at midday in Maho village.

Simon, the Maho catechist, his wife, Diane, and two of their children, Simon-Peter and Debi, beneath the yam house of their Hemenaha garden.

Two cousins, Felicia, and Lucila, bringing firewood to their husbands' mothers.

Men and boys repairing a fishing net at high tide.

Female mourners applying charcoal paint on the day of the funeral of a senior affine.

Women cooking yams and fish behind the village houses in preparation for the feast of Hanyalogi.

Redistributing food at the feast of Hanlekeleke.

The "corpse" of axes at the feast of Moni.

Female mourners surrounding the "corpse" of food, "matched" by object wealth.

A widow is beautified by the *tohan segaiya*.

The tally of unit-value wealth on a path of skirts at the close of the feast of Moni.

Women cutting a sago cake into slices for the feast of Vetantan.

Throwing the spear of debt at the feast of Gebyuwas.

A scene from the Maho village beach at low tide.

might expect from increasingly mobile and uncommitted *totolamwau* in upcoming generations.

For men, the increasing allure of "polygamy" (*boawa*, for which the Sabarl playfully substitute the English term "double"), is directly related to this situation. First, provided they are natural or classificatory sisters, two wives come as cheaply as one in terms of bridewealth—and in all of the three polygamous Maho village marriages in 1986 (up from one in 1976) this was the case. Also, a man stands to gain *tovelam* recruits in the form of children's spouses without increasing his own workload as a *tovelam*. Sabarl women are not generally pleased by this trend, and some have threatened to take a second husband on the model of a woman at Tagula, who is legend: by the rules, *boawa* marriages can go either way.

Edmund and Melissa were launched on their lifetime partnership of "support" (*labe*) and "complementarity" (*gaba*). Yet it remained for Edmund to give one additional item of wealth to his senior affines to "seal" the marriage contract. This item was a canoe, and it would make, as we shall see next, a significant difference to his identity as married man.

Six

Mobility

A marriage does not "come of age" until a man is able to present a canoe to his wife and her people, claiming the paternal right of "direction" over their children. Among young men there is a feeling that, until they can manage to do this, some other man could slip in with a canoe and steal away both wife and children—which incidentally has never happened as far as I can determine. A young married man once commented to me: "When you lie awake at night and you can't sleep, you are worrying. Always you are worrying about only two things: canoes and gardens. It is always these: canoes and gardens."

The "direction" of children consists of the right to shelter, nurture, guide, and support them as long as they live, and in other ways elicit the strong affective ties that will make them want to reciprocate care as adults. This is the root experience of giving "from the heart" (*henununwana*)—without obligation, on one's own initiative. A canoe allows a man to buy in to his future security, assuring him *continuity of influence* through generational time and a future for the memory of the patriline not automatically enjoyed by males within a (nominally) matrilineal descent system. In one man's words: "If I do not give a canoe, my memory cannot travel." Canoes, he says, are like children in this regard. And in most people's eyes, like children they function as mobile "retrieval cues" for the achievement of a marriage.

Marriage is an especially meaningful achievement to men, who are viewed as failures by the "scarce" women of Sabarl if a marriage collapses. In a divorce, it is the man whose "bad ways" are first suspected to have caused the problem, making him an unattractive prospect for remarriage. At the most basic level, a "bad" person is a nongiving person. Thus, by giving a canoe a man covers himself against that accusation at the very least.

In fact, a woman's grounds for divorce or separation on such grounds as physical abuse or neglect shrink considerably once her husband has delivered a canoe, although harsh treatment of women or children can make a man very unpopular—as well as a target for sorcerers and *waunak*. One day I was walking along the beach when ahead of me Bari flew out of his house with an ax in his hand and began chopping furiously at his wife's canoe. He had caught her, I heard later, with another man. In Sabarl terms the reaction was perfectly understandable. Someone who had lost control over his wife revealed the lost control of a part of himself by taking an ax to their marriage canoe, and although no one approved of his "wild" (*bekik*) behavior, they felt this way was better than being violent with her.

The gift of a canoe is a significant achievement in part also because producing even a small canoe is an elaborate project. There are several ways of acquiring rights of ownership, or more exactly "direction," over a canoe. A man can sponsor the building of a new canoe or gain control of the canoe his sister or sister's daughter receives in marriage. A man or woman may also inherit a canoe at the death of a relative or spouse or purchase one outright from a seller—although in both cases I was told that a man will ultimately "direct" the canoe, as women "direct" food. Additionally, people may secure rights of "usufruct" (*yavayava*) by assisting in the canoe's construction, maintenance, or repair or by contracting to charter or borrow it.

Manufacture

Typically, building a large (twenty-foot) canoe without plank sides costs the sponsor and his helpers three to four months of actual labor time, over a period of one to two years. At certain stages, such as cutting the tree for the dugout and dragging it out of the bush to the sea, villagers from several islands may participate. For example, Titipopwa and Danla, two Manilobu clan "brothers" from Mamanila, were building large canoes from trees on their land at Panatinani. Gathering to help them were seventy men, thirty women and as many children, from the villages of Maho, Hebenahine, Tandeyai, and Noholaha on Sabarl, as well as from Mamanila. All the contributors were either "relatives" (*tutuiu*) or junior affines of someone in the work party. By helping with the hard physical labor (in the case of men) or cooking for the men (in the case of women), everyone there was earning the right to use the canoe in the future, especially in an emergency. Similarly for caulking, and for lashing the outrigger to the canoe, the entire population of the village gets involved in one way or another, earning themselves emergency access rights to the finished canoe.

During the manufacture of these large canoes, the degree of cooperation I witnessed, cutting across differences in clan and place and across individuals' agendas, was extraordinary for Sabarl. Apart from major mortuary feasts or government-imposed work projects, these were the only occasions when personal interest merged with something like pure community spirit to generate an affecting image of unified purpose. People seemed delighted—and somewhat surprised—by the sight of themselves working together toward a single goal, and all at one time. They cooked together, ate together in public, and made of these occasions "secular feasts" (*sulili*).

In the days before pacification, Sabarl were known for their small, fleet attack canoes: low outriggers with bush pandanus sails. The first plank-sided sailing canoes (*sailau*) were acquired late in the nineteenth century when Sabarl warriors murdered the crew of a fleet of Panaeati raiders. Lacking hardwoods as well as a continuous tradition of building plank-sided canoes, Sabarl are today still largely dependent for *sailau* upon the Panaeati, whom they like and trust no better than in former times. What continues to perplex me about this trade relationship is that other options do exist. The Panaeati themselves are believed to have stolen the techniques of canoe building from the Utian (Brooker islanders). Utian migrants settled parts of Sabarl, their descendants have traded sporadically in other items, and they continue to build *sailau* for export, though on a much smaller scale than the Panaeati. One problem is that the Utian are not very visible in Saisai waters other than during droughts or famines, when they come in search of water or sago.

Unlike the canoe-exporting societies in the region (see especially Berde 1974; Munn 1983), Sabarl use almost no magical techniques in their own manufacturing process. The men I spoke with alluded to (but would not pass along to me) magic words to impart fleetness. These spells are applied with the whitewash and matte-black charcoal paint that are said to make the dugout resemble a shark.

The fleetness Sabarl seek seems less a goal of the outward journey than of the journey home. In discussions on the subject, the emphasis was on returning, on being drawn back to sources as opposed to striking out. Magic spells applied to the carved pigeons on the points of outriggers have the aim of urging canoes to flock together; of preventing a fleet from becoming scattered. However, magic words are also used in connection with the carved and painted "sequences of signs" (*luluwoli*, glossed as "writing") that specialists apply to the gunwale and prow, and conceivably these could have an opposite goal. The "vocabulary" of these motifs is today quite limited. Once again, I was unsuccessful in obtaining any samples of magic words, and it may well be that a woman would not have been told such secrets under any conditions, the "business" of deep-sea voyaging and fishing being one of the few preserves of exclusively male magical knowledge. This is so despite the pride men take in the technical skill of Sabarl women as deep-sea navigators.

Stories from Ancestral Times

It is not surprising that some of Sabarl's favorite narratives extol the value of creating space for everyone in the work agenda, since everyone counts in times of crisis.

I discussed earlier the Katutubwai tale "The Girl Who Dressed as a Boy," where the woman who later gives birth to the heroine finds no room in the canoes of her village mates, fleeing the island and the specter of death.

In another version, a boy hero slays not only Katutubwai but an eagle and a crab as well. These are archetypal images of death when they appear in Sabarl narratives: the cannibalistic monster, the carrion-eating eagle, and the "hot" red crab with the image of a person in the creases of its shell, which sorcerers use in their homeopathic rites. The boy cleverly tricks and kills the eagle and the crab. Then he makes a canoe of the giant's body, giving it the wings of the eagle as a sail and the crab's shell as a bailer. With the banishing of untimely death from the island, everyone returns to live eternally in peace.

In such narratives, canoes figure most strikingly as coded messages that death has been "finished" (deconstructed) and recomposed or reformulated—literally transformed into something useful, as an enabling vehicle of new social beginnings. The recomposition clears the way for the reunion of the generations and the return to "one place" of the scattered society that is itself a coded reminder of the disintegration and shame that forgetting social obligations can engender. This message comes to contemporary life in cultural patterns of purchase, usufruct, and inheritance.

Purchase

The process of purchasing a canoe is called *leau*. Currently the term refers to the sequential payments of many types of wealth to the seller of a canoe from its buyer, conducted in the spirit of commodity exchange (as opposed to the construction of ongoing relationships). However, the roots of *leau* lie in the days of interisland raiding and the large-scale exchanges of wealth between leaders of places on guardedly friendly terms with one another. *Leau* in these days, still within living memory, had the effect of continuing relations between ambitious and competitive men, and it took a very structured form. Consider the following description by Anselm, a current clan leader:

> Yankok is a big man at Nigahau, and he has one shell necklace [*bak*]. I see this and ask Nigahau people to *leau* this *bak*. When Nigahau brings the *bak* to Sabarl their canoe stops in front of my house. Yankok and some of his friends bring the *bak* and hang it outside the house—it doesn't matter where. It is a sign that this is *leau* business inside. Then I take ten ax blades (*tobwatobwa*) out to their canoe. After this the men who have been waiting in the canoe come inside my house. Inside there is a path made of mats, and on the path are maybe thirty ax blades, in their [decorative] handles. The Nigahau people stay three or four days. We cook for them; we make sago cakes and pudding and kill a pig. They return home with the ax blades. Then two or three years later, I receive word that they are ready to call back the *leau* [*leau gongon pahavina*]. My brothers and I go to Nigahau with nothing in our hands. They cook for us and give me forty *tobwatobwa* plus four. Then I either give them one *bak* as *golase* [closing gift] or it is my turn to look for more *tobwatobwa*, and so it goes on. If I die before the *leau* is closed with a *bak* and I still owe my partner *leau*, my son will give him two ax blades to claim [*posela*] my debt or what is owed to me. Then later he can open *leau* with this man for himself.

Leau in past times was a fame-making strategy for individuals and their "places" (hamlets, villages, islands). Through it the strength of an individual's support could be relayed to outsiders in the concrete form of valuable objects that were at once the lures and the trophies of bloody off-island raids. As such, *leau* was essentially an extroverted gesture, indicating first the value then placed on expanding social networks (see Belshaw 1955:30), but also the importance of constructing an image-shield of wealth against attacks by neighbors who were continually assessing the degree and quality of coordinated support a man might muster. A decision to *leau* was furthermore read as a sign that the organizers more than accepted the risk of sorcery that any grand gesture invited—that they felt secure enough in their knowledge of protective magic to risk challenging would-be attackers.

One effect of *leau* was to disseminate valuables along the Chain. For example, people talk about feeding stone ax blades and such through the renowned Motorina woman Labayoni, who would pass them along to her *leau* partners on Misima, who in turn carried them north to Muyuw and into the famous *kula* exchange system of the northern Massim (see Leach and Leach 1983).

What remains of this earlier meaning of *leau* to Sabarl (see also Berde 1974; Macintyre 1983) is the large-scale nature of the prestations, the image of collective strength that such giving conveys (although nowadays with less emphasis on place than on clanship), and the prestige a person gains by coordinating the project and "winning" a canoe away from its seller.

When I was in the area in 1986, Bruce, a young man at Bwailahine village on Panatinani, was preparing to take possession of a strikingly sleek *sailau* canoe from the Panaeati. The Panaeati had already accepted a number of payments from him (and from two other buyers on neighboring islands, unknown to any of them). They had also offered the canoe to the Catholic mission for an exorbitant price. The scandal eventually erupted, and Bruce's father made it clear to all involved who the true buyer was. Bruce's father and father's brother were powerful men, with considerable experience in *"leau* business." Bruce had wisely asked them to do the negotiating on his behalf, believing himself "too young to be taken seriously," and promised his father's brother a very large pig as a consulting fee.

One year after Bruce's father had approached the Panaeati and given them a down payment of fifty bundles of sago plus a pig and one long *"leau*-sized" ax blade, he and others were helping Bruce to prepare for the final delivery and the closing gift of another long necklace, two more pigs with tusks, another long ax blade, four baskets of garden food, another fifty bundles of sago, one basket of lime, and K200. This wealth was the contribution primarily of his father and father's brother, his mother, his brother and sisters, and his mother's mother. In addition, his mother's mother's sister came down from Sabarl to help him cook for the Panaeati's outrageously long stay in the village, bringing food from her gardens, as did his wife's mother and father and her clan "brother" (MZS). Since Bruce had married a Maho village woman who was "helping" in her role of "junior affine" (*tovelam*) to Bruce's senior relations, and since Bruce was purchasing the canoe to give to his wife and her matriline, their expectation was that the canoe would be kept at Maho. The expectation was heightened by the fact that Bruce's father and father's brother were junior "brothers" of his wife's father. Thus there was a strong possibility that Bruce's father and father's brother would be "lent back" the canoe by his wife in her position as *tovelam*. What this stood to earn her was not only a "strong" position in her husband's natal village, but a strong claim to be buried, and to have her children buried on her lineage's land on Sabarl—advantaging any heirs hosting their mortuary feasts from that quarter.

I never learned the outcome of this particular story. When I left, Bruce had taken possession of the canoe, which was still under his "direction" pending an "acknowledgement gift" by his wife's people. But even after the acknowledgement, the canoe would continue wherever it went to "carry" Bruce's name, publicizing his accomplishment and that of his father's line as a mobile, circulating "memory."

Charters

Any person can "charter" (*hinavai*) a canoe from any other, regardless of clan or place affiliation. However, the practice is most common among place mates. Men especially charter large and glamorous canoes to make a favorable impression on trading partners. This also benefits the canoe's director, whose name "travels" with the canoe. When the person returns, he or she may offer the director one of the valuables obtained on the journey, in the hope of opening a partnership. If the canoe's director is interested in forming an ongoing trade relationship, the valuable suffices as a "canoe charter fee" (*waga temalikina*). Otherwise, traditional ceremonial foods will be cooked and given to the controller in payment, "closing" the contract.

Infrequently, Europeans such as myself or resident schoolteachers from outside the culture area will charter a canoe for money and stick tobacco. There is an increasing awareness of the advantages of making a canoe available on this basis. In 1986 I paid K25 and a row of tobacco for a journey form Sabarl to Nimowa (twelve hours on that day, four hours in good weather). The fee is variable but tends to climb about the time taxes are due. Particularly as more Europeans move into the Misima area in connection with gold mining there, charters are being encouraged by the local Catholic missionaries, committed to heightening awareness of the meaning of money and the tendency of outsiders to exploit those who are ignorant of it.

Loans and Inheritance

There were once three brothers who between them "directed" the resources of the island of Dadahai: its garden and residence land, its reefs, its sago stands and betel nut trees, its coconut plantations. Brandon was their elder sister's son. Whenever they needed support—and especially when sponsoring a commemorative feast for a member to their clan or supporting their wives' clans in sponsoring feasts—Brandon "helped" with generous gifts of pigs, food, and valuable objects. Indeed, his support was so generous and constant that the uncles gradually turned over to him all their landed holdings and control of the reefs.

One by one the aged uncles died, and at the end of their mortuary feasts Brandon would "help" their widows and children repay the dead man's paternal clan. This assistance had the effect of refreshing his claim to his inheritance. After the last uncle died, he reinforced the claim by building a house on his property in the village and living there part of each year.

The consolidation of all these holdings was accomplished at the final feast of the last uncle to die, when Brandon inherited power of direction over his large canoe, *Navava*. Immediately Brandon "lent" back the canoe to the uncle's widow and her children, and at the same time he indicated to the eldest uncle's eldest son, whose name was Diho, that he was giving him an option of buying back all of his father's property, which he could meanwhile use. Thus Diho used the canoe to assemble wealth from trading partners and off-island kin, and used the land to muster food resources, in order eventually to sponsor a "property purchase feast"—a Tagalekeleke—with the hope of taking control from Brandon of all of his father's property. The "purchase" would in this case take the form of "repayment for the loan" of the canoe, the land, and the reefs. Such "loan repayments" are called *powon lase* (or simply *powon*).

The interesting thing was that in talking about the transaction, people spoke as if the canoe alone were being transferred. The reefs and land, I was told, were "inside" the canoe: this was a "bundled" property. Also, they called the canoe by the name of the dead man's widow, although neither she nor her clan had ever directed it. Canoes and landed property have in common a compelling force as "memories" of marital partnerships. As the tales of a productive marriage are said to be "grown" in the gardens and groves of the couples who have worked there together, so canoes call marriages to mind—the "evidence" of the union is carried through space and time across the waters each time a canoe is transferred at the death of one spouse or the other.

However, the person who directed *Navava* controlled not just the visual reminder of a marriage, but more specifically the "memory" of one man's achievement in gaining control over what that marriage had yielded in the form of children, shelter, and food: in other words, his nurturant identity. There is no mystery why the children themselves were emotionally motivated to capture *Navava* away from their off-island cousin. The canoe embodied their hope of moving between clans what theoretically stays within the clan: namely land, reef, and their own allegiances.

Once again, I never learned the outcome of this Tagalekeleke. Brandon may not have accepted the amount of wealth the widow and children offered for the "canoe" he inherited. Certainly his own clan heir, who helped finance this building of the house on Dadahai, would have had a say in the matter of accepting or not accepting his future legacy. Although a man's children must be very "strong" to win their father's property away from his clan heirs, *they will always have the right to try* for what would be their supreme public achievement in life. For them, time is of the essence, since unlike claims within the matriline, this right will become diluted in subsequent generations. By contrast, if Diho's Tagalekeleke is successful, Brandon and his heirs will relinquish their rights to use *Navava* or any other of the rich resources "inside" it. However, their descendants will always have the right to reinstate the claim.

It is believed that such packaged legacies were far more common in ancestral times. However, the loan of a canoe at death is a common form of *powon*. To mark the canoe as a loan rather than a gift, Brandon floated it over to the widow and her children on the day following his uncle's death, with wealth on board: two ax blades, K10, and a pig. The wealth "cleared" the canoe of death's pollution. It would have to be repaid.

There were three possible scenarios for the loan repayment. In one that we have come across already, the loan is returned on the initiative of the borrower, with interest—that is, Brandon would receive more wealth for the canoe than he sent along at the time of the death. However, if Brandon had suddenly needed the canoe or its wealth, for example, to repay a more pressing debt of his own or to fulfill an unexpected obligation, he would have forfeited the interest as a kind of penalty for doing the asking (as we have seen in the case of land and object wealth). A third scenario would include a death on the side of the borrowers. For example, if the widow died before repaying Brandon, he would expect the immediate return of the canoe, along with a great deal more wealth in interest from her children than he would have received during her life.

Death works differently on a loan when the lender is a spouse, and it is quite common for a spouse to inherit a canoe and lend it back to the clan heirs. The circumstances of this maneuver usually involve heirs who are senior to the dead person (e.g., older siblings, maternal aunts or uncles). If the spouse dies before the repayment of the loan, the heir will be expected to return the canoe immediately, accompanied by the exact amount of wealth that went with it: that is, without interest, "like you were giving it back on the day you got it." Death in this case makes the widow or widower's people "forget" time, since a clan heir would never be expected to lose wealth on a loan of a kinsperson's property.

Yet for all the calculation, it is well to remember the feelings involved in making these decisions. I spoke with a widow, Anna, who was eager to lend her canoe away. It reminded her of her husband, of all their trips, she said, to the garden and the sago stands, and it made her feel sad. As long as she used it, people would see the canoe on the sea and think of their marriage. If she remarried, they would continue to think of that marriage until her new husband gave her a new canoe. As she told me this, there were tears in her eyes.

In overview, we can see that *powon* with canoes and *powon* involving other portable wealth and land operate in much the same way, except for the emphasis on ritually removing pollution that emerges in the context of canoe transfers. The sense of this lies not only in the close links of the canoes with personhood (ancestors were sometimes buried in their canoes), but as with the myths of Katutubwai, in canoes as transitional objects at death.

Images of Mobility

As we have seen, there are primarily three forms of object valuables circulating in the Saisai area: the chama-shell necklace (*bak*), the ceremonial stone ax blade (*tobwatobwa*), and the wooden or turtle-shell limestick (*gobaela* and *hiyenga*, respectively) strung with chama-shell beads. Like canoes (and also like people), these objects are classified linguistically as "animate." That is, they cast an animate-category "shadow/reflection" (*kanukanunu-*) as opposed to the mere "shade" (*pwapwalulu*) of objects that do not circulate.

Their affinity to human mobility is expressed iconographically, such that every object invites overlying readings that collapse into one another formally, images of the person and patterns or vehicles of movement. Thus, for example, the mushroom-shaped limestick may be "read" as a human body or a human face when held upright, a canoe when inverted. The part of this object that on a "canoe" is identified as the *tanatana* or "gunwale" represents the "arms" of the body, the "forehead" of the face. One reading obviates another that is the potential reading of another moment, of some other individual, from some other perspective, or in some other context. Similarly, the triangular holes identified as the "person who guides" the canoe are "all the holes of the person" in the upright position. The shell beads strung along the crescent's rim are the "islands" the canoe moves between,

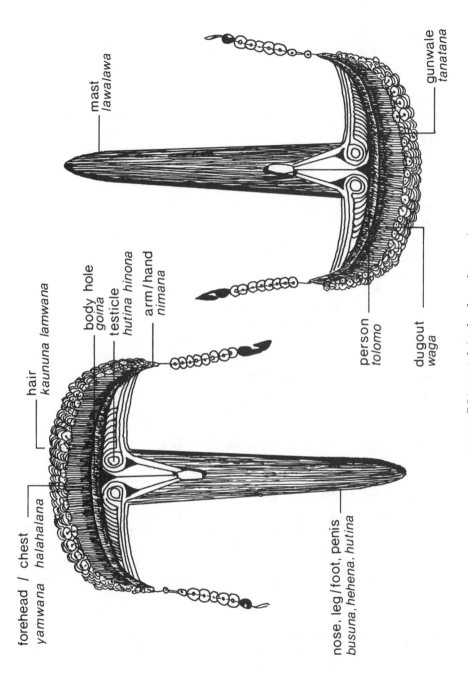

forehead / chest
yamwana halahalana

hair
kaununa lamwana

body hole
goina

testicle
hutina hinona

arm/hand
nimana

mast
lawalawa

gunwale
tanatana

person
tolomo

dugout
waga

nose, leg/foot, penis
busuna, hehena, hutina

FIGURE 7 Limestick (*gobaela* or *hiyenga*).

cent's rim are the "islands" the canoe moves between, but the "hair" of the person when inverted. Redundant imagery works to create identification of the distinct symbolic clusters more immediately than any sequence of acts (phrases, dances, ritual actions, etc.). But it also creates a sense of the absent alternative: the latent image that the current or salient meaning "covers," such that the latter becomes a way to find what lies beneath and to recover it to memory. That canoes retrieve "memories" of persons, and vice versa, is the coded inscription of the limestick.

The shell necklace or *bak* is less obviously anthropomorphic in the minds of Sabarl themselves, it seems, and in its current form its connection with canoes is somewhat more oblique.

On the simplest level, there is the helmet-shell "head," which transforms the necklace from a married woman's ornament into an object of wealth. A necklace with a head is said to acquire a "voice" in the form of shell chimes. Although it appears at first that the head is what makes the object "more like people," closer questioning reveals that the *bak* is in fact an icon of two-directional movement. The strands are divided into an "out" and a "back" side by a clasp that symbolically "turns" the flow of the valuable shell beads "back toward home" (*hiyeba iyomwe pahavina*). The clasp itself is on some necklaces an "eagle's beak," on others a gold-lip shell "canoe." In this case, various readings are inferred from narratives that Sabarl say shed light on the "reading" of the necklace. One such narrative we have already encountered: the story of the bird and the snake who created the ring of islands, which the two strands may be seen to represent, as they represent also the snake itself in the birds's beak.

There is also a section of the necklace known as the "bush fowl's legs" (*kulihi hehena*), twin strands connecting the pendant to the necklace. In a myth of the same name, a young woman is tricked into climbing a betel palm that takes her to the top of the sky. Here she marries a reef heron and sets up a home. Her parents miss her and sponsor a competition for the birds of the world, offering a *bak* to the one who brings her back to them. It is a total surprise when the ponderous bush fowl—the "ancestor bird"—succeeds. Her grateful parents wind a side of *bak* round each leg, turning it red. This story was brought to my attention by a woman who was explaining the different parts of a *bak*. Several people who were listening had never considered that the story might refer to the "out" and "back" sides of the *bak* and were intrigued. The bush fowl in the story functions as an image of paternal support in recycling the woman back into reproductive life, just as a widow is recycled by her husband's cousin "father," who has

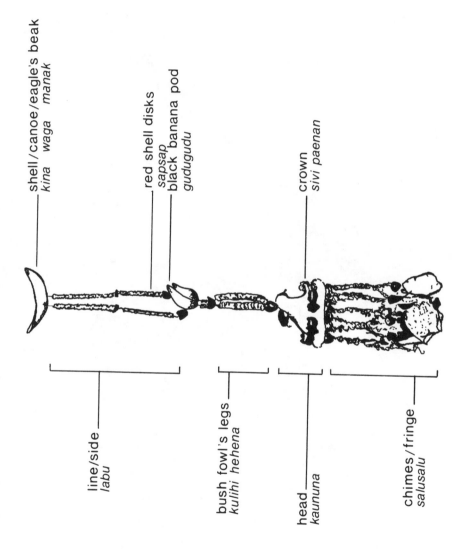

shell/canoe/eagle's beak
kina waga   manak

red shell disks
sapsap
black banana pod
gudugudu

crown
sivi paenan

line/side
labu

bush fowl's legs
kulihi hehena

head
kaununa

chimes/fringe
salusalu

FIGURE 8 Ceremonial shell necklace (*bak*).

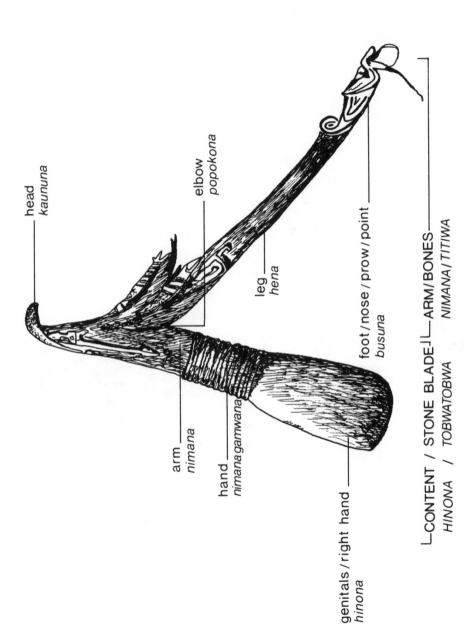

head
kaununa

elbow
popokona

leg
hena

foot / nose / prow / point
busuna

arm
nimana

hand
nimanagamwana

genitals / right hand
hinona

CONTENT / STONE BLADE ┘└ ARM / BONES
HINONA / TOBWATOBWA   NIMANA / TITIWA

FIGURE 9 Ceremonial ax (*tobwatobwa*).

the job of releasing her from mourning; and just as on another level the maternal line is recycled past a generation break through its children. The eagle's beak and the canoe are identified as vehicles for turning" death around. The necklace images the "path" of human endeavor, broken in the middle—that is, opened out to new possibilities.

The same "out" and "back" movement is read in the *tobwatobwa*—the stone axes that are the primary currency of the area. In my opening remarks, I mentioned the story of Enak the Creator, whose memorials are scattered around the archipelago in rock formations shaped like axes, canoes, pots, and so forth. Sabarl regard these representational images as sacred "proof" of the truth of the creation, literally the "hand mark" (*nimana muina*) of Enak, which if they were vandalized would cause the islands to sink beneath the sea. All indigenous artifacts recall this original relationship, but the "arm" of the *tobwatobwa*, with its richly layered iconography, in many ways epitomizes it.

The ax as a whole takes it name from the stone blade. The blade is the *hinona*—the "content" or "vital substance" of the valuable, the object of value in economic terms. But as we have seen in the context of the physical person, *hinona* is also the term for "genitals" and the "right hand." The flat wooden handle or "arm" (*nimana*) displays and "supports" (*labe*) the blade (and is in turn supported by it in certain sacred rituals, as I will later explain). Its shape is said to suggest "bones" (*titiwa*). The handle is traditionally carved from red *mwadawa* wood (a species of teak), associated in myth with red maternal flesh and in verbal exegesis with the matriclan.[1] Likewise, the "head" (*kaununa*) of the handle is carved in the primary emblem of clanship, the head of a "bird" (*man*) rendered in profile. Thus, as "bones," "flesh," and "head" the wooden haft is a representation of the "body" of the social person: the person as clan member. The blade, as *hinona*, broadly represents the reproductive potential of the singular person.

Other body parts appear in the more specific names of parts of the handle. The long section of the handle is the "leg" (*hena*), which ends in a carved "point" (*busuna*) identified alternatively as the foot, the nose, or the prow of the handle. And here we have a clue to the object as canoe, for the carving at the point, as on the prows of all Sabarl canoes, is the head of a snake. The shorter section is the "arm," with fiber bindings at the "hand" (*nimana gamwana*).

Keeping in mind the importance of *hinona* to the physical person, we are now able to glimpse something of the significance of the *tobwatobwa* blade, for in effect the object is identified with persons through the very essence of their physical existence. This connection becomes clearer once we consider what *hinona* as a medium of biological productivity has in common with *hinona* as an economic force—namely, its association with heat: the heat of sexual intercourse that generates conception; the heat of aggressive physical labor associated with axes as implements and weapons. The *tobwatobwa* blade embodies heat symbolically; it is even described as heat generating or "greasy" in certain contexts. Thus *hinona* is a link in the production of new people, new objects, and new social ties (through exchange)—in short, in a fabrication process that at once distinguishes the person and prepares the ground for his or her membership in a clan-based society. Literally containing this heat is the "arm" as body, the "arm" as canoe.

I have talked about the ax blade as "content" and "reproductive substance." It is also, of course, a crafted stone, once quarried and shaped in regions to the north and traded south over time—except that many Sabarl do not view it as such. It is widely believed that the blade is a natural object that grows "like shells" (also like people) outward from the center. The spawning grounds are thought to be shallow estuaries at the westward end of the Calvados Chain, significantly, pools where "cool" fresh water (*bwai*) and "hot" salt water (*soga*) intermingle. Eventually the growing blade takes on a triangular shape.

However, the hafted ax as a whole is perceived not as a static triangular shape, but rather, as I have implied, as an image of action and directed movement. I first became aware of this when a Sabarl man commented that *segaiya* "looks like *tobwatobwa*" and drew the shape of the arm in the sand. We had been discussing his special nurture relationship to the cross-cousin "father" who called him "my child." Rendered graphically, these exchanges "look like *tobwatobwa*": a lateral movement of wealth items from the father's side (the left side or "arm" of a person) to the mother's side (the right side) as gifts to the paternal clan at the child's *segaiya*. This "reading" gives a great deal of significance to the turning point of the action and the bend in the handle: to death and the "child" on the one hand and the "bird's head" and "elbow" on the handle on the other.

As I mentioned earlier in discussing incestuous relationships and the paths of descent (chap. 5), an elbow is the part of the arm that "makes it strong." There is also the saying that when a person is drowning, his "elbow" will save him: a reference to the special *tubu* called "elbow"—the mother's mother's brother's son or daughter whom one is not allowed to marry. One reason for this proscription is that one would be marrying one's mother's cousin "child," or figura-

tively speaking one's own sibling: oneself, in property terms. Returning to the theme of support, which is the special function of the
MMBS/D in the parable, we can see that *tobwatobwa* "elbows" represent the turning point in the vital movement of reciprocal giving (rendered in fact in the *tobwatobwa* arm); also, the point in an individual's
societal existence where clan-based tensions tend to articulate. This
same movement is perceived as the ideal route of durable valuables,
that is, away from the person, clan, or place and, importantly, back
again. It is also the circular route of the mythical bird and snake, the
most prominent motifs of the *tobwatobwa* arm, whose mortal competition left its mark on the world as a ring of islands.

The importance of materially embodied images of mobility, and
in particular the salience of canoes in Sabarl thought and social action,
cannot be overemphasized. It indicates the cultural value placed on
mobility as an index of group and personal viability and on social circulation in general. As with circulation in the human body, the circulation of landed and portable wealth, and the circulation of human reproductive substance through the three-clan system, there is nothing
automatic, nothing given, about the course of a marriage, of a political
or subsistence career, of one's material holdings. Social life must be
"turned" to one's purposes. Canoes symbolically summarize the process, less as static images of containment than as the pattern of "cor-
raling" the artifacts of social achievement. In this respect they stand
for individual organizational prowess and foresight, while at the same
time incorporating some of the basic schemata of Sabarl cultural organization.[2]

Overall, durable, circulating wealth represents the relational person displaced—that is, in movement. Such objects are "read" not only
as fixed representational images, but as kinetic "evidence" of a course
of social relationship. Thus the arm of a ceremonial ax may be seen as
the representation of the body of a person or as the bidirectional "path"
of exchange between cousins and as the dispersal and reclamation of
wealth; the lengths of a ceremonial necklace as the legs of an ancestor,
or as the "out" and "back" movement of women through the developmental cycle, away from home at marriage and back toward home at
death.

From this perspective a "memory"—a "trope-ic" cultural construct, materially embodied—can be seen to incorporate images of,
and be subject to the forces of, its own unmaking. The intersubjective
reality of this situation is the topic of the next chapter.

Seven

Fame and Diminishment

On Shyness and Shame

The subject of shame has received considerable attention in recent psychological[1] and anthropological[2] literature. Such studies reveal the extent to which "shame"—whether considered as anxiety or fear of disgrace, or as the affect of contempt directed against the self, as the stance of respect or reverence assumed toward others, or as some combination (Wurmser 1987)—is variable across, and also within, cultures (Rosaldo 1984:149). Yet researchers in this area do share common ground in positing, first, that shame represents a withdrawal from sociality (usually in response to feelings or perceptions of subordination to someone whose negative evaluation matters to oneself [Lewis 1987:108]); and second, that this withdrawal takes the form of a flight away from others and into the self—the inference being that such behavior is wholly undesirable and unrewarded in cultural terms.

But the depiction of shame as a phenomenon where the self is invariably central requires some modification for Sabarl, as does the related view that social separations are likely to be dysfunctional—that they tend to create dangerous holes in the social fabric.

My discussion of these points begins with the components of a "shame complex,"[3] for which the Sabarl gloss is *mwalina. Mwalina* can mean either "shyness-embarrassment-apprehension" or "shame-humiliation," conditions related dynamically as prospective shame and as consummated shame.

Prospective shame (Sabarl will say "shyness" in English) is a set condition of ongoing social diminishment, where social asymmetries are "forgotton" (whether inadvertently overlooked, deliberately left unacknowledged, or displaced) only at great personal cost. Basically, it takes a death in the relationship to put this condition into reverse. In explaining "shyness," people often point to the example of children who are sent to request tobacco or betel nut on behalf of some adult, usually as part of teaching them the etiquette of "asking" (*wanun*). Shyness, in general terms, is the condition of those who feel only circumstantial, conditional efficacy or empowerment in the face of interactions they find attractive or potentially beneficial.

On Sabarl, the cultural expression of shyness is most developed within the junior affine/senior affine relationship. Indeed, the junior affine (*tovelam*) condition can be viewed as the contextual background of shame, establishing a cultural predisposition to being shamed that moments of acute exposure (Wurmser 1981; Lynd 1958) precipitate. In this latter type of consummated shame, the shaming incident can be "officially forgotten" quite straightforwardly, by payment of a fine. Nonetheless, it is consummated shame that invokes the specter of a response that can endanger society (e.g., willful isolation, general withdrawal, affectively charged disconnectedness), a specter foreshadowed in the deliberate separations of junior affines from seniors—where, however, separation is perceived as having positive social value.

In other words, prospective shame, as a variety of cultural interdiction (Wagner 1977), inhibits the indiscriminate flow of social relations, working against the collapse of critical cultural distinctions. In the case of *tovelam* "shyness," *mwalina* defines kin categories not by contrast to some "natural" order, nor by delimiting "public" and "private" spheres (cf. Fajans 1985), so much as by setting up relations of opposition that are analogously related to other such relations (the most obvious example being marriage proscriptions). Conceived thus on the level of process, nonseparation—not separation—is the original problem for society. It is the problem, for Sabarl, of Enak's perennial pregnancy in the time before time mattered—of a world without producers, but also without consumers: without the texts, that is, of reproduction and exchange.

The problem is addressed in avoidance "customs" that create "breathing space" in social relations. These shame observances are predicated on approaching seniors as superior to oneself and being approached by them in turn as an undistinguished member of a junior work force. Yet here lie the roots of cognitive cultural dissonance. For within this relationship, persons are subordinated and evaluated grossly, on the general grounds of service, whereas elsewhere within other relationships the likelihood exists of their being judged more subtly and positively. For example, one may be seen, and see oneself, as a strong leader, as a senior affine to be reckoned with vis-à-vis one's own *tovelam* work force, as a responsible parent, and so forth, and simultaneously as merely a *tovelam*. Furthermore, in addition to one's current self one sees one's future self—one's social potential—in this empowered senior other: the purely senior affine one could someday become when one's own senior affines have died.[4] Thus from a developmental perspective the person, as a self-other, pays respect to the potential in himself or herself in cultural expressions of shyness. (An analogical relationship is revealed in the respect persons show to cousin "fathers" as their future undertakers, while being shown respect as "fathers" themselves by other cousins.) This complex intersubjective reality creates the dissonant tension that constitutes shame as a cultural dynamic. Indeed, an interesting expressive point in this regard is that, until very recently, junior affines who contributed a hardwood post in the construction of a senior's house would inscribe the post with their totemic "signature": their "memory" endures only when displaced to the realm of those who subordinate them.

Yet there is another element to consider here: that in Sabarl society, where personhood is relational (where the person is basically construed as a self-other), shame may be reflected back onto the self by the other *as if originating in both partners.* From this perspective we can appreciate how the danger is as much that a superior other will overstep or contravene the rules of relationship—diminishing all that he or she represents and devaluing the *tovelam*'s history of service— as that the person subordinated by age, weakness, and such will in some way transgress. Shame can work from the top down. Thus it is not any one individual who stands to lose "face" (cf. Goffman 1967:5), but rather the relationship in question.[5]

This brings us to a final point concerning the paradoxical twist to consummated shame: that withdrawal or temporary isolation may be distinguished in a way that actually enhances the social image of individual transgressors; that is, persons who go against the rules brazenly enough and stand out to take the social criticism can find themselves admired for their audacity. Shame, in short, can convert to fame. And when this occurs, the particular relationship being held up to social scrutiny in a negative light is obviated by a new or revised relationship of the transgressor to his or her "disciples" (*pankiviliu*). I was amazed to observe this effect when a Maho man—a leader with a reputation for sorcery—broke into the house of his beautiful lover (some years later his second wife) quite shamelessly one night while his wife slept just two doors away. The next morning his wife ordered him out of his house until he produced an ax blade as a penalty fee. Yet people spoke admiringly of his braveness. For one thing, he had taunted any *waunak* who might be a supporter of his wife and her kin. By aggressively becoming the agent of his own shame, he had cancelled out the reflexively critical eye of society at large, casting himself, in effect, as his own judge.[6] Such behavior inverts subordination, which often (as in this case) is linked to overtly expressed "anxiety" (*hatebwalebwalenga*) and "fear" (*matot*) of the magical potency of those who take liberties, by those who do not have the social support or temperament to challenge the conventional structure of legitimate authority.

Sabarl construe the difference between shame and "inner feelings" (*nuwanuwatuk*) of guilt in terms of the memorability of shame behavior versus the private recognition of wrongdoing. Thus, whereas shame, as a witnessable phenomenon, can be "officially forgotten," not until Sabarl were introduced to the Catholic concept of confession was a means made available for "forgetting" guilt. That currently the difference is not stressed between having God as a witness and having a member of one's own society may indicate a move away from the moral premises of relational personhood and toward a more individualistic personhood on Sabarl.

"Forgetting" Shame

I came upon Jonah alone on the beach in front of his house one afternoon, looking ostentatiously "downcast" (*yamwana ipuyowa*, literally "forehead/mind lowered"). He was squatting with his head bowed and his forearms resting on his knees, in the pose of a man exhibiting shame to the passing world. Later I learned that Jonah had returned from the garden a few hours earlier, having heard a rumor that while he was away another man had "opened the door to his wife's house." His pose was an announcement to the village that Jonah had confronted his wife and was refusing to live with her again until she and her lover had paid him *sas*: a "penalty fee" to "cover" the shame. But if he continued to sulk beyond a reasonable time, the elders of the village could demand a "peace offering" (*paen*) from Jonah (a pig is most appropriate) for his part in disrupting village routines. If nothing else could, I was told, the squeals of his pig would bring him back to his senses—or more exactly, back to the sense of himself as a mature, relational human being.

It follows from the contagious nature of any shame scenario that "covering" shame proceeds by formally constructing a new "memory" of the relationship. This reconstruction takes the form either of *paen*, which is a gesture of smoothing over relations, or of *sas*, to correct wrongdoing. Gestures of *paen* are not always or even usually one-sided.

Two men have exchanged "bad words" (*iliwa ngakngak*) in private: the one who began the exchange will give the other perhaps one or two ax blades and a K10 note to resume relations, and the other will reciprocate (sometimes with a bit less). Two women have argued loudly enough to disrupt the neighboring households: a lineage leader or senior person in their hamlet will call a public meeting for them to perform their reconciliation by shaking hands and exchanging ax blades—*paen* "to calm their excited hearts" (*hatiena iyut*). They will also be expected to compensate neighbors for their distress.

Displays of angry withdrawal diminish the force of the image of strength and solidarity that Sabarl feel protects them from attacks by enemy outsiders. To disrupt, in effect, is to endanger. Indeed if Jonah, for example, had fallen ill shortly after discovering his wife's affair, his recent contact with shame would have figured in local explanations of the cause of his illness

As distinguished from *paen*, a *sas* or penalty fee is demanded of persons who are recognized as having elicited shame by violating specific rights, rules, or sensibilities of the larger group. For example, in the case of "slander" (*wasangak*), *sas* is the only legitimate reparation for "spoiling the name" of the lineage and clan of which the victim is perceived to be a living "memory." The same is true when a death has occurred in some hamlet of the village: to signal the direction of the hamlet by the dead person's clan (and by the dead in absentia), and also to warn outsiders that normal life has been frozen by pollution restrictions, clan seniors erect a "no trespassing" sign (*hivi*) on the beach in front of the dead person's house.[7] Any trading partner so unwise as to pursue an interest there could be fined heavily by the ruling clan. In effect, the *hivi* publicizes the intensification and dominance of prospective shame within the life of that quarter.

There are few more serious transgressions than the failure to "respect" the name or property either of the dead or of their living representatives. Sails are lowered and canoes solemnly punted past hamlets, sago groves, coconut plantations, or wherever a *hivi* is displayed; voices are soft and postures stooped when people pass "forbidden" places. In short, they take much the attitude before a *hivi* that they do before senior affines.

Thus the passing world shows shame in the presence of death, as if the shameful behavior of all of human life had come to this. This notion, that cultural responses to mortality give expression to the experience of vulnerability in life as well as respect for those who appear invulnerable, is important. For through it we begin to perceive how shame is practiced as a countervalue that something like negative space—the holes in the net of human relationship—reveals by contrast the value of positively manifested cultural guidelines.

Shame, Fame and the Search for Food and Wealth

Hanna had come to a difficult decision. It was February, well into the "lean season" (*suwai*), and food supplies were low. It would be four months at least until even "early" gardens could be harvested. Powerful southwesterlies had brought cyclonic winds and torrential rains, interrupting sago production. Hanna described her husband as "depressed" (*tomipahab*). Their child was just recovering from pneumonia. They would soon have to feast the villagers who held nightlong vigils outside their house to guard against attacks by evil spirits.

Hanna hoped to find additional food, and money for rice and tea, without involving her husband. She wanted to save him the shame of asking for such basic things. One of her uncles lived at Mamanila (on Panabarli) and had enormous gardens there. But she worried that he might think less of her for not planning properly for household emergencies such as this one: this could hurt her chances of asking him later for garden land.

However, Hanna had put away an entire basket of lime parcels that she had manufactured the previous season. She decided to sail with her teenage son to Bwailahine village on Panatinani and exchange the lime for food from her "namesake" (-*valesa*) there. Because Hanna was doing her namesake the ongoing favor of bearing her name with honor, there would be no shame in asking her for food, especially in exchange for lime. Hanna's plan was to then continue to Nimowa to sell the remainder of the lime for money and to purchase rice from the trade store there.

Hanna's plan was perfectly appropriate to a Sabarl woman. Nonetheless, the enterprise was distasteful to her husband. With his "name on her canoe" as its donor, he would not be immune from the taint of shame that clung to all such "subsistence journeys" (*hahalau*). He suggested to Hanna that instead he undertake a different kind of voyage— a journey "in search of fame" and wealth (*lobutu*) to the home of a trading partner. He would say that he was looking for a valuable pig (which in truth they would shortly need to repay another trading partner who had lent them wealth in the past). But he would also bring along Hanna's lime, in the hope that this partner would act nobly ("act like a big man" [*guiau*]) and save him the shame of asking for food by first asking for lime. In the end, Hanna persuaded her husband that she should accompany him and organize the lime exchanges while he conducted the more prestigious negotiations for wealth.

The delicate business of circumventing the shame of requesting necessities is a Sabarl islander's preoccupation. Typically, adults face decisions such as Hanna's once or twice a year. Sabarl lime, the harvest of the "bones of the serpent," has long been employed by women as the medium of preference for reducing the shame of requesting food. Indeed it is said to be the hot, high-grade lime that first drew other islands into trade with Sabarl at a time when warfare was endemic. Currently, trade circuits formed and renewed by exchanges of lime for food, betel-nut ingredients, domestic accoutrements, tobacco, and money tie Sabarl into supplies of the low-prestige necessities of social life more securely than any other type of exchange. The surplus commodity of women, lime is complemented in this respect by surplus sago traded outside the Saisai area primarily by men for prestige pigs, ax blades, and clay cooking pots from Motorina and Utian. Sago is also used as partial payment for canoes, as described in the context of *leau*.[8]

The circuitous trade routes are echoed in the circuitous etiquette of "requesting" (*-wanun*) and "offering" (*toto-*) wealth. The proper way to ask is to raise the point of the visit, then "talk around" it (*lihu bwabwanaga*) for hours or sometimes days while the host decides whether to offer what his guest is seeking. Not surprisingly, it is within the sphere of prestige exchange that the art of eloquent asking is culturally elaborated—that is, in requesting removed from the cultural constraints of shame.

The "story" of seeking renown through asking—the plot of converting shame into fame—was invariably described to me as a cultural performance as prescribed as any ritual sequence. I was told:

> We begin by arriving in front of the house of a trading partner (*tutuila*). We stay inside the canoe, grooming ourselves. If we possess "magic oil for asking" [*bunama*—perfumed oil containing an ancestral relic] we put it on our lips [to] "grease" our words and "sweeten his or her feelings towards us" [*nuwalia ipaposa*]. Then we approach the house. They spread a mat in front of the house, and we give them a "solicitary gift" [*wot*] of betel nut, tobacco, or mustard. If our partner is a male, his wife will go inside to prepare our "visitors' food" [*buligi*]. If our business is with her, we nonetheless talk with her husband, and he will confer with her in private afterward. Then we move inside to eat. They sit off

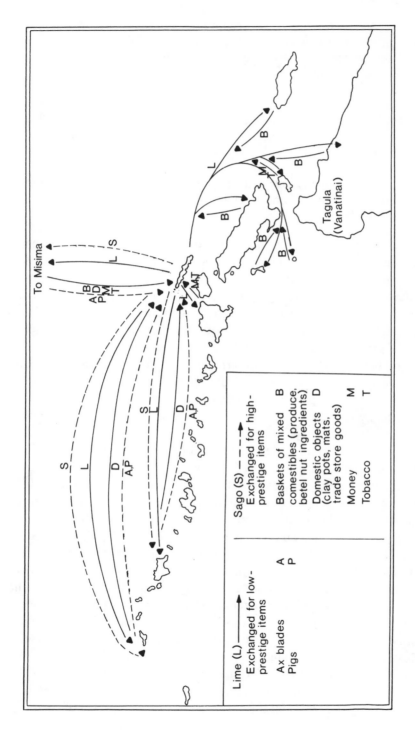

MAP 4 Lime and sago exchange paths.

to one side, not eating, keeping us company. They will not allow us to discuss business while eating; they fear we might become distracted and put aside our food before we have truly finished. Then sometimes we "go for a stroll" [*dodogan*] or "take a nap" [*hiyena*], or else we "joke" [*yo-kayelu*] or chew betel nut to stay awake and start talking again. Then we say we must leave. They will offer us a small "consolation gift" [*huluwen*], perhaps a pot or dish or a K2 note. Or else they will give us what we came for. Then they "return" [*lase*] our solicitary gift: they tuck betel nut and such into our basket, and they give us cooked "food for the journey" [*kanali*] and see us to the canoe and "on our way" [*pawaleli*].

Although partnerships may continue over years of exchange, re-producing the relational conventions upon which society turns (Weiner 1980), Sabarl explicitly conceive of them as episodic transactions, bounded by the "opening" and "closing" of a "path" (*hiyela*) between partners in a single exchange of gift and countergift. Both prestations are referred to simply as "path" gifts. Relations are usually launched by the gift of a large ax blade, which is said to "create the path" (*hiyela iginoi*) between the transactors (the anthropomorphic canoe iconography of axes is interesting in this respect). The gift creates a "debt" (*vaga*) that binds people into relationship until the path is "closed" (*golase*) by the return gift. The return gift is described as "the return part" of the path.

Ideally, a person is left at the end of a "path" exchange with an object special enough to "draw" new partners. In other words, from the wealth itself spring the shoots of a new transactional history, just as new stories open out from ancient ones retold. In 1979 Fred allowed me to use his house during my stay in Maho. In return I gave him, among other things, an air mattress. After I left, a minister based on Tagula arrived at Maho for a visit and slept on Fred's mattress. On his way home, he stopped by his sister's house on Panatinani and told her about the wonderfully comfortable thing. She showed up at Maho the next day and asked Fred to exchange the mattress for a very large pig she owned, named Meat. Fred agreed, and Meat's fame brought one canoe after another to Fred's door. He acquired a new partner with Meat, and meanwhile, another pig from its original owner. At the time of my visit in 1986, their relationship was still very active.

Converting shame into fame through asking is largely a process of masking the vulnerability that comes from not having surplus wealth enough to offer first. Who is and who is not in this position is revealed most often on the occasion of death, when only those persons with "command presence" enough to call in their debts on time can offer their "support" at exchange feasts sponsored by others. Furthermore, the gratitude of recipients for being spared the shame of asking is a generating force of the loyalty that any kind of debt-based leadership turns on.

Punishing the Guiau

A scene from the field (1977): One day I was passing by a newly cleared garden on Hemenaha Island when I noticed something unusual about the yam house next to it. Sabarl yam houses (*nakanaka*) are typically simple, boxy structures set on posts. They resemble rudimentary residences, and people use them for storage and for overnight camping. Hanging from the floor supports of this one were two long yams, curled in the middle like ribbons. I asked a young man who was resting nearby to tell me about them. What he said was that these were the "arms" of the yam house: one was red—the right arm or "mother's side."; one was white—the left arm or "father's side." Together they "directed" (*logugui*) the new garden. Then he continued:

> "And if the garden is good, we put them inside the house with the harvest. We know they have directed the garden as a venerable woman [*selaki*]. They are a venerable woman because they have many children. But if the garden is bad we punish them. They have been a bad leader [*guiau*]. We decorate them [to look like a leader], and then we leave them to rot and we throw them in the bush. They die so they cannot come back to the garden [giggles wickedly].[9]

Recall that the first Sabarl settlers, arriving there from other islands in times of endemic raiding, found in Sabarl a coral fortress and rich fishing grounds. Sabarl see themselves coming into being as a people at this time of convergence, when achieving renown was a matter of demonstrating bravery and skill in raiding for food (primarily preprocessed sago) and valuable objects (secondarily) and attacking the bodies of their enemies spiritually with sorcery or poisons. Successful persons in these terms were the "great men"—literally, the "brave men" (*saksak*)—of Sabarl, defined as such by their unmediated risk taking.[10]

It was Sabarl women who first and most regularly ventured out to trade for yams,[11] often in enemy waters. These women established the pattern that exists to this day of voyaging long distances in search of food and luxuries acquired for lime from partners and off-island kin.

Thus, as men aggressively seized fame and security, women wove exchange-based safety nets for times of famine and drought. A few "big women" (or "true women," *vanakau suwot*) emerged in the process—women whose interests extended to the acquisition of unit-value wealth (pigs, stone ax blades, red shell necklaces beaded limesticks and belts) and who, legend has it, could stop a raging battle by flinging down their skirts between the warring men (see Lepowsky 1983). All these women were said to be innately possessed of supernatural vigilance, mobility, and aggressiveness and were generally assumed to be witches.

This dual archetype of the sorcerer-warrior and witch-entrepreneur underwent a practical transformation when the Saisai area was pacified in the early to mid-1940s. However, the model survived in the image of the *waunak*: the murderous spirit of a living person, whose cannibal raids on the human body and reciprocal exchanges of human "pig" are believed to generate death and indebtedness.

We know that male *waunak* (*saksak*), who are thought to have acquired their skills by apprenticeship to known sorcerers, are the organizers of corpse-exchange feasts in the spirit world and the orators at meetings where the identity and fate of future victims are decided. In their most lethal form they are known as *bibiloia*—beings who have learned the secret of materializing their spiritual selves. By contrast, female waunak (*yoyova*) fly to spirit meetings in packs, their identities disguised by the swarming density of their nunbers. The most feared *yoyova* take the form of "hot" shooting stars.

Throughout the pacification period, "big men" (*guiau*) were developing exchange relationships as representatives of their communities in *leau*: large scale public prestations of community wealth. *Leau*, as I indicated earlier, was basically an incremental delayed-reciprocity competition involving displays of booty. So it was that beyond their own "image management," such leaders were in charge of projecting the defense image of their local group: that is, they "ruled" the imaging of collective, coordinated strength through the management of artifact evidence of it. Interestingly, the term *guiau* is still reserved for those persons whose holdings of food or wealth allow them to show initiative through noble "offers" (*toto-*) that save others the shame of asking for things.

With the relegation of physical combat to the realm of imagery and symbolic action, there came a shift in the cultural valuing of aggression—from wholly positive in the former context, where it was closely linked to subsistence enterprise, to equivocal in the latter "modern" one. And as risk taking lost its essential motivation in survival, so, arguably, greatness itself—and standing out generally—took on ambivalence (or else the ambivalence became accentuated; it is hard to say which).

I am suggesting that this ambivalence is at base gender linked, reflecting the nature of the primary "work" of contemporary men and women of note (most of whom also have knowledge of "*waunak* business") in political exchange. The work involves them respectively in the management of durable and ephemeral objects of wealth and their comestible wealth counterparts. Specifically, men manage "unit-value" shell and stone objects as well as unit-value pigs and surpluses of the sago that was once the main object of raiding; women manage "bulk wealth" (*palo*), especially surplus mats, skirts, and baskets "piled" together and heaps of surplus yams from gardens they plant and harvest.

The main occasions for ceremonial exchanges of wealth are mortuary feasts (*segaiya*). *Segaiya* are sponsored by lineage leaders in clan territory within the hamlet or village. Men and women who distinguish themselves as organizers on these occasions emerge as "hamlet leaders" (*yawan tologugui*). Ideally these leaders are husband-wife teams. "Like a dugout and his outrigger," such couples represent stability within the village. If beyond this a man manages to acquire a deep-sea canoe (one large enough to carry his hamlet members in an emergency), he joins the ranks of the big men: he controls the symbol of encompassing security.

Thus, the "great" and the "big" are coexistent realities for Sabarl today in the unseen realm of imagery that mimes a convergence of conditions and gendered patterns of production in the "root period" of Sabarl settlement. The empirical realm has meanwhile come to be dominated by the mode of mediated exchange, which men have come to stand for by their control over permanent, unit-value wealth.

On one level, then, one could speculate that "punishing the *guiau*"—punishing the yams that direct the garden—is a gesture of annoyance with big men in general who forget their roots in the feminine model of production, behaving like rampaging great men and threatening the peace of the realm of the yam fields.

*

In surveying the eleven occupied hamlets of Maho village, I discovered that nine of the sets of corulers were married couples and the rest were

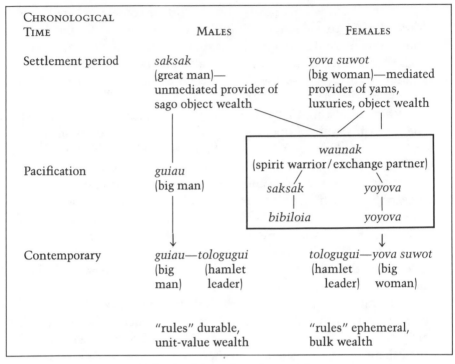

CHRONOLOGICAL TIME	MALES	FEMALES
Settlement period	*saksak* (great man)— unmediated provider of sago object wealth	*yova suwot* (big woman)—mediated provider of yams, luxuries, object wealth
Pacification	*guiau* (big man)	*waunak* (spirit warrior/exchange partner) *saksak* *yoyova* *bibiloia* *yoyova*
Contemporary	*guiau—tologugui* (big (hamlet man) leader)	*tologugui—yova suwot* (hamlet (big leader) woman)
	"rules" durable, unit-value wealth	"rules" ephemeral, bulk wealth

FIGURE 10 Leadership and gender models reconstructed.

siblings. This meant, of course, that a fair amount of the time people directed hamlets settled by ancestors other than their own. Given the stigma attached to uxorilocal residence, I expected that most nonclan corulers would be women. In fact, women directed the homeplaces of their own ancestors 36 percent of the time. Now, as we have seen for garden and sago land, and for property "bundled" with canoe transfers, residential land may in fact move back and forth between clans by means of land-purchase feasts (Tagalekeleke), as well as in mortuary-related transfers. Such transfers are especially likely to occur when a man's children wish to remain in his house (usually with their mother). But unless the purchasers belong to the founding clan, prestations must forever be made to clan representatives at the death of the current title holder. In short, that women in a significant number of cases direct quarters they can claim to control by clan right means that they and their children are in a very strong position politically within the village—even if their husbands have formally purchased the land. It is in such situations that children, for example, may sue to have their father buried on the spot where he was living. If successful, they keep his "memory" within calling distance, as well as grabbing away from paternal kin the glory of hosting his mortuary feasts.

Whatever their strengths individually or as a unit, a ruling pair will need an extraordinarily strong support network of junior affines and siblings (and here we see the advantage of married-couple rule)[12] if they are not to rely on the clan leaders outside the settlement for help in marshaling the material resources and labor they need to host even modest commemorative events.

Conversely, persons seeking influence and leadership beyond the limits of their own settlements are expected to be very "generous" (*kaukauwawa*) when other settlement rulers need assistance. But beyond this they are also expected to anticipate the needs of others and to offer guidance and resources before being asked to do so. In exchange, they stand to win emotionally indebted followers who, "because his name is on your things," carry the message of gracious support wherever they go and wherever they redeploy the wealth that was offered to them.[13]

Once their "renown" (*biyagu-*) is established in this way, leaders can simply send for the people and objects they need to support them on public occasions, rather than having to leave their base of support at home. As leaders "remember themselves" to more and more people in more and more places, making their presence in the lives of others concrete in the form of wealth, they gain not only followers but more opportunities to acquire landed resources in recognition of their history of support. In this way leaders ramify their base of power through land—enhancing their security through the quintessential vehicle of it.

Ultimately, then, the counterforce to the centripetal "power of place to draw" people and things into relationship on commemorative occasions is the centrifugal force of ambition to disperse them. As leaders and rulers gain renown for "collecting the words" of their constituency, so also material evidence of support ramifies their renown, broadcasting their reputation. However, extending one's name, one's wealth, and one's landed resources also brings major risks. First, those same emissaries who carry one's name can easily "spoil" it (*halam iyopengekn*) by behaving shamefully while representing one elsewhere. "People see these people and they remember you," and negative remembrances "make a person small again."

But more important, persons who "stand out" (*-mililase*) from others are also stepping away from the secure ground of group identification. This not only moves them out of earshot of the "discontent" (*sihawagnakgnak*) of close support relations who are feeling neglected, but also separates them from the protection that a group identity confers by masking their vulnerability as mortal individuals. Having stepped out of the shelter of collective identity, leaders say they feel the essentialness of knowing protective magic—the self-manufactured shield of those who "stand out"—believing they would soon be dead of envy-inspired sorcery without it.

Their comments reminded me of the Sabarl tradition of staining the teeth with betel juice. This is done by chewing betel nut and lime with black *tali* seeds (Melastomaceae: *Melastoma*) until the enamel is coated a gleaming reddish black. Once a part of coming-of-age rituals for boys and girls, blackened teeth are considered beautiful "because they make the teeth look like all one tooth," and "make the teeth stronger." Blackened teeth "don't fall out so easily." Collective activities that project an appearance of coordinated, unified strength likewise make people feel stronger, by bringing them to an experience of the force of their own collective image. But separated by ambition or achievement from the seamless mask of sociality—being memorable and distinguishable—persons "standing out" confess to feeling bare. Their cultural response is to coat themselves with magic words and knowledge, and with the beautifying feathers, shells, and cosmetic paint that convey their confidence and suggest the invisible presence of a strong (or wished-for) following. Returning to the story of the "bad" yam leader, prettily decorated only to be thrown away and left to rot, it is not entirely without smugness that ordinary people watch outstanding ones fall sick and die as, inevitably perhaps, their leaders fail them.

What this example demonstrates is the important difference between the positive Saisai value of "independence" or "self-rule" (*totou logugui*) and the *guiau*'s self-promoting generosity with its goal of generating a following—the difference also within the range of ambition between the comfortable status of hamlet directors and the uneasiness of those seeking fame beyond it.[14]

Successful leaders detach themselves from the negative aspect of extensive power when they remain at home (demonstrate stability) and send out alter images to other places: as "seers" (masters of rhetoric) whose reach is turned to the good of the community, and in concrete form as the wealth objects and offspring that carry their name farther in space and in time than they themselves expect to travel.

The Story of Taviavia

There is a very popular Sabarl narrative that profiles many of the features of the shame/fame syndrome we have touched on so far.

While his mother and father are away at the garden, a young boy, Taviavia, named for the weeping sores that cover his body, approaches a net-mending party on the beach in his village. The women have prepared a feast for the male workers, who will soon embark on a fishing expedition, and all the villagers are eating. But they chase away young Taviavia because the appearance of his skin and the stench of his sores are offensive. His parents return from the garden to find him crying alone. The following day the fleet leaves for the Manuge reef (a famous haunt of sorcerers). But Taviavia and his mother have gone before them. One by one, the canoes are drawn to the reef and wrecked. As they are drowning, the men see Taviavia, soreless now and resplendent, sitting with his mother among the birds (the clans) of the world, high on a great *mwadawa* tree (the tree used for manufacturing canoes) that has risen from the reef. Taviavia's father marries all the village widows.

Along the same lines as the story of the girl who was left behind by village mates to face Katutubwai, this is a story of the cataclysmic consequences of forgetting about shame. Young Taviavia, the very image of the painful exposure that subordinates suffer in their condition of shyness, approaches the group to ask for food (which he should have been offered as a matter of course at this feast for the "homeplace"). The scenario itself exposes the critical flaw in seeking primary allegiances at the superficial level of place—building, as it were, on the shifting sands of conditional, context-dependent loyalties: shyness and shows of respect at that level invite abuse. As we see by the outcome, which is a happy ending at least for Taviavia and his father (the relationship created through a woman), place-based allegiances stand in contrast to relations that articulate at marriage, with their foundation of shame in the enduring supports and complementarities generated by clanship. Indeed, it is the matriclan (here, a mother-son unit, since the story is one of masculine revenge and rule) that triumphs over shame and converts to fame. The medium of this conversion is the complex symbol of the red *mwadawa* tree, which elicits images of the red clan blood and the marriage canoes that are themselves archetypal signs of circulation (that is, the circulation of blood and of wealth). Supported by clanship and marriage, persons can rise above their shyness, distinguish themselves, and glorify their clan. However, the process of conversion has roots in the acquired, illegitimate knowledge of sorcery.

It is likewise a theme that aggressive action is an alternative to "depression" (*tomipahab*). One young man explained depression as being "like the sores are on the inside." Persons who are chronically moody, withdrawn, and enervated (the gloss is *lumaluma*) may in fact be spoken of as "*taviavia.*"

All in all, to ignore prospective shame is to risk the collapse of crucial distinctions on which society is based and through which it renews its values. The admonition is to seniors—to the inherently empowered—more than to the dominated, that the danger inheres in shyness's converting to fame at the cost of the destruction of place-based solidarity. The only possible way of "covering"—of officially forgetting—the ultimate shame of social abandonment is, figuratively, to officially forget (kill) those who are the living reminders of this terrible possibility and who carry it on into the future. The only "memory" that endures when all traces of place-based abandonment are gone is that of the matriclan in masculine profile.

*

In part 2 I have suggested the basic dimensions of social relationships on Sabarl. These relationships are constructed in exchanges and transfers of valued things that reveal how Sabarl persons anticipate their own disaggregation in their everyday lives. As we turn now to consider mortuary acts as the process by which these constructions are officially forgotten, and by which an openness to new relations is created in their place, we embark on a journey of Sabarl society itself, reframed as a cultural collage of particular histories and memories.

Part Three

The Person Performed

I knew when dark-haired evening put on
her bright silk at sunset, and, folding the sea,
sidled under the sheet with her starry laugh,
that there'd be no rest, there'd be no forgetting.
Is like telling mourners round the graveside
about resurrection, they want the dead back.

Derek Walcott

Eight

Segaiya

Projective Remembrance

We turn directly now to the subject of *segaiya*.[1] The term refers to the mortuary feast series as well as to the central exchange feast within the series, honoring the paternal matriclan. Yet the concept of *segaiya* goes beyond the commemoration of individuals. For *segaiya* is an act of restoration: people are reconstituting, symbolically and collectively, the relationship they have lost as a part of their own historically situated identities; collectivities of persons are being restored to themselves. *Segaiya* thus rewrites the relation of society to the social person, creating a fictional, multiply authored "memory" from the stuff of "custom." It is in this sense that *segaiya* commemorates memory itself.

As we move through the series of feasts, the broad theme is projective remembrance: the fabrication of a future for the dead within the feelings and thoughts of participants; the fabrication also of a sense of order, control, and security in the face of mortality; and finally, the fabrication of a present perspective on enduring cultural values.

An essential requirement of projective remembrance—the creation of a future text on the theme of personhood—is that it be a "proper" performance. Let there be no mistake: we are concerned here with the dramaturgy of memory, where theatricality is an essential feature of memory making. (I will discuss this further in the concluding chapter.) However, *segaiya* is a dramatic performance without "roles," at least as we commonly think of them. That is, the actors are not so much taking on another identity and function within the frame of the stage as coming into themselves in an expanded sense (e.g., as living embodiments of their clans). They are also detaching from themselves in a final way—severing bonds of relationship that return them to an unencumbered, contractually free social state vis-à-vis the deceased's 155 survivors. Thus Sabarl are engaged in reconstituting social selves, not shedding or donning social masks.

In addition, projective remembrance entails what might be termed "achieved redundancy": the layered repetition of personally and culturally significant forms and processes that generates an experience of continuity, largely through the perception that time and space have collapsed. This is essentially a matter of doing things in a particular way because one has done them before in an everyday context, and of using particular things on this occasion (e.g., types of food and objects, songs, dances, words, dress, cosmetics) because they were used before. It is the fact of a prior, localized experience that accounts for the significance of these objects and actions in commemorative practice and endows them with affective force: the fact of using or doing things again in reference to this particular relationship *for the last time* is what endows key elements of the performance, beyond cultural meaning, with personal meaning. In other words, we are concerned with a symbolic process of making meaning *seem* continuous for individuals as for societies. So it is, for example, that persons who have lived away from Sabarl culture for any length of time find their experience of *segaiya* an empty one if they return for a visit, no matter how well they remember or how well they are coached in the rituals and ceremonial etiquette. The reason is that they are merely acting this continuity.

Last, projective remembrance involves returning the physical person to the living, in symbolic forms that are socially useful. In *segaiya*, survivors exchange and redistribute material substitutes for the dead in the form of things that were used in life to extend their influence through space and time. Thus we are also concerned with generativity: the potential for the next generation of heirs or trading partners to add "new shoots" to the story of social growth that the dead person lived.

The Feasts in Sequence

What follows is a rendering of the main events of commemorative feasting, as people pointed them out to me. I shall be emphasizing not so much the level of disputes and strategizing and political machinations as what Sabarl people wished me to record—the significant actions that comprised *paga*, or "custom." I have witnessed all the events mentioned here from one to five times. Thus my understanding is uneven, and uneven in a different way than is the understanding of those who happened to be available for commentary and discussion. But about what counted as "custom" there was consensus, and it is *paga* that provides the framework for what follows.

We begin, then, with a profile of the "typical" death of a notable male elder. Where gender alters the shape or content of events, it is noted and discussed. The expectation among Sabarl is that men will die earlier than women, mainly owing to their greater exposure to sorcery and witchcraft in their generally more public life careers. Women who follow their husbands shortly afterward to the grave also conform to a pattern that Sabarl anticipate and find sad and somewhat beautiful. However, women in politics invite the same risks as men, and their commemorative feasts, or those held for a child of a notable man or woman (someone within that person's own personal "domain")[2] are not essentially different from the following account.

The Agents

Segaiya activities focus on the deceased and three key figures who represent the core of his social world: his father's, mother's and spouse's matriclans. These are the people who, in their separate ways, have nurtured the person during his lifetime.

The Paternal Clan Representative

Representing his father's clan is the special patrilateral cross-cousin (FZS/D) with whom the person shared a ritualized feeding relationship throughout most of his lifetime. This is the cousin he called either "my father" (*tamau*) or "my substance/force eater" (*hinona ihen*) and who called him "my child" or "my sago pudding" (*no moni*). With the death of his "child," the cousin "father" assumes the title of *tohan segaiya*—"*segaiya* eater." It is his (or her) primary responsibility to prepare the corpse and bury it. In this capacity the *tohan segaiya* stands apart from the maternal and affinal clan representatives, although he is allied with the later as "affine" in other respects, as I will discuss shortly.

The Maternal Clan Representative

The maternal clan units who sponsor mortuary exchange feasts are known as *totonewaga* (sing., *tonewaga*), and they stand for maternal clan direction and dominance. Representing this unit is the chosen clan heir, most commonly the sister's son or surviving senior sibling of the deceased. The heir is someone the dead man was expected to support and "look after" (*matahasik*) and who supported him in other ways. The heir's relationship to the deceased never entailed a ritualized gift contract, with its object of manufacturing a relationship between clans. Nonetheless it would have involved the expectation of reciprocal respect, carried on the prospect of a flow of property and food between them. In other words, the relationship would have developed through a shared consciousness of mutual gain, with mutuality based on the bond of blood as well as on convergent personal and social goals. It is on the basis of same-clan identity that the heir would often have substituted or worked for the deceased and is now obligated to take responsibility for publicly overriding the generational rupture that has occurred—for example, by taking his name or otherwise symbolically collapsing social distinctions between them.

The heir's duties consist mainly of "looking after the memory" of the dead person: coordinating prestations of memorial wealth and organizing the schedule of activities for the three major clan groups—particularly in connection with feeding off-island visitors. In terms of social identity, it is as if another version of the dead person were hosting his own funeral and overseeing his own commemoration. For it is the memory of the heir's performance at deathtime that continues in place of the dead, so that heirs invoke the latent image of the dead throughout the rest of their lifetimes. In return, the mother's clan representative asserts his right of control over any property, especially land, that was not transferred to clan mates during the dead person's lifetime. He also has the right to demand further payments toward consolidating transfers to nonclanspeople.

THE WIDOWED SPOUSE

Representing the junior affines or *totolamwau* (sing., *tovelam*) is the widowed spouse. Her affinal position would always have placed her in service to her husband's senior clanspeople and obligated her junior relations to support them materially with *muli* (affinal support) on ceremonial occasions. She displays her self-effacement and "shame" to them now in her deathtime identity of primary mourner. In effect her shame becomes her prison. Her body and face masked out entirely by charcoal paint, she is the living image of human vacancy to which the death of her husband has reduced her in the eyes of senior affines. Throughout the early feasts especially, the long shadow of affinal rule cancels her identity, rendering her socially a nonperson. Her appearance also recalls the image of the unrecognizable female *waunak*, and as such she represents illicit consumption at the scene of death.

During her confinement, the widow is expected nonetheless to be sending covert directives to her children and siblings and generally orchestrates the complicated business of obtaining pigs and valuables that, over time, will purchase her release from further economic obligations to her husband's kin. To the extent that she accomplishes this, she is freeing herself to remarry.

The widowed spouse shares with the ritual "father" a relationship to the deceased that is constructed through "feeding," across differences in blood. This shared position becomes the basis of a collapse of their separate identities into one affinal unit, achieved during the mortuary feasting. It is also represented in the dead person's *tovelam* work force—the junior affines brought into relational being to him through the widow.

Thus, underlying the triadic clan structure of Sabarl society and the premise of interclan symmetry is a dyadic structure, based on the asymmetry of "others" vis-à-vis the maternal matriclan. The control of the clanspeople over the affines during mortuary feasting creates an asymmetry that renders all affines junior, regardless of their generation. We have of course been cued to expect something like this in observing how the seniority of fathers is displaced onto their nieces and nephews when they become "fathers" symbolically: their acts of nurture, anticipating the postmortem situation, obviate generational differences. And we can now see how spouses, in their *tovelam* servitude, are similarly directed by this final asymmetry of clanspeople over the "other."

Alongside the widowed spouse and the ritual father, "otherness" operates on a less inclusive level through the *seveseve*, who are the "close junior affines" of the deceased—for example, a man's children (or a dead woman's children's spouses). *Seveseve* may even host certain feasts when they are making claims to land. Finally, there is the circumscribing asymmetry represented by the *tubu* audience: the ancestors and soon-to-be-ancestors, the living elder *tubu*, who are thought to be watching the proceedings very closely in case they are called upon to contribute wealth.

Clan-based relationships are only one kind of dyadic identifier. Cutting across them are the place-based dyads: "us" ("people of the village," *tonhiyeba*) versus "others" ("guests," *bwabwali*). Thus clan distinctions will carry through in those feasts where, for example, the object is to lift a taboo on people of the village rather than to "straighten" relations between clans. But they may be "covered" or obviated by the necessity of feeding and caring for the dead person's trading partners and off-island kin. As events that emphasize social divisions within the community, those exchanges or distributions that are clan oriented are usually scheduled to occur before visitors arrive to witness them.

To summarize, on the most inclusive level the relationships of *tovelam* (affine, junior) and *tonewaga* (maternal clansperson, senior) are the lowest common denominator in social organization in *segaiya*:

those who support and bury and incorporate the singular person. Since a person is not allowed to marry within the matriclan, the *tovelam* and *tonewaga* represent the precondition, beyond procreation, of social and cultural reproduction. *Segaiya* rituals, exchanges, and distributions stage their intercourse and deliver the promise of this interactional order. But it is a promise fulfillable only by extension to "others" as "guests" (*bwabwali*) by "people of the village" (*tonhiyeba*), in a process of seeking and drawing home valued things that are used to construct and deconstruct "memories" of the dead.

The Death Scene

Lying in the central open room of his house, a man is dying. Close kin have surrounded him, some already crying. When they hear his "death rattle" (*garlgarl*) they begin to moan, and their weeping becomes louder. Gradually males (other than the closest kin among them) leave the house, and female relatives and friends stream in. The moaning grows louder, more stylized, as others are drawn to the scene. Soon the only sounds to be heard are the descending chants of mourners overlapping their voices in waves of open grief.

The widow is center stage in the chorus of keeners. It is her role to dramatize grief as primary *hagabwe* or "female mourner" (masc., *sibwauwa*). The role becomes her ritual title as well as her most conspicuous identity in the months and years to follow. The period between her husband's death and his burial is the time of the "longest sleep" (*hiyena mwenewa*) when she lies beside him, clinging to his body, weeping over it and caressing it.

As inside the house the sea of women weep or sleep or talk softly together, outside the "organizers" (*tonlogugui*), mostly men, discuss the details of the following day's activities. The atmosphere outside is morose, and behavior is restrained. Soon people begin to appear strained and unkempt, though only junior affines take on the formal mourning attire of shame. Women are scrutinized and are particularly fastidious in this regard. Painstakingly, they blacken their skins with itchy charcoal paint (*taudum*), quickly repairing any spots rubbed off. They leave their hair uncombed and don "heavy" fiber mourning skirts (*yogayoga*) or else black cloth ones. Men are significantly less articulate in expressing their shame; they smear their bodies roughly with pieces of charcoal and let their beards grow out, and they usually wear dark or black shirts and "laplaps," trousers, or armbands. Meanwhile, the maternal and paternal clanspeople remain relatively well groomed and aloof.

The dramatic separation of women and men into interior and exterior space at the moment of death enacts an important dichotomy in Sabarl social organization. The message, however, is not entirely or even primarily about gender. Although it is women who are inside wailing (and widowers likewise, "feminized" and subordinated by their grief), the important contrast following death is that of the flow of tears and sounds at the scene of death (inside the house) with the restricted behavior and long silences at the scene of the reconstruction of social life (outside the house). The persons acting out this contrast are actually inverting a gender stereotype that depicts women as "cool," cerebral, and rational and men as "hot" and more prone to "wild," emotional behavior. Symbolically, the charged interior brings the house alive again through grief, while outside, social life is paralyzed by it.

Thus the theme of the period following death's disorientation is "out of chaos, delineation," with private and public, intellectual and physical, feminine and masculine, maternal and affinal aspects of personhood having already emerged. The delineation is etched in social space by the contrasting movements of aggregates of survivors: centripetally toward the house interior (withdrawal into the realm of flow), centrifugally into the exterior space surrounding it (the realm of interaction), where the "death house" (*tomata na yuma*) becomes functionally fused with the dead person as the orienting object of social action.

The widow leaves her husband's body only to relieve herself, and then beneath the heavy concealment of skirts and capes, with a large smoke-blackened basket covering her head and shoulders. Women of her husband's clan walk slowly ahead of her and behind her on the way to the bush, holding a pandanus sleeping mat (*baloma na lam*, "mat of the dead") over her head like a roof. This unfolded mat recalls a time before bedsheets and coffins when the dead were wrapped in their sleeping mats to be carried to the grave. In effect, then, the widow leaves neither her husband's body nor the shelter and confinement of the death house, both represented by the mat. She is said to be caught by her senior in-laws "like a fish in a net." But besides ensnaring her, confinement is said to protect her against *waunak* attacks on her weakened spirit. The costume, the guards, the mat, the wailing performance, the death house: all can be viewed as a complex mask for a state of potent pollution—images of the burdensome taboos that cloak this time and this place.

Solu

At some point during the second day, a helmet-shell trumpet sounds at the village perimeter. The sound is significant, first, because it opens the period of restoration, and second, because it signals a shift away from the level of individual feelings and toward collective action.

The trumpet heralds a procession of the junior affines, carrying a single large pig and a red shell necklace as an "appeasement offering," or *solu*, to the senior clanspeople of the dead. This gift is the first of several ritual acts "to wash their dirty hands" (*nimabikina*) of a shame condition that death has made an acute problem. They hang the necklace outside the door, where it remains while pigs are delivered beneath the house by affines from other villages and islands. At times a canoe may be offered in place of the *solu* necklace. When this occurs it is "forbidden" (*sinosino*) to use the canoe interior until the taboo is ritually lifted, "since the body of the dead man sat there." Any infringement would result at the very least in boils on the ears, whose shape canoes recall.

The hours pass, the pigs' squeals from beneath the house mingling with the wailing inside. The clanspeople meanwhile remove the *solu* necklace and begin preparing food in their own homes for visiting outsiders. Cooking so close to death amounts largely to private hospitality gestures on the part of close kin villagers for any visitors they have taken in. As such it has no ritual significance, although it is framed within the context of "deathtime" (*gabub*), which imparts solemnity to the preparations. However, the mother's clan representative does have two important symbolic acts to perform. First, he goes to the dead man's garden and does whatever task is appropriate for the time of year (planting, harvesting, etc.). This assures the ancestor that he need not return to his garden—that it is being tended in his absence. It also "opens" the garden for use in feeding visitors. The heir repeats this chore for coconut plantations and sago groves, ritually cutting down a tree. Then he returns to the village, where cooking is under way by people of the place who are not in a state of pollution—the mother's clanspeople, with father's clanspeople "helping." Most of the burden falls on the unmarried girls, who work extremely hard splitting firewood and preparing food. Their work is made more awkward by a ban on carrying loads on their heads—a sign of "respect" for the ancestral pate. Bearing loads on their shoulders, they work like men.

Later in the day the food is quietly distributed under the guidance of maternal clanswomen. Pieces of uncooked pork for the affinal pigs "complement" (*gaba*) the basic garden foods the maternal clanspeople supply, with both sides contributing sago. The food is eaten quietly inside the various houses as evening approaches. These private gestures demonstrate that the village and the core of kin who represent it

(as affines and clanspeople) are still socially "alive." Also, the appeasement offerings that remove the taboo on eating pork and the "opening"
of the dead man's food resources are the first in an intricate series of
acts to "lift" (*lekeleke*) the layers of deathtime restrictions.

Meanwhile the cousin "father," the *tohan segaiya*, is preparing
the corpse. The mourners cry a little less as they watch him chatting
softly to the widow while he shaves the dead man's beard and cuts the
hair, reserving the tufts to distribute afterward as relics. Then he
washes the body in hot water and dresses it in "best clothes" (almost
always unused European ones) before anointing the exposed parts with
coconut oil. The oil is followed by a scent mask of herbs and baby
powder,[3] intended to overpower the stench that is regarded as the only
"true" sign the person is dead. Red shell chokers (*samwakupwa*) and
small necklaces of black and white beads are tied round the neck.
Then the face is painted with black-and-white designs that identify the
spirit to his clan in the afterworld.[4] The word for painting the face is
the word for matriclan (*hun*). This is not just a gesture of identification,
but one of respect for others past and present who are the person's
collective aspect. Face paint in other words acknowledges the history
of contributions of blood and food to the person and its effect of "positive transformation" during life. Finally, a stone ax blade is placed
under the head, and the mouth is covered with other forms of currency—paper kina notes, a black lip shell "spoon" (*kepu*) or a red lip
shell (*daperli*).[5]

Thus the body is made into an effigy of the social person—an
artifact, displaying the accoutrements of status and youthful beauty.
This project visually equates the dead person with an ancestral ideal,
counteracting (at least superficially) the travesty of the physically decomposing individual. It is at this point that a ritual expert, usually
from the father's clan, conducts a summary divination (*luwabwa*) by
waving over the body a small pandanus bundle with diagnostic substances inside.[6] The bundle is hung in a secluded niche in the house
and later examined privately for signs that could indicate the cause of
death. These days, divinations have no public consequences.

By dawn on the third day, with a few close kin still en route from
jobs on the mainland, people are growing anxious that the decomposing corpse will pollute the entire community. Women make loud spit-
ting noises, protesting the odor as they pass by the house. At last the
decision is made to transfer the body from its sleeping mat to the coffin
the cousin "father" has either purchased or made and to cover it with
bedsheets. By now the corpse has become the centerpiece of a "dis-

play" (*paisela*) of wealth constructed by the mourning women. They have suspended long lengths of cloth from the crossbeams above it and hung long shell necklaces that chime softly. Ceremonial axes and "bulk wealth" are piled all around. A pot of cooked garden food is placed near the head, made fresh each day by a clanswoman. All these things will "fill his canoe" (*na waga hinona*) on the journey to the afterworld, though only as "images" (*kanukanunu-*): the physical objects will be quietly recovered by their owners while the body is being interred.

But first the coffin must be filled with wealth and luxuries that will in fact be taken to the grave. This is the work of the widow and children, in a performance of abandoned, hysterical giving. Sobbing and wailing, they attempt to cram too many precious things into the coffin. The *tohan segaiya* gently restrains them, while trying not to interfere with their expressions of grief. In the end, while bundles of sago, ornaments, clothing, valuables, and small luxuries such as soap and betel nut are "piled" up over the corpse—lending the alternative name of Palo ("Bulk Wealth") to the burial day—seldom does more than one ax blade remain inside the coffin, together with some personal domestic items too intimate and polluted for use by anyone else. There will also be a seed yam placed at the head of the corpse "where his left hand can carry it" to an afterworld garden, and over his right shoulder a cooked sago pancake, "because his right hand knows how to eat." Last, at least in theory, his wife's skillet, a concave potsherd (*kulubagewa*), is placed over his face. This, according to ritual experts, is the "most important" item in the coffin, even over food, "because without it the person could not cook" in the afterworld. Ironically, it is usually forgotten.

Following this segment of the burial activities is an open-air mass behind the house, presided over by the local catechist or the priest if he is available. Junior affines then carry the coffin to the grave (*heli-waga*) at the village edge.[7] The widow follows weeping, physically supported by her children; the rest of the community comes behind. The coffin is lowered, then a handful of sand is sprinkled into the grave by the cousin "father," I was told, to spare the widow the pain of hearing the earth strike the box. Still, the soft sound inspires fresh weeping and the widow is led back to the house before the father's clanspeople fill in the grave. The fresh grave is covered "like a house" by an open mat "roof," propped up by a spindly fence intended to keep animals away. A ritual expert may at this point dust the top of the grave with powdered lime, creating a field where the name of a sorcerer can be written in the night. If no name appears, there is apt to be little further talk of sorcery—at least in pubic.

Inside the house the widow is crying quietly over the place where the body lay, when suddenly the dead man's children appear, enraged and sobbing, sticks and boards in hand, and begin to batter the walls and supports. Lamps are shattered and floorboards splintered as people gather to watch from a distance, showing flickering signs of sympathy mixed with flinching uneasiness as valuable objects are dramatically demolished. Once the house would have been destroyed completely. Among Sabarl, this rarely happens today.[8]

*

Primarily, people have two incentives to organize and carry out after-death activities according to "custom." One is to morally validate themselves and their kin and village—to prove themselves "true" persons in the social sense, that is, persons who can "recognize" a moral code and have feelings for other human beings. This is a complicated business of making themselves memorable as they set about "finishing" the memory of the deceased *that they themselves were part of* and thus, paradoxically, killing off a part of themselves. In this sense their participation is a sacrifice that conflates donor and recipient; that is, the distinction itself is the sacrificial gift.

However, what reinforces this attitude is the belief in what the spirits are capable of doing for and to the living in return. The time between death and burial is tense and anxious in this regard; the environment is thick with tales of sightings of the dead persons's restless spirit, of the *waunak* attracted by the stench of the corpse, of startling *baloma*. The burial night is especially dangerous, for it is then that the spirits of *waunak* are thought to gather and feast on their victims. Accordingly, only those who have died "natural" deaths—for example, in very old age or after a lifelong illness—are thought to truly rest in peace.

The Feast of Hanyalogi

On the morning following the burial a new phase of commemoration begins.[9] The strain of the previous days has lifted, to be replaced by almost palpable relief. It remains to begin "lifting" the pollution that has paralyzed normal activity for the junior affines since the time of the death and to continue the process of "washing dirty hands."

This process involves all three clans in a set of rituals and exchanges known as Hanyalogi, literally "Fish Eating," to lift the affinal taboo on local fishing and on eating food from the sea. Before the feast can begin, the widow herself must be released from the maternal clan net and ritually washed of the pollution that has prevented her from touching food since her husband died—making her dependent in an infantile way on the clanswomen to spoon occasional tidbits into her mouth. The ritual, called "bringing down" the widow (*papagolau*), is enacted at the edge of the sea, where she exchanges ceremonial axes with the maternal clanswomen who have been guarding her. Turning to face the widow, the clanswomen hand her their axes and splash her with purifying seawater, after which she hands them hers. The gesture is said to mean "my weapon is yours and your weapon is mine," and it symbolically cancels enmity between the widow and her deliverers— but likewise collapses the foundations of their relationship. The widow is now free to move about the village and oversee food preparation for the feast to follow.

Hanyalogi is launched when the mother's clan representative escorts a group of junior affinal males to his own clan's canoes and "opens" them for use in catching fish. This likewise, I was told, opens the canoes as the "ears" of the villagers must be opened, so that they can learn to speak again in normal (rather than hushed) conversational voices. The affines leave to go fishing and, when they return with the catch they anchor the canoes in the lagoon and remain sitting quietly on board. The mother's clan representative wades out to them and spears a small fish from the catch. Shouldering the spear he returns to shore, where he is joined by several young men of his clan. Together they file through the village with the little fish skewered on the spear, the leader and his followers chanting loudly (and not without embarrassment) in "call and response" (*hoiyalayala*) until they reach the veranda of the death house. Their shouts "open the voices" of the people of the village, so that they no longer need to speak in lowered tones. Meanwhile the widow's group has prepared hot food, which they give to the men in exchange for the fish. Each member of the group, male and female, has taken part in each step of the food preparation, queueing up to toss a piece of yam into a pot, scrape a coconut once or twice, and so forth—symbolically reengaging in the nurture process. The maternal clansmen then carry the food to the canoes, where the fishermen eat before bringing the catch to shore to be distributed. A mother's clan representative oversees the distribution.

PIPIWONA

The first portion of the catch goes to the father's clan representative, whose clanspeople participate in cooking it, together with the other feast foods, inside the *tohan segaiya's* house. Thus begin preparations for the ritualized exchanges of Pipiwona. The name is a reference to the etiquette of "breaking food into pieces" before eating, in the fashion of the *pip*, a small fruit-eating bird. Interestingly, widows released from mourning, like infants and mothers making their debuts in the village after postnatal confinement, wear *pipiwona* designs on their cheeks and foreheads. Likewise, this phase of the feasting is the first formal gesture of reentry into society of the widow's group as persons capable of reciprocating nurture.

When their scouts have determined that the father's group has finished preparing their food, a member of the widow's group formally approaches the *tohan segaiya* and asks, "Are your things ready?" The *tohan segaiya* responds by having his helpers carry the cooked food into the death house. He himself follows. The ambiance is gay and relaxed as the *tohan segaiya* takes pieces of the food in his hand, makes a gesture of encircling his own face with the food, and places the food in the mouths of the widow's group, as the dead person's father did "when he gave the person food as a baby, with his hand." The members of the widow's group return the gesture, using utensils that they afterward give to the *tohan segaiya* along with a small amount of money (20 toya on average). By the end, everyone is joking and laughing and messy. This continues until each person in the widow's group has fed and been fed by the *tohan segaiya*. Long before the end he is so full that he waves the food away. Then the members of the widow's group carry the food they have cooked to the house of the *tohan segaiya* and each group retreats to its separate house to eat—although not before the ritual "father" has taken a plate of food and eaten from it as he walks around the village perimeter, "opening the place" to eating together in public.

I was told that along the lines of the previous seaside exchanges "to bring down" the widow, the message of Pipiwona is "my food is your food and your food is my food." Beyond this, however, what is enacted at Pipiwona is the collapse of generational distinctions between sources of nurture created through marriage and the creation of a nurturant unit through death. The more explicit effect of Pipiwona is to move the widow out of confinement—out of the womb "net" of the maternal clan's domain. The maternal clan, in other words, delivers her, on the model of the first ancestor, out of a timeless mythical existence, back into mortal, durational time. She is cleansed like a newborn and fed like an infant by the *tohan segaiya*, as if she, and not her dead husband, were being born again. And indeed, this is a familiar pattern in mortuary rituals worldwide (for this Durkheimian perspective, see discussions in Huntington and Metcalf 1979): that survivors' cultural conduct echoes the progress and perils of the dead in the journey to the afterworld and death rites in general echo on the level of structure the rituals of birth. However, such identifications are cultural setups in the Sabarl context, for the relationship is born, as it were, to die.

That this process parallels the simultaneous delivery of the junior affines, the *tovelam* work force, from their servitude to the dead is significant in gender terms also. The performed contractions of maternal clanswomen's normal activities within the death house, imaged even in the implosive force of wailers collapsing onto the body, form the basis of a structural and emotional empathy with the widow's clan as they deliver the *tovelam*. As we shall see, this mode of delivery contrasts with the *tohan segaiya's* delivery of the widow's group in the subsequent feast of Moni: a masculine delivery, acted out with explosive aggression.

Throughout this period the mother's and father's clan representatives continue to share a central role as the restorers of life—though life in a new form—to those whose routines the death has touched. The period of appeasement ends on this note.

Over the next few days, the visitors from other villages or islands pack their things and move their canoes from the beach to the lagoon, preparing to depart. The village grounds are swept. And for the clan representatives—the widow, the cousin "father" and the heirs of the deceased—the search for food and wealth for the second major feast begins.[10]

Between the Feasts

We have seen that in many respects the death house is an epicenter of deathtime (*gabub*) activity. However, the pattern of peripheral action following a death is not analogous to a straightforward ripple effect. For though it is true on the most general level that fewer people are involved the farther they live from the dead person's home village, death is the catalyst of realignments of political and spiritual power in other places simultaneously, so that public attention jumps back and forth between different critical points and persons of interest throughout the island community. Thus attention may converge on a potential heir who moved away, or on the canoe she borrowed and sublet to someone elsewhere. And wherever the objects of interest wander, they pull along with them the force of deathtime restrictions. Time reverts to the moment of death wherever these objects of high ambivalence, usually in more or less taboo states, are or go. The effect is to ignite throughout the island community discrete, small-scale incidents of ritualized exchange aimed at lifting taboos and otherwise reestablishing rank and order. For example, Hanyalogi may be performed in a number of villages other than the one where the dead person lived, to release those affines unable to attend the burial (because they were sick, had no transport, had no food to contribute because gardens had failed, were too old to travel, etc.). Gradually these events decrease in frequency as the various death predicaments are resolved; gradually also, new obligations and growth of new relationships are instigated.

There are a variety of peripheral deathtime interactions, alike in that they tend to be more idiosyncratic, less formalized, than the central events. These fall into two broad subcategories according to whether the interactions are in spirit or in the flesh.

The spiritual variety has primarily to do with interaction between living and dead survivors—especially the living and their ancestors. For example, an old man dreams a conversation with someone who has died several islands away and relates it to village mates at a public meeting. His story has the effect of drawing attention away from the scene of the death and, if he has told it convincingly, becomes a subject of widespread speculation—"carrying his name" from island to island exactly as if he were a central actor at the scene. Or a daughter of a dead man reports having seen her father's hand at her house on Tagula. Her story travels with her there, and wherever she sails in search of valuables for the subsequent feast, and wherever her children go on her behalf.

Peripheral material exchanges are primarily about repealing taboos, settling inter vivos disputes, or soliciting valuables from trading partners for the feast to follow. These peripheral exchanges, material and spiritual, are important. For through them deathtime invades the everyday time between feasts—in effect making death business everyday.

The Feast of Hanlekeleke

When several months later the major clan representatives have amassed sufficient food and wealth, the time of the feast of Hanlekeleke ("Lifting the Food Taboo") is announced from island to island by messenger canoes. Hanlekeleke is primarily a place-centered feast, variously described as lifting the taboo "on eating pork together [in public]," "on feasting in public," and "on cooking in public," wherever the survivors reside—wherever the memory of the relationship survives. People will not have sailed much farther than other Sabarl-speaking places in search of wealth. The object is to draw home those who are away making gardens or sago or working and residing elsewhere in the Chain.

On the day of the feast, the deep, hollow sound of shell trumpets announces the approach of canoes carrying pigs. Throughout the previous week, the mother's clan (*tonewaga*) "directors" have stockpiled firewood, coconuts, water, and food as well as rice from the local trade store, and a ritual expert has bespelled them to ensure that supplies will be plentiful enough. Garden food in particular is believed to multiply itself under magical influence where it is stored in the house of the hosts. Also, the widow's clansmen and junior affines (*totolamwa-*) have gone fishing with nets the night before. Once again the maternal clan heirs preside over the events, jointly with the paternal clan *tohan segaiya*. Both will be honored by the widow's clan and the *tovelam* work force.

When it appears that everyone has arrived, the mother's clanspeople deliver supplies of food to each affinal household as well as portions of fish and pork from paternal clan donations. In the public space behind each house, stone ovens are assembled and fires built for the large clay pots of vegetables, pork, and fish, and for the sago-coconut pudding that only men can prepare. By midafternoon each household has finished cooking its allotment of maternal and paternal clan food.

The focal events of Hanlekeleke are prestations of wealth to the maternal and paternal clanspeople from members of the widow's group suing for release from affinal obligations. The feast is "opened" by the *tohan segaiya* when he presents five (sometimes four) ceremonial axes to the widow's clan, inside the death house. The axes are named for his services as undertaker and constitute a request for reimbursement.[11] Immediately, couriers vanish with the ax blades, taking them around to other members of the widow's group to assess their value against the group's holdings. Unless it is determined that they can match the ax blades with ones of equal value plus one or two extra, the *tohan segaiya* is asked privately to wait for the delivery of his wealth until the subsequent feast.

Either way, the stage is set for the exchanges that follow. They begin inside the death house with women of the widow's group assembling piles of "bulk wealth" (*palo*) over the spot where the body previously lay. This is the first of three "corpses" (*gimbane*) of wealth, assembled only to be disassembled shortly after, in the space still imbued with an affecting power from contact with the actual body. Typically there are two piles: one for the cousin "father," the *tohan segaiya*, and one for the maternal clan heirs. The "corpse," in short, is symbolically resurrected—but not, significantly, as an androgynous totality. Rather, the dead person has been symbolically decomposed by junior affines and presented as a return gift to his parental sources.

Recalling the story of the young woman who was chopped to pieces by a jealous husband, only to be resurrected by her grandmother from a ceremonial platter, each *palo* has as its base a large sago cake (*bwebwai*) in a round wooden platter (*nohai*). On top of the cake the women arrange objects of ephemeral domestic wealth (skirts, mats, baskets, cloth), building a mound roughly the height of an adult person. Purists will say that only these items are appropriate as *palo*. Yet far more common is to layer raw yams on top of the cake as a kind of "padding" and to build the other items around them. Also, women nowadays always include clay cooking pots, store-bought pots and pans, and eating utensils—domestic items that are semidurable. Finally, money and pieces of gold lip shell may be tucked into ceremonial axes and placed on top of (or sometimes beside) the pile for the *tohan segaiya* as a further promise of repayment for his undertaking services.

The piles comprise the collected contributions of those persons who wish to be released by one or the other of the parental representatives. However, to contribute bulk wealth to the paternal clan is on this occasion optional, since the focus of Hanlekeleke is on the maternal clan's nurture contributions. Whether a junior affine decides at this feast to contribute wealth for the *tohan segaiya* or for the clan heir, or some wealth for each, depends partly on his or her material resources. But it is also a matter of which "side" one wishes to acknowledge this gift by returning something the affine needs or wants. For example, one may choose the ritual "father" because he has agreed in advance to acknowledge the *palo* with land. In this case the affine would usually wait until the subsequent feast, which honors the paternal matriclan more or less exclusively.

The only persons with little flexibility in the matter of *palo* are those children of the dead (*seveseve*—in the case of a deceased female, her children's spouses) who wish to make a bid for their father's residential property for themselves or for their mother. These nonclan hopefuls must at some point present *palo* to the clan heirs and include ax blades and other durable wealth objects alongside it. A prestation of this type is called *lam golgol*, "rolling up the mat" of the dead person. *Palo* is presented in the usual way, heaped up in the center of the dead man's house. Then, in addition, durable wealth is rolled in a pandanus mat, which is tied at the ends "as if the dead body were inside." I was told: "Instead of the house, you give them only a mat for their memory," the "grease" or increment of durable wealth in place of the ephemeral body with which the *palo* and the house are both associated. The maternal clan heir will take the wealth away to his own house to count it. If the payment is judged sufficient, the transaction is closed—at least while the memory of it survives. Otherwise more wealth will be demanded at subsequent mortuary feasts, or else at a Tagalekeleke, a feast to lift the taboo on transferring land, held specifically for the purpose of clearing debts to the land's previous owners.

Returning now to the feast at hand, we find that the *tohan segaiya* is the first to be called to collect his *palo*. He and his helpers enter the house and take it away to redistribute it. The "father" himself keeps only the ax blades (their handles are returned to the owners) and the gold lip shells and money. The rest is divided among clan mates and supporters who "helped" him cook for the previously held Pipiwona. The maternal clan heirs collect their *palo* next and retreat to divide it likewise.

At this point a blast of the shell trumpet calls the affinal women to the public area behind the death house for "combining" (*hotowoi*) food they prepared earlier in the day. Together with their *tovelam* "helpers," they converge on the clearing, their baskets of cooked food on their heads, in what amounts to a parade of most if not all of the village women. A leading maternal clanswoman (the dead man's sister or niece) awaits them. She is seated at one end of a long palm-leaf "path" (*hiyela*). The *tovelam* women seat themselves around the path and remove from their baskets empty enamel basins, which they place on the leaves. Some bring along wooden platters. Amid teasing and laughter and the loud bossy voices of the elder clanswomen, the women begin tossing food into each other's platters and basins until it has been equally "distributed" (*pwala*). With the casual vigilance of poker players, they conceal the contents of their own baskets and appraise what the others are contributing, often—with characteristic *sabsabarl* frugality—not contributing all they have brought along. Finally they remove their own dishes from the path, now filled with other people's food, and return to their houses. The food is said to reward the women for their cooking services during the Solu period. In fact, no woman of the place would be left out of any sizable *hotowoi*.

While the women are engaged in "combining," the men are removing pots of pork and of sago-coconut pudding and large wooden platters of sago cake from the public cooking area and placing them on palm mats laid out in front of their houses. To this is added the food from the *hotowoi* (with some especially nice foods held back for the

children and women to eat inside the house). Then a maternal clans-
man sounds the trumpet for the second time in a call to *"hanlekeleke."* This sends *tovelam* males off to find men from one of the other
clan groups to sample a spoonful of each of the foods displayed in front
of their houses, "lifting the taboo on public feasting" (although we
note that in fact "togetherness" is displayed by males alone). A community prayer, led by a church representative, is sometimes offered at
this point (this was a rather recent innovation in 1986). The men afterward eat a small portion of food, squatting around the mat and dipping
shell or metal spoons into the pots, then pause to shout "thank you"
(again, in unison) to the maternal clanspeople, who watch from behind
their houses without eating. The remainder of the food is removed to
the house interiors for the women and children and for people to return
to as they become hungry later in the evening.

In the final prestation of the Hanlekeleke, food is returned to the
junior affines by those who received *palo* earlier. The exchange scenario is in many ways a complementary development of the individually enacted nurture rituals and exchanges of Solu, where the *palo* that
the widow's group contributed to the coffin was acknowledged by
cooked food supplied by the heirs.

On one level these exchanges establish the parity of givers and
receivers in the gift and countergift of bulk for bulk, ephemera for
ephemera, *muli* (affinal support) for *muli*. Yet on another level, they
render transactors distinct within their sameness. For by accepting the
comestible transformations of domestic labor, the affines symbolically
act out their shame as consumers.

The Feast of Moni

It is usual for a year or two to pass before the feast of Moni or "Sago-
Coconut Pudding" is scheduled for harvestime. This is the feast alternatively called Segaiya. Preparations for Moni are more elaborate than
those for the feasts preceding it, and people express this in terms of
how far they are willing to sail to obtain the wealth they will need for
the occasion, which in this case is to the farthest reaches of their trading networks.

Moni is regarded as quintessentially *segaiya*, the most important
of the mortuary exchange feasts. Its primary objectives are, first, to pay
final tribute to the *tohan segaiya*, the paternal clan representative, for
past contributions to the dead "child," and second, to honor the paternal clan as a vehicle of release for the junior affines from subordination
to maternal clanspeople. These objectives involve the widow and the

tovelam work force, now "working" for the maternal clan heirs, in elaborate distributions of unit-value objects and pigs, food and bulk wealth. However, the real theme of the feast is "helping" in itself, since affines are themselves assisted by the maternal clan in paying off the cousin "father" and by the paternal clan in paying off the maternal clan heirs if this has not yet been done.

On the night before any outsider "guests" are due to arrive in the village, the maternal clanspeople hold a "trial" exchange or "rehearsal" (*hamtohon*) inside the house of the clan heir. The object of the exercise is to assess the wealth and level of support of clanspeople of the place—the core maternal clan group—against the estimated resources and expectations of the paternal clan. On this occasion the maternal clanspeople (the *totonewaga* hosts) commit themselves in advance to contribute wealth by laying their ax blades down on a "path" of mats. The path extends from the front to the back door, dividing the main room of the house.

Events in the "rehearsal house" are cloaked in secrecy, and only members of the maternal clan are allowed anywhere near. Exceptions were made for me, and I was asked on several occasions to spy for the opposite side. The persons assembled are almost always male, many of them representing women (sisters, wives, daughters) whose names they pronounce as they commit their ax blades. The heirs must decide at this time if they can match in size and quality the blades the *tohan segaiya* uses to make his claim for remuneration. Although heirs often spend the remainder of the day and night convincing people to contribute a bit more lavishly than they had intended, feasts are never actually canceled at this late point for lack of material support.

The following day begins with the usual feast-time preliminaries—stockpiling of supplies, blessing of the village with bespelled ginger, methodical sweeping of residential space by women and girls—as the guests begin to arrive. Like the Hanlekeleke, the Moni is officially "opened" (*posisi*) by a delegation from the paternal clan, led by the cousin "father." The delegation is received by the clan heir inside the death house, where the *tohan segaiya* either presents the heir with five stone ax blades fitted into ceremonial hafts or mentions the five blades he wishes returned to him from the Hanlekeleke. As before, the blades are named for the *tohan segaiya's* undertaking services.

In anticipation of the cousin "father," the clan heir has once again laid out a path of mats and placed at the "front" of it (near the back of the house) one very large ceremonial ax, the "leader" of the wealth that will follow. This ax is called Tuut—"Thunder"—in reference to the powerful voice of a leader rallying his supporters for battle. Tucked into the haft underneath the vine binding is a tiny bundle containing two miniature ax blades, the ancestral "mother" and "father" blades of *segaiya*, and a bit of ginger. The blades have been bespelled and urged to "rub together" to produce new ax blades for the maternal clan.[12] Of the unit-value wealth, only ax blades are thought to be capable of parthenogenesis, and their association with paternal substance is interesting in this context—an expression of the dreams of males for reproductive self-sufficiency in the sphere of political economy, as women and the "garden's children" reproduce the clan base of Sabarl society.

The *tohan segaiya's* axes are placed on the path behind the leading ax, and he departs. Then a call is put out to maternal clan supporters to come and "match" (*patapatal*) their ax blades against the *tohan segaiya's* on the path. One at a time, they enter the house by the front door and, under their heir's watchful eye, each removes an ax blade and puts an identical one in its place, carrying off the original in his personal basket. When the maternal clan contributors have matched all five of the paternal clan blades, the heir removes the substitute blades to a room or some hidden nook in the back of the house. Any clanspersons who arrive at this point may leave without contributing wealth to the path, although some make perfunctory gestures of trying.

At this juncture the clan heir summons the *tovelam* work force to add their wealth to the path of mats. One by one, the male *totolamwa-* (junior affines, plural) enter the house and lay down wealth, announcing as they do what debt they are repaying to the dead, or on whose behalf they are contributing and why; afterward they remain by the path. By the end there is a line of overlapping *tovelam* axes behind the heir's leading ax on the path of mats. Ceremonial axes form the "spine" of path displays, although ceremonial limsticks and money may be added also. In effect, then, the axes are a tally in object form of the maternal clan's continuing support force, aggressively imaged as the wealth weapons brought to the heir's support on this occasion. The concrete measure of his influence as a social person, it represents an update of social relations—relations that could well have preceded his birth, could continue on well beyond his death, and now must be re-established.

This is a moment of no little truth in a Melanesian society, where political power is mercurial and persons oftener than not achieve notability according to their persuasiveness at critical moments. However, beyond the distinguishing character of the heir, the action on the path of mats is influenced by his performance as the present embodiment of an ancestral personage. It is this "convergent personhood," a product of pulling together historical relationships and sequences of commitments and of ordering them as overlapping moments of support, that is constructed in the artifact procession (and later deconstructed, as I will shortly describe).

A NOTE ON AESTHETICS

Beyond the somewhat arbitrary point when "enough" valuables are on display to represent the maternal clan honorably, the aesthetics of the path, including proper decorum on the part of contributors, are as important as the quantity of wealth assembled there. In relation to *segaiya* numbers are elusive, having always to be appraised against unpredictable variables: an ancestor magically produces an ax blade; an aunt "finds" a necklace to contribute at a critical moment. And always the strength of an opposing group similarly involved in the mysteries of prognosis cannot be reckoned with any confidence. Order, on the other hand, and attention to the details of appearance are prerequisites for success on the "path" exchanges no less than when people organize and adorn themselves to impress trading partners or tidy up their gardens or perfume themselves to entice yams to grow.

Sabarl liken the "line" (*yaho*) of wealth to a procession of supporters moving along a path behind their leader, "evenly spaced, orderly," "all of them heading in the same direction," not "askew" (*galawin*). More than support in numbers, the image is a complex one of unified, coordinated, directed movement—the "evidence" of agency, of an organized mind. Such displays are directed to the followers themselves, at the point when they are making the decision whether to support the heir as they did his predecessor. The transformation of discrete relationships and discrete objects into an effecting publicity of community strength is what the heir must accomplish on this occasion.[13]

There is another aspect to consider in this regard—the appearance of the *tovelam* contributors. Normally these men are concerned to look their best in the presence of in-laws. However, now they are obligated to display their shame and nonsociality on their dirty skins,[14] with guests from other places looking on. The path activities present an opportunity to assert the self on a characterological level in the form of beautiful objects, against their own dishevelment. But there is another goal: namely, making the objects themselves more powerfully effective by contrast to their donors. Thus the junior affines may give the impression that they are socially dead, but their wealth tells another story entirely. Ax blades are polished and sometimes even perfumed with scented oil, their wooden handles freshened with "bright" earth paints or trade-store enamels; they flutter with paper money and pleated pandanus streamers of the type people tuck into armbands or weave into skirts for dancing.

For most men, it is through their involvement with the surface appearance of valued things that they move from acting out an image of control to actually effecting control over the cultural and personal constraints of the moment, moving from the level of ideal images to the assertion of character that will influence others to remember them. This tendency is very different from the way female affines re-image themselves in displays of "bulk wealth" (*palo*). The object of the *palo* displays is to give an impression of things "too numerous to count"—a jumbled profusion of wealth. As in the overlapping ax blades, the rhetorical power of *palo* lies in the imaging of collective force. But it is an unorderly force comprising indistinguishable units. The piles of *palo* thus visually restate the unkempt appearance of the junior affinal women. That the objects themselves are substantively (not merely cosmetically) fresh and new makes them no more memorable individually, but the freshness does project a fresh future for women beyond death (the potential of matrilineal continuity), something merely "added on" to durable objects.

What is interesting about the rehearsal house "path" of wealth is that we see for the first time in the context of *segaiya* material "evidence" of how men appropriate and "direct," "straighten out," women's productivity (as ephemeral wealth) in order that it become not a freestanding aesthetic and economic force, but a "support" for their own mode of productivity (the procession of durable objects). These alternating relationships—equal and complementary, unequal and rivalrous—are expressed and constituted, constructed and deconstructed, throughout the *segaiya* series.

THE "CORPSES" OF FOOD AND AXES

It is at this point, with the wealth of the living on display, that the dead are approached for donations. Signaling the *tovelam* work force to leave the house, the maternal clan heir removes the bundle containing the miniature "mother" and "father" ax blades, tucks it into a mat from the path, and sets it aside. He then removes to the back of the house the five axes matched by clanspeople with the *tohan segaiya's*. There, in absolute privacy, he sets about building a "corpse" (*gimbane*) of axes, propping them against one another with the "heads" (the bird's-head crest at the joint of the handle) facing in the same direction and inclining to the apex, balancing them on their blades and points. The *tovelam* wealth is placed around the pyramid. The mat that contains the miniature blades is then set up as a screen that hides the corpse from view.

With the maternal clan heir sitting as solitary guard, the "corpse" of axes is at this point left alone in the house to "reproduce," much as harvested food was magically urged to self-multiply before the feast of Moni began. Then, later in the afternoon, the construction is disassembled and the wealth is removed to the path and again laid out on top of it and counted. Any increase (there is always some) is attributed to the ancestors. If the Moni is a large-scale event—that is, if the person who died or any of the clan representatives has a large following—the *tovelam* work force may once again file into the house in another wave of giving. When at last it is clear to the maternal clan heir that no further economic "help" is forthcoming, he marks the blades on the path with a lime-paste X to keep track of them during the subsequent exchanges. He is then joined inside the house by clan mates, and the affines leave to join the widow, who now sits quietly outside, where yet another "corpse" is taking shape—this one made out of food.

The "corpse" of food is assembled by the junior affines in the public area behind the death house. It includes five items: a pot (*huye*) of cooked yams (*punlau*), a pot of sago-coconut pudding (*moni*), a large sago cake (*bwebwai*) on a wooden platter (*nohai*), a blackened basket (*yogowa bibikina*) of uncooked yams (*laha*), and a conical banana-leaf bundle of seed yams (*suluwalata*), set in an unused cooking pot. The food is covered with mats, fiber skirts, enamel dishes, and pots in a display of the massive defensive force that can be formed by merging "bulk wealth" with its comestible wealth counterpart. Then the widow, together with those junior affines who have chosen the paternal clan representative to release them from their mourning, seat themselves in a ring around the food. All are dressed in mourning to some degree, and a few, including the widow, are draped in heavy fiber capes (*nubnuwob*) and wear personal baskets or enamel plates on their heads as "mourning caps" (*gumwagumwa*). Thus the widow, the *tovelam* work force, bulk wealth, and food—that is, all valuable people, things, and food subordinated to more highly ranked people and things—are offered up for consumption: "memories" of "shame."

At this point everyone who is not inside the death house or seated around the food begins to gather in the shade behind the house—the maternal and paternal clanspeople sitting separately near the edge of the clearing. Suddenly the dead man's sister (or some other clanswoman in this category) begins hurling insults at the widow and her group. She paces and shouts, advancing toward them threateningly, her clan mates chorusing abuse: "You are weak and lazy"; "You never served my brother"; and so forth. The widow, meanwhile, begins shouting back: "You are always tricking us"; "We give you support, but you never deliver." She too has moved away form the circle, striding, torso inclined, toward her husband's sister until they are shouting in each other's faces. Seemingly just short of blows, one or the other finally cracks a smile, and the two burst into laughter and embrace warmly. The chorus of insults, some of which have become quite personal, gradually trails off on cue. The fury of persons on both sides of relations of inequality has been acknowledged and symbolically "finished." After this charged and very convincing dramatic performance it takes some time for people to quiet down and return to their places (onlookers were concerned to point out to me that the women were only "pretending" [*semibwa*] to argue) and there await a second confrontation, this time using valuables in place of words.

From inside the death house the maternal clan heir suddenly appears at the back door, armed with a ceremonial ax. Shouting more abuse at the junior affines, he and other clansmen rush down the ladder into the clearing, brandishing valuables as they swarm among the pots of food, people, and wealth. Still shouting, they toss their valuables onto the ritual foods or lean them up against the seated widow and her circle. Money is roughly tucked under the rims of the mourning caps, where it flutters over the eyes of the mourners—some, especially the widow, all but buried in objects. Gestures are sometimes made as if to cut the widow's neck before relinquishing an ax blade to her. The affines, meanwhile, take this sitting down, though they may fling light insults at their "attackers."

As the heir and the other maternal clanspeople retreat, the ritual "father" prepares to collect what is coming to him for his past gifts of *titiwa* or "bones" and for his services as undertaker. His prize is the consumable "corpse" of the "child," reconstituted as wealth. Beyond a supplementary product of a cross-sex couple, this artifact supplements society as the "addition to the identity" of its maternal and affinal units. In short, the "corpse" is a symbol of *segaiya* itself: the necessary nurture surplus in Sabarl life.

The *tohan segaiya* approaches each person in the widow's circle and, one by one, removes the valuables propped against her or him and returns with the wealth to his group at the edge of the clearing. There he "matches" (*patapatal*) the valuable against one or more of the same kind from his own collection of paternal clan wealth and returns the latter to the person in the circle. This is a payment "for the grass skirt being so heavy," a formal acknowledgement that the affines have suffered a burden of grief and shame on account of the death—by implication clearing them from any suspicion of guilt in connection with the death. Alternatively, he may arrange to return a piece of land or some other property, as negotiated beforehand. Afterward he removes the remaining valuables, as well as the shame-permeated fiber capes, skirts, and caps.

The items of mourning dress are regarded as catchments of pollution: the cap "catches the dirt from the hair"; death clings to the fiber cape, which is "like the beard of the dead man." In effect, then, the cousin "father" publicly purifies the widow's group as he did the corpse, initiating their social rebirth by returning them to the premarital condition of clan artifacts of paternal and maternal nurture. Later a woman from his clan completes the job by washing off the widow's mourning paint and exchanging her long fiber skirt for one cut short on the spot to signify reentry into sexuality. She also trims the widow's hair and glosses her body with coconut oil, paints her face with the designs of a firstborn child, and covers her in flowers and beads. It is commented that old women are made "new" again by all this, and people do remark genuinely on their beauty.

Meanwhile the *tohan segaiya* himself removes the five ritual foods, each one "complemented" (*gaba*), and symbolically armed, with an ax. The axes are said to "add grease to the food," adding the masculine increment of wealth that strengthens it as a gift and, beyond this, completes the prestation as a person substitute. The "father" is given back his "child" in a form that cancels the indebtedness of the "child" he helped to strengthen and grow with gifts of food and wealth during his lifetime. He is given in addition the corpse of the widow, that is, the corpse of their relationship. Also, speaking economically, he is assured of recovering his investment of five opening ax blades, since uncomplemented food is not considered acceptable on this occasion. However, it may happen that the blades he receives are inferior in quality. For example, the "father" may not be able to match the affinal blades. If he sees this happening, he will usually vanish from the scene and send in a substitute (in the case I observed, a female sibling) to act on his behalf and buffer his shame. He will later be expected to make good his side of the bargain, but this will be done outside the formal framework of the *segaiya* series.

When all the polluted "bulk wealth" has been removed along with the ritual foods, the *tohan segaiya* makes a final tally of his wealth by laying out the durable, unit-value items (*gogomwau*) on a "path" composed of the skirts he has removed from the mourning affines.[15] He calls out: "Where are the 'matches' (*lopatal*) to my ax blades?" Then, looking down, he makes a show of delightedly discovering them on the path, alongside the *tovelam* blades marked with Xs. Once again, however, not all paternal clan representatives are satisfied with the amount or quality of wealth on the path. Indeed, bitter arguments between paternal and maternal clan heirs may occur at this point. There are only two ways of resolving such matters successfully within the terms of *segaiya*. Either the maternal clan representative tosses in the large Tuut ax blade that "led" the path, or arrangements are made to hold another Moni. The former happens more frequently.

Each durable wealth item, regardless of quality, counts as one unit on the path of skirts. The number in this final tally is what circulates through the interisland community when people speak of the success or failure of the Moni. Meanwhile the bulk wealth, like the food, is absorbed into the patriclan and vanishes without a trace from the oral annals of *segaiya* past.

Vetantan

It is common for several years to pass before the next and final commemorative feasts of Vetantan, "For the Weeping Women," and Gebyuwas, "Burn to Clear," which nowadays are often combined. But though the chronological interval may be considerable, a bridging feeling persists among survivors that certain important matters remain unfinished. Thus, following a Moni there is less observable evidence of death's hand, to be sure. In terms of physical appearance and observable expressions of grief, things seem quite normal; deathtime taboos that at one time altered the rhythm of everyday life and restricted available space have usually been lifted. Then too, other deaths have generally intervened, creating their own distracting epicenters and reverberations. Nonetheless, most major economic issues are yet to be resolved, keeping survivors bound within a burdensome consciousness of the dead: as one widow put it "like we are still wearing our heavy skirt."

The Vetantan revolves around one primary distribution where pieces of raw pork and sago cake are presented by maternal clan heirs to women of the widow's group, acknowledging their pain and the "work" of mourning. It is "opened" when the heir blows a shell trumpet, drawing the women to the back of the death house for the distribution. He awaits them there, standing either on the veranda or on a high butchering platform erected nearby, while underneath him a swarm of village dogs lick the blood from the dirt. Calling each woman by name, he hands down the slices of cake. Each one has a "complement" of bloody pork on top. Pork and sago cake served in this style are called *genita*—"human flesh." They are said to be "payment for their eyes" or "like tears from their two eyes." An old woman told me: "One eye cries for the dead man's clan, one eye for the in-laws." The tears, in other words, are shed for the death of the marital relationship. It is the state of that marriage that is symbolically referenced at Vetantan and served back up to the women in the form of pork—the maternally constituted flesh of the dead person—and sago cake—the enduring affinally constituted bones of the widowed spouse, but "cooked," brought back to life, given new "value" (*mola-*) as a source of nurture.

This is an important occasion for female affines as well as for the *seveseve* (children of deceased males; spouses of children of deceased females), who are bidding for land controlled by the maternal clan. For having asserted through tears their relationship to the dead, they must now reinforce and substantiate the returns they expect from it. They do this by "helping" to supply the maternal clan with pigs and sago for the feast, alerting the heirs to expect a serious bid for land at the final feast of Gebyuwas.

Of course, as in all relatively long-range economic strategies, planning for critical Vetantan contributions can easily become entangled with tactics related to intervening goals. For example, when Diane's husband's maternal uncle died, Diane, as a *tovelam*, purchased a small pig for the uncle's Vetantan. She did this because the uncle owned garden land that Diane had been "using" for some time and wanted transferred to her children. For several years Diane fattened the pig. But one day the uncle's son (the cousin "child" of Diane's husband) came to ask if he could have the pig to purchase a canoe from the Panaeati. He wanted the canoe as bridewealth for Diane's younger sister. He promised to "remember" the pig at his father's Vetantan. It would have been foolish for Diane not to part with the pig. She was gaining not only a *tovelam*, but rights of access to a large canoe—all without relinquishing her claim to the land on behalf of her children. Of course, her husband could have claimed the land as a clan heir (although he had others competing with him for it), but his children would then have had to compete with their cousins later on. As it was, their clans would be strengthened significantly by a long history of payments, particularly the mortuary payment "for their grandparent's memory."

Gebyuwas

With the feast of Gebyuwas, or "Burn to Clear," the focus of control shifts from the maternal clan heirs to the widowed spouse and the *seveseve*. The goals of the feast have primarily to do with landed property, including the continued use of residential space and garden land by domestic family survivors. Thus a widow must host a Gebyuwas on behalf of her children as a claim to their father's garden and sago land and residential property and so she herself may remain in his house. In Sabarl terms, the children are expected to repay their father's maternal clan for eating food from his gardens and taking shelter beneath his roof. Meanwhile, a widower sponsors a Gebyuwas for the right to keep his children with him and working for him in the fields. The issue in either case is who will "look after" (*matahasik*) the dead person's land: his most prominent "memory" after other "marks" of social personhood have been erased or scattered.

However, if the Gebyuwas is about the use of the estate, it is also about its destruction. For more than releasing the hold of the dead man's clan over his property and freeing it for reproductive use by affines, this phase of commemoration "finishes" the spiritual and emotional hold that his property still has over persons closely related to him. "Finishing the memory" is enacted by burning personal things that until this time have been stored inside the death house. From their place in the eves at the back of the house, they have exerted the power of material reminders to "direct" the thoughts and behaviors of those who live there. At the same time, one of the dead person's own pigs, which "sleeps" inside the house the night before and represents his corporeal remains at the feast of Gebyuwas, is burned along with them, removing the most affectively charged symbols of his domestic presence.

The exchanges that precede the burning rituals involve for the last time both "people of the place" and "guests." To prepare for them, for months the widow and children as well as the maternal clan representatives have been planting surplus gardens and stocking their houses with sago and garden produce, as well as sending the work force of junior affines sailing about specifically in search of pigs. Gebyuwas exchanges center on bulk wealth and food (rather than on durable wealth), particularly objects symbolic of the widow's productivity at home and in the gardens, and these things will be needed in abundance to accomplish the exchanges and present an image of ongoing reproductive strength to outside visitors.

By the day of the feast, the central room of the death house is piled high with mounds of food from the dead man's gardens; the rafters are lined with sago from his groves. Members of the *tovelam* work force have added their own sago bundles, hung along a long pole (*kewa*) that runs the length of the house beneath the ridgepole. At the "front" of the pole is a very large bundle of sago supplied by the children—in the position of the maternal clan heir's "leading" ax on the path of mats that laid out the axis of exchange at previous exchange feasts. All in all, the house resembles more a garden storage house (*nakanaka*) than residential space, and indeed, this is what it is called on the occasion. Once again, the maternal clan heirs take their place inside the house, alongside the children. When all is ready, an heir will formally ask the *tovelam* work force, "What are your plans for all this food?" and they will respond, "It is for you."

This is the cue for the exchanges to begin. At the death house, maternal clan heirs position themselves on the back veranda, blocking entrance to the house with their bodies as if preparing for a siege. The impression is not inappropriate. For outside on the beaches a *tovelam* work force from each of the guest villages is organizing bulk wealth and food with which to storm the maternal clan stronghold. A sapling is cut and hung with items of "bulk wealth." Basketfuls of food are amassed, and more poles are hung with sago. Pigs are tied by their feet to poles and taken up onto the shoulders of the men.

With the blast of a trumpet, men, women, and young people of the work force launch their assault on the heirs by "dancing" food and wealth—their collective "affinal support" (*muli*)—up to the back door of the death house. Heading up the procession is a man with a spear called "Debt" (*Vaga*); behind him is a man brandishing the bulk wealth sapling and then men carrying pigs and sago and finally women with basketfuls of food. Drawing near the house, the spear bearer sends the spear over the heads of the maternal clanspeople and into the roof of the house, symbolizing the power of debt to socially slay them. This act "kills" the relationship between affines and clanspeople by killing the "memory" of the deceased: in one man's words, "so that he [the deceased] cannot get up to give again." The food and wealth are then aggressively hurled onto the platform as the affines shout, "Eat! Eat!" I was told, "They are angry at having to give so much again, because this time they will not be repaid." Meanwhile the maternal clanspeople hustle the food inside the house and, tying the pigs outside to the house posts, shout at their backs, "Our ancestors's value" as the affines withdraw and a new wave of affines from another village prepares to advance.

The clanspeople retaliate by quickly matching each piece of garden food exactly with food from inside the house and sending a delegation back to where the affines have retreated. The garden food the *tovelam* work force receives is thus exactly what they gave, but different. And it is this food from "people of the place"—the heirs and their *tovelam* and *seveseve* suppliers—that is later cooked and distributed to feed the visitors, as in previous feasts. The same performance is repeated for each of the affinal groups present, the maternal clan retaining only the "bulk wealth" and pigs, to be killed alongside the dead man's pig on the following day. However, the ritual pig that is burned with the dead man's basket spends his last night trussed and lying inside the death house, near the back door.

The final ritual exchanges occur the next morning. After the pig has been removed from the house, speared, and suspended for singeing, the dead person's children emerge from the back door, carrying his basket and sobbing, "Always before we saw your basket inside the house and we thought you were there. Now we burn it, and maybe you're not there anymore." Inside the house the heirs cry quietly, prevented from showing shameful tears in public. They hear the children call out to them, "Do we burn this or not?" The question draws them outside, where they respond, "What are you burning inside?" and reach in to remove the hidden ax blade. Then the pig and the basket are burned as the children continue to cry beside them. When the fire has burned itself out, the heirs place an ax blade inside a large clamshell that was once the feeding dish for the pig. The children remove it, and the clanspeople "overturn the clamshell" (*sipwahom ali sopwakile*), signaling the end of the burning phase of Gebyuwas.

When dusk approaches and everyone has eaten, the sound of drums will suddenly be heard in the vicinity of the death house. People gather excitedly to watch as a double row of maternal clan males emerges dramatically from some hidden spot in the village, beating large and small drums (*sidae* and *lodidi*) as they approach. Their faces, frozen masks of seriousness, are elaborately painted and their bodies glossed; streamers and flowers flutter as they move, and they wear fancy dancing skirts tied on the left, in the style of men. Behind them clanswomen follow in rows, branches from the bush tucked into their armbands or held out ahead of them. Near the house they form a circle with the men facing inward. They stop, and a male leader starts up a dance song (*laos*). The men join in, lunging inward and out again, the drums dipping, as the women dance around them counterclockwise in a dance called *sobu*. The words are simple images of things fondly remembered—a canoe or boat trip, a woman, fine weather. The songs and dances will continue all night as the clanspeople "close the place" with their "final drumming" (*sidae mwamwawaina*). This was described as "like covering over the hole of the grave that the first feast opened."

No one will dance on that spot so long as they remember this event and the person it commemorates—the memory lives on through the observance of the blank space. For although Sabarl themselves speak of "erasing" or "unraveling" (*maleleka*) the material "marks" left behind by their ancestors, and go about this deliberately, "finishing" is also a project of creating open space—of bringing into being a sense of felt and active "absence" or "vacancy" (*wasim*) as the traces of the person are eradicated.

To repay the maternal clanspeople for dancing, yet another *palo* or "bulk wealth" presation is made by the children and the *tovelam* work force, "emptying the house" of pots and mats and baskets and skirts and all kinds of domestic luxuries, hung from or piled up around a sapling with tobacco on its branches. Canoes will sometimes change hands at this time. The affines also cook for the dancers during the night. If the clan heirs are not yet satisfied with the amount the children and the *tovelam* work force have given for control of the land, they will ask for a Tagalekeleke (a land acquisition feast) sometime in the future.

Certain activities optionally follow the departure of the visitors as a kind of postscript to the Gebyuwas. If the large sago bundle that the children supply has not been burned by this time, the burning will be staged as an act of *nibwe tongpase*, "gathering up the charcoal." This refers to the custom of gathering in partly burned wood from individual fires to make one communal fire before leaving a campsite. The maternal clan heirs burn the sago with whatever "bones" remain from their gardens and groves, for the people of the place. If the sago burning is postponed until a later feast (a sign, for example, that the Gebyuwas food exchange was in some way unsatisfactory), the additional feast will be known as Wasi Nakanaka or "Clearing the Yam House." As explained, this is "like planting time, when you don't need the yam house any more. It is finished, like a person."

In this rendering of *segaiya*, I have deliberately kept "dramatistic" (see Burke 1969, 1977) language to a minimum, for reasons I have already stated. However, it should be noted that, as in a play in acts or a song or dance, no one would ever plan to stop in the middle of such a project or to leave out important parts. To violate the aesthetic would be dangerous—tantamount to destroying a "memory" created by Enak. Indeed, it is through the dialectical nature of the commitment to the entire series of feasts on the part of persons who are socially absorbed as well as idiosyncratic agents that *segaiya* continues to function as social architecture. Yet likewise, the wholeness of *segaiya* is experienced through varying degrees and kinds of attention to its parts. This is no static script or blueprint. The flow of events is paradoxically composed of fragments and the spaces between them, subjectively "written" into memory and edited out. Persons are not merely performers, but also interpreters and, beyond this, inventors of new identities for themselves in a nonstatic society. Thus the limits of the dramatistic metaphor are important to keep in mind as we move on to consider the closing theme and imagery of personification.

Nine

On a Concluding Note

In these pages I have shifted the focus of mortuary analysis away from the dead and their survivors as separate social categories and toward what Leenhardt (1979) first recognized as the "relational" aspect of Melanesian personhood: the self as defined and experienced through an array of significant relationships with others, past and present, living and dead.

From this perspective the meaning of cultural acts of remembrance and forgetting lies not so much in people's going through the motions of social solidarity or of expressing beliefs in some hypothetical worldview, as in doing *for the last time* what they have done before in forming themselves vis-à-vis an other in common. Such significant repetitions[1] are structured to perpetuate, but also to edit, the memory of the relationship. In this way people effect what might be termed the "phased closure" of those social experiences: the progressive cauterization of a previous interactional "flow" in rituals, exchanges, and private acts that clear space for new relationships. In other words, what occurs in *segaiya* is a cultural reframing of commonplace interactions (gardening, trading, giving or sharing food, and so forth) that lends them significance beyond personal experience, but not regardless of personal experience.

What is critical to appreciate here is how in the course of this reframing, a *segaiya* series—a "memory" containing memories—employs concrete "evidence" of what a life and a death have come to in social terms, but without reducing a life to this. Such cultural artifacts are the sources of the "generative schemes" (see Munn 1986; Wagner 1986a) inculcated in Sabarl memory as cultural "dispositions," "habits," or "conduct,"[2] the "models of and for" Sabarl social behaviors, values, and tastes. Controlling the dialectical forces, the culturally constructed tensions, of convergence and divergence in particular is a central goal of Sabarl personal and public life. It is a goal realized through the conduct of one's commitment to a whole array of analogous values and countervalues: anchoring and mobility, solidarity and initiative, collectivization and individuation, homogeneity and salience, among the most important. These are the templates that, contained within the circumscribing mnemonic structure of *segaiya*, are restorative of Sabarl cultural life.

It makes sense, but seems remarkable nonetheless, that the most important signs of a healthy social history—food (pigs or produce) and items of wealth (individually valued or in bulk)—operate as tokens of value in the same symbolic terms. As we consider this subject more closely, it will guide us through a summarizing profile of Sabarl personhood as a process wherein the cultural production of self-other relations proceeds by way of, and can only be appreciated in context of, cultural consumption.

Personification

In his critical study of economic processes in clan-based and class-based societies, Gregory defines reproduction as "the conditions necessary for the self-replacement of both things and people," a "wholistic concept which includes production, consumption, distribution and exchange as its principal elements" (1982:29–30). He goes on to discuss "personification," more specifically, as the process of converting gifts of things into personal relations, largely through the consumption of those things. Consumption, then, "permits the survival of people, first by providing their nourishment and secondly, through their sexual relationships" (1982:33).

Gregory goes on to distinguish between people gifts and thing gifts within clan-based economies. As these gifts are consumed, they must be replaced: people through marriage transactions, and things (objects and comestibles) through economic ones. This explains why, for example, the symbolic equation of food consumption and sexual union is widespread in Melanesia (as throughout the world).

In the Sabarl case, "marrying," "complementing," and "matching" things are central to mortuary transactions, as we have seen. In the feast of Moni, the symbolic intercourse and subsequent conflation of the "corpses" of objects and food makes the point dramatically. Objects are said to add "grease" to the food. Consuming objects and food alike releases the reproductive potential of particular individuals and of the community.

However, a closer look reveals certain discrepancies between the local Sabarl picture and Gregory's marriage-centered reproductive model, particularly with regard to consumption. To begin with, the very merger of objects and food that symbolically sparks regeneration at the Moni indicates an important ranking in the relationship of people, food, and objects over and above the dyadic relationship of people and things. Food, we recall, does not become "more like stone ax blades"; ax blades become more like food, and both of these "more like people." In short, the relation of people to things is not the whole story of reproduction.

The implications of a ranking of people-food-objects are far reaching, and far from exhausted here. But certain points are usefully made in relation to *segaiya*. First and most evidently, food—raw and cooked, gift and nourishment, for use in exchange and for immediate consumption—can be seen to occupy a place at the very center of Sabarl social reproduction. And where the food is, the women are, or more precisely the subordinate, "shame-intensive" position of widowed spouses, encircling (in a sense, circumscribing) the corpse of food, literally on the same level, the primary objects of consumption. Subordinated women and food share this position as the motivational core of the personification process that, as we recall, is the basis of reproduction in gift economies. Of course this situation, where women in effect personify personification, makes special sense in a matriclan-based society.

The place of women and food in turn reveals that the consumption of wealth objects is in a secondary (supplementary) position with regard to economic motivation. Managing objects becomes a way of enhancing and fortifying social reproductive processes. Beyond this, however—and this is the paradox—certain objects represent within the triad of people-food-objects the value of rank itself and of permanency in the social order. In other words, these objects have permanent rank as neither food nor people do. We can see how these objects of permanent, individual unit value would be the appropriate tools for rhetorical self-embellishment, being less like people than food in the former respect, but also closer in the latter respect to imaging the value of those who stand out in society and represent it.

Yet to accept that the consumption of things (food and objects) is a necessary condition for the production of people—to accept this definition of the personification process—is to get only half the story of reproduction as Sabarl live it. The other half, encoded in myth and religious practice, is that people consume other people as well as food and objects. We have seen, for example, that "eating" refers to sorcery, and that the eating away of human energy sets in motion separations of bodily substance, enabling their recombination and reuse. In the tales of Katutubwai, new life (the trickster children) passes through the devouring monster before overcoming it. *Waunak* babies are swallowed by their mothers and dead bodies by the *waunak* themselves. The placental "first skin" of newborns and the putrefying image, the last skin, of corpses are consumed by dangerous fish at the threshold of new existence. "Eating," legitimate or illegitimate, constitutes *the* precondition of new, or further, life. But although on Sabarl consumption is associated more generally with sexual union than with marriage (Gregory bypasses this distinction, but see Bloch and Parry 1982), it is far more strongly associated with dying and death.

Thus the ranked order of people and things that are featured wealth on Sabarl is actually a ranked list of "edibles"—people, food, and objects—that subsumes the relationships: people:food:: food: objects. "Personification," then, might be better understood as consumption that converts food and objects and people into *other* people.

To recognize the central place of death in social reproduction, alongside productive sexual union (its structural counterpart) is to bring the "personification approach" into line with other analyses of Melanesian gift economies where death and regeneration are basic to understanding indigenous philosophies of exchange (see especially De Coppet 1982; Wagner 1972; Weiner 1976, 1980). However, it is well to keep in mind that death transactions are never complete until the widowed spouse (see also Watson 1982) and all persons brought into relation with the dead through consumption have also died and been officially "forgotten."

The "Bones" of the Matter

With this understanding, we are now able to get some distance on the central theme of paternal nurture as the Sabarl perform it within *segaiya*.

Strathern has observed that "many matrilineal systems [in the Massim] are interesting in their conceptualization of nurturant paternity . . . in terms of productive labour which creates debt" (1984:53). She cites specifically Weiner's work on Trobriand reproduction (1980) and Damon's study of Muyuw kinship and exchange (1983).[3]

However, among Sabarl symbolism of paternal nurture is particularly elaborate in relation to the problem of "memory" it addresses: namely, the termination of paternal substance within a matrilineal social system and the attendant need to construct a continuity. Thus, as paternal substance in one form (for example, in the blood) terminates, other forms (for example, objects and food) are brought to substitute for it, as they must in order for paternity to be acknowledged as making an ongoing difference to society. This substitution can be seen as being in the interest of a cultural order wherein clans exchanging women are considered symmetrical (though never explicitly stated by the Sabarl, this is given by the system) as well as of reducing the particular asymmetries of wife givers and wife takers.[4]

We have observed that men as brothers produce the bare bones, as it were, of Sabarl society when they produce dry-lean sago for sisters and mothers, standing to inherit, most importantly, a *wisebua* (bridewealth) necklace for their efforts. Indeed, the traditional style of bundling sago into "husband/wife" pairs (also said to be "like testicles") may be seen as a reference to the power of masculine labor to generate reproductive partnerships.

Men symbolically mark the potentiation of their reproductive "reach" when they complete in *segaiya* the process begun in the groves: transforming dry-lean sago into greasy-sweet sago-coconut pudding for their sisters and, on another level, transforming patrilateral relations into pigs and ax blades—adding the fat to the feast. In these terms, the *segaiya* feast and ritual series can be thought of as a person performed, its "flesh" provided by maternal clan hosts and its "bones" and "fat" by affinal males.

The theme of male potentiation is summed up in the act of feeding the sister's deceased husband's "father"—ideally an act of feeding one's own father's clan. This translates on the sociological level as a man coming into a position of strength when his sister's husband dies. Ultimately, then, by giving sago pudding to his sister's husband's "father," he is returning to his own father's clan a mature version of the "bones" given him.

With regard to symmetry and asymmetry the picture is all the clearer because the action takes place within a single generation. To summarize from the point of view of a male person, he is from the start and forever a dependent "child" vis-à-vis his father's clan. This is acknowledged by the part he plays in *titiwa-segaiya* exchanges early in life and in his efforts to turn the tables by giving *powon* (loans with interest) to his father through his mother as he grows older.

At this point he also begins to recognize his dependence on women of his own clan for bridewealth—a dependence enacted by his labors in the sago groves and his efforts to strengthen his relationship with his mother's brother, again with gifts of *powon*. He moves from a point of dual dependency to ternary dependency at the marriage either of himself or his sister, when his energies are further divided by the demands of senior affines. When he starts thinking of children, the additional gift of a canoe is his bid for a shift in the balance of power between him and his wife's people. If his sister's husband should die, his dependency will be reduced. However, if his wife dies before him, he returns to parity with her kin only when he chooses to remarry—indebting himself to yet another set of relations if he does not marry "properly," that is, within her lineage.

In short, although Sabarl cross-cousins do not marry, in the ideal scheme of things a person's "father" and "child" will be members of his or her father's clan. Even without marrying into one's own father's clan (although this happens frequently enough, as we have seen) one is keeping things in the family through death exchanges begun in childhood. The paternal clan receives sago pudding from its nurture investment in the child's wife's brother, and it receives ax blades from its nurture investment in the child—exactly as if the child had married into his own father's clan.

We also see the emergence of gender at the core of alliance-based giving, not as the result of a process of sibling separation by gender-based labor (cf. Damon 1983), but rather as a process of sibling coordination and the articulation of distinctive spheres of contribution. Yet as a "code for the conceptualization of difference" (Strathern 1984:50), gender is pervasive although not always dominant in the acknowledgment of paternal nurture, a process in which the splitting of males into fathers and uncles, juniors and seniors, is in fact critical. Overall, we seem to be encountering among Sabarl what Giddens has called "the coordination of movement in time and space; the 'coupling' of a multiplicity of paths" (1979:205), not all of which are gender-linked. In the final instance, and in their own terms, the challenge for Sabarl lies in the practical and "balanced" negotiation of the paths of life.

Closure through Opening

At this juncture we need to be clear about one key point of personification and its relation to consumption: namely, that the new collective "memory"—the person performed as *segaiya*—is constructed *in order to be officially forgotten*; "corpses" of food and axes are assembled so that their deconstruction can be witnessed, shared in, and "written" into the public record. To speak, as I did in the Introduction, of a deconstructive inflection in Sabarl society is to recognize how actions of representing social life are informed by actions of "directing" the cultural response to death. More than imitating life, *segaiya mimics death.* This becomes apparent when we shift our perspective on the feast series once again, away from a focus on material evidence and toward the acts of "clearance" accomplished by means of them. For in these acts of "finishing the memory" (bringing it to closure), new ground is opened for sociality beyond it.

*

We have seen how performed memorials inscribe the value persons have to others onto the landscape of social history; how this process casts the living and the dead alike not merely as performers of social roles, but as agents of social reconstruction. Survivors thus "write" (enact) with sung or formally spoken words, gestures, and valuable objects, in a succession of voices and images both current and ancient, a kind of text of texts symbolic of the events that gave the person a memorable social profile. And in the process they create a useful (and newly usable) identity. Since this process is one of fabricating a memory and constituting social value in terms of it, the effect is to impress into consciousness an image that "ossifies, petrifies, and blocks" further development and manipulation of that memory *in the public domain* by establishing "an artificial limit, an arbitrary law, a subjective finitude" (Kristeva 1980:57) in the manner of writing everywhere. *Segaiya* is the enacted text of a "finished" person, historically situated.

The Channeled Person

We come, then, by way of discussing *segaiya* as "writing," to a critical observation of its paradoxical effect. In the corpus of feasts, the "person performed" is construed not as a bounded figure nor as a coherence of substances and forces: indeed, the disassembling and redistribution of a material coherence is the most memorable part of the feasting, as people carry away parts of the "memory" to other times and places. Rather, the performance of personhood is experienced, and the *segaiya* agenda stated explicitly in terms of, achieving openness of place and society *on the model of channels of knowledge in the physical person.* Taking the major events in sequence, we see how the ears of the social body are opened at Solu to "gathering words" (to organized thought, as against the formless flow of keening emotion); how the mouth (at Hanyalogi and Hanlekeleke) is opened to exchanges of food and words; how the sexual organs are opened to intercourse (at Moni, with the flow of sago-pudding "semen"); how the eyes (at Vetantan) are opened to new prospects of support and complementarity, until finally all boundaries of person are removed and the person is only an opening—an active absence or "vacancy" (*wasim*)—as the yam house is symbolically "finished" (at Gebyuwas or Wasi Nakanaka). This is the essence of ancestorhood: to be all-knowing is to be all-open.

In short, people enact an image of the channeled person (as opposed to the sealed-off protoperson in utero, on the model of Katutubwai getting nowhere in Enak's womb) as a potential permeability—an ideal image of circulation, both corporeal and social. The fenestrations and positive signs of fenestration in aesthetic objects (the triangular holes in the limestick, the painted triangles between canoe motifs, etc.) refer to this same valued feature: the openness and distinctness/delineation not so much of things or people as of knowledge they contain that others furnish or elicit. And in the sense that circulating wealth is a "memory" displaced, it represents *ancestral power as an analogue of debt:* the "positive negativity" that is the precondition and the artifact of social exchange. Selective forgetting ensures that social entanglements that could compromise this ideal image are struck from the public record.

Underlying our awareness of *segaiya* in these terms is a view of Sabarl personhood as relational and dialogical. If in practice the self is a self-other, realizable only by way of others (others' voices, others' images), incorporating them, and capable of social action only in respect of this reflexive knowledge, the person performed as *segaiya* is at once the dead and the survivors. *Commemorating others is a process of commemorating self.* But conversely, as relational persons delineate an image of the dead, performing for the last time the summarizing signs of social activity and social growth, they effect the constriction of their own social domains, becoming agents of the loss of a bit of their own history—"officially" forgetting it. By their own authority as participants in "writing" the text of relationship to the dead, they edit out a part of their own identity.

This awareness of an absence of an aspect of self is also the precondition of new acts of social extension and new stories of life (new exchange partnerships, new kin relations, the manufacture or acquisition of wealth, the production of children, and so forth). Creating new connections masks or obviates—displaces and rewrites—the self-other, the ultimate text. In the case of the dead, what is "finished" is corporeal existence, which becomes displaced onto magical substances such as *muho*, to be rerouted through the gardens of the living. In the case of the living, it is the memory of the relationship apparently left behind, displaced onto new vehicles of meaning (children, canoes, and other objects of wealth) as a supplement or increment to the relationship.

These new stories form around an essentially political reality, which is the deconstructive tendency of paternal matriclan units to act as "challenging voices" (Bruner and Gorfain 1984:56) to the writing of the text as a preestablished and conventional "happy ending" for the maternal matriclan. In other words, by challenging maternal claims to an inherent right of control over memory in the form of new vehicles of meaning, they represent the centrifugal force of the unrepeatable. When this force is lent the profile of a persuasive individual—when it is delineated in the person of a leader—incidental challenges, easily forgotten, become transformed into a salient locus of "memory" where the successful challenge comes to stand for the absence of a norm. Wagner (1986a:219) talks about this aspect of commemoration in reference to Barok mortuary imagery: "Symbolically, [the result of the mortuary cycle] is obviation: beginning with individual death, it moves, through a series of transformations and dialectical cross-implications, to a point of resolving (i.e. "killing") social meanings and of actually 'cooking' or killing the dead." And Munn (1986) makes a similar point for Gawa: "Mortuary rites thus involve the creation of a temporary memorialization so that, paradoxically, forgetting can be generated . . . [166]. [They create] both closure and potential" (180).

Yet for Sabarl, "finishing" is more than a matter of "forgetting" or "killing" the dead. The process goes beyond canceling out objectifications of the dead as bodily beings and the "falling apart of social ties and selves" (see Munn 1986:66, 166). In this respect, editing a memory out produces, as I mentioned earlier, a *positively valued negative space*. Meaning, that is, is not "killed" or canceled by successive meanings, stories by successive stories, images by successive images. Rather, previous writings remain an active absence beneath or alongside the masks of superseding ones. New stories occur, new signs or texts are produced over and around (in respect of, informed by, in spite of) their antecedents. And in an act of congruency with their ancestors, the living make statements and gestures about surviving in spite of having "finished"—selectively and officially forgotten—that part of themselves that is "present in absentia."

Segaiya makes ancestors (new persons) as it makes memories: as positive absences ("negative signs" of personhood). Its enactment sends new stories, like new shoots, out from the body of the dead. It also creates Sabarl as a people who can write without European tools and skills, which are likewise officially forgotten, obviated, rendered obsolete by the multivocal complexity of the occasion.

Personalizing Memory and Forgetting (or, The Bright Spot on the Floorboards)

The mnemonic function of narrative is likewise displaced onto *segaiya*, which is the more trusted vehicle for keeping open the channels of interisland contact, since it demands occasional presence, continual updating, in a world of perennial separations. I was told once: "We don't have a story of *segaiya*, because we do it all the time."

Sabarl epistemology puts us at odds with authors who suggest that words are "the preservation technique par excellence in non-literate societies" (Bourdieu 1977:186–87).[5] The suggestion is that, through words, people succeed in objectifying—rendering detachable from individual memory and therefore analyzable—the cultural inheritance. Words are exactly repeatable, reversible, not "attached to the situation."

Yet as we have seen for Sabarl, spoken words have no such automatic authority, not as ancestral stories nor even as eyewitness accounts. Indeed, it is quite the other way around—understandings gained from participation in public performances, whether passively or actively, are more trusted than anything conveyed through the mediating sight and talk of others.

This is not an isolated attitude in Melanesia. In those many societies where "talk is cheap," and even where it is not, the objectification of cultural values tends to be entrusted to other forms of action and their material artifacts: iconographically elaborated forms of wealth, paintings and carvings, masquerade or self-decoration complexes, and the like.[6]

In the Sabarl view, the value of "memory" is determined precisely to the extent that it is indeed "attached to the situation"—of the moment, applicable to matters with which people are currently concerned.[7] Selective forgetting ensures relevance and likewise gives rise to an impression of connection to the past.

The experience of connection is not always pleasant. Indeed, more often than not I would hear how "painful" the effect of "memory" can be. Among the most "heart piercing" memories (*hatieu ipoi*) are the casual evidence of a person's hand on the world, as it were, executed "in passing" and not as a sign intended to be remembered at all. A gash on a tree where your young wife sharpened her bush knife, her footprint on the path to the garden, a shell that she attached to a shingle "just for style." Commemorative feasts give persons access also to this personal dimension of remembrance, less through the model acts of "custom" than by increasing awareness of absence—forcing a confrontation with previous experiences and buried significances.

One outcome is a Sabarl tendency to nurture painful remembrances "unofficially" long after acts of custom have removed the concrete signs of the person, beyond the time of official mourning that establishes the absence as a matter of history. We especially find people creating their own personalized acts of postscriptive, or negative, "memory": Simon will never use sugar, believing this was the cause of his small daughter's death. Mari avoids wearing red out of respect for a dead cousin's preference for the color.

Observances like these keep fresh the sense of emptiness as an inner reality. Personally projected clearances, they break up the course of life like invisible "no trespassing" signs, silent interdictions that keep the dialogue going between the dead and the living as inner voices—ghost authors. As mentioned earlier, there are spaces in Maho village, totally unmarked, where those who remember that someone's memorial dance was performed there will refrain from dancing or singing, "out of respect." The significance of the space, its capacity to affect behavior, and the space as such vanish along with those who project it; they reemerge in the same place or elsewhere under the gaze of different persons with different memories. Social behavior, temporal orders, the social landscape itself are redefined by the invisible agency of an "active absence": the experience of nonactivity special to active constituents of a human history.[8]

This sheds some light on why ephemeral memorialization is so enduring on Sabarl: by disassembling, scattering, uprooting what the dead have built up in the course of their lives—marriages, houses, gardens, or whatever—and washing over material artifacts with the dissolving solution of social action, space is created for a more profound, because more personal, memorialization process.

To consider cultural remembrance subjectively as a kind of productive forgetting overturns most of the assumptions by which we conventionally approach not only memorialization but symbolism in general (see also, and notably, Casey 1987, on perdurance). Indeed, it represents a paradigm shift in the more usual (Durkheimian) depiction of death as rending holes in the social nets of small-scale communities (see Blauner 1966) and of mortuary events as a mending process. For here the holes and space making are ascribed positive value; they are integral to relational interweaving rather than its nemesis and contribute to a meaningful personal life. And it is in this respect that the mortuary response is to mimic, not contradict, death. We arrive, then, at the central problem of form this book addresses—why people go to such lengths to assemble relationships, and on mortuary occasions displays of relationship objectified in artifacts and food, only to decompose, disperse, or abandon them afterward.[9]

Segaiya throws people back to experiences in their past and out of the frame of current affairs as much as it focuses past experiences in the present through mimesis. In the sense that it guides persons through this creative process of fragmentation, *segaiya* as a mnemonic structure has some of the attributes of montage or collage—or more exactly, of an assemblage made up of "found objects" from past relations.[10]

*

I have tried to convey how the feasts of *segaiya* are occasions for the experience of absence, by way of consumption, indebtedness, and diminishment constructive of social futures and personal potentialities for Sabarl survivors. As death draws people home from wherever they are to the "bones of the serpent," *segaiya* concentrates individual memories there, erecting at their source a social experience of remembrance and forgetting among disparate personal ones, drawn from the texts of everyday life.

A young man explained to me once that *segaiya* was like a bright spot left on the floorboards after a mark is scrubbed away. Such images are the heart and mind of the matter. And of course they say more about memory than any story of Sabarl I might be able to tell.

Appendix

Narratives

The following narratives are more detailed versions of the most important summaries included in the text. During my first field trips to Sabarl, I collected nearly two hundred narratives, exchanging for them stories from "Amerika." Most of the Sabarl tales were recorded in the local language, and though I could usually follow the plot, I engaged translators for greater accuracy and for nuance and commentary. Translation turned out to be the work of women who could organize time away from their children and other domestic responsibilities. Women generally had a better command of English than men, partly from using it often in casual intellectual play with each other and with their children. Diane Melia, Nola Mary Diwole, Pepetua Weniye, Lucila Danole, and Nancy Ema contributed considerable time and effort to this project, working singly or together, their voices weaving in and out of the translated text. Their comments and my annotations are included in brackets. Younger storytellers sometimes asked to speak in English, both "for practice" and to avoid criticism by their elders, and I have noted these instances.

The Story of the Bird and the Serpent

The heroic bird in these narratives is generally identified as the *manak* or sea eagle (*Haliaeetus leucogaster*), which Sabarl regard as the most highly developed of the birds that eat fresh meat and carrion, a category that also includes the *bwanebwane* or black-breasted kite (*Hamirostra melanosterna*, termed a "buzzard" in British nomenclature, but not to be confused with a vulture), and the *hiohio* or Brahminy kite (*Haliastur indus*), whose white head and breast make it resemble the sea eagle. One translator suggested that the heroic bird might be a *koukou*, or large Papuan hawk owl (*Uroglaux dimorpha*), and in another version, from Misima, the *boi* or reef heron (*Demigretta sacra*) was named. (Sources: Pizzey 1980; Slater 1970.)

1. *As told in English by Josephine, head teacher at Maho school in 1976–77, whose home is on Tagula*

The largest snake in the world lives under one bush in a hole at Western Point [on Tagula] and frightens all the animals there and some people. Small birds fly around the snake's hole to antagonize it, but it cannot catch them. People ask them to tell a huge eagle to get that snake. The eagle replies, "All right; tomorrow you fly around the hole and sing and sing until the snake comes all the way out." The bird tells his mother he will be flying far away and not to worry about him. Next day the birds sing and sing until the whole snake comes out; then the sea eagle grabs it in the middle and flies round and round with it for days until it dies. He continues to fly with it until the flesh is rotting. Pieces of flesh fall into the sea. They become the first islands—the Trobriands, Murya, Misima, and others. At last it drops the bones, and that is Sabarl: two rocks at the end are the eyes, and the white blood is the fringe of white beach all around. After this the eagle returns home. He tells his mother he will go for a short walk because a giant octopus on Yele has challenged him, saying he wants to meet this bird who is so proud. Small birds relay the message. But the octopus has four arms beneath the water that the bird cannot see. With the other four he pulls the eagle down, and he drowns. His feathers float onto the beaches of all the islands. From each feather springs a small bird, a *bwanebwane* (black-breasted kite). Each bird goes to visit the eagle's mother, who says, "You're not my son. My son is the largest bird in the world. Go away." She pours whatever she is cooking on them, making them different colors [these kites have rust-colored patches]. Finally she knows that her son is dead. She dies of sorrow.

2. *As told in English by Sigi, a Misima man living on Panawina*

One man got married, but they could not have children. Another day the wife said, "My husband, today we go to our garden." He said, "I have a headache. You go alone." She said, "All right, you stay here." She did not see the rain come up—a heavy rain, big flood. She went down where the flooding was and saw a mango tree there and mango fruit. She took some for her basket and held one in her hand. She held on to it and floated out to sea. She floated out and then found a log and used it to paddle around to the other side of the small island named Ponowan [she was straddling the log.] She went up to the island and was already pregnant. She thought, "Here I am pregnant, and no house." She went to live under the trees. When she was hungry she ate the mango fruit. When she finished, she threw the seed on the ground. One night it grew big. On the second day it flowered. On the third day it bore fruit. She ate it and then went to fish in the sea. There was no fire, so she put the fish in the sun to cook. Time passed, and she was ready to give birth. She gave birth to a bird. She did not feed the bird at her breast but only fed him food. He grew into a sea eagle [described by this teller as a large *boi* or reef heron]. Very quickly the bird grew and began catching fish from the sea. When strong enough, he flew to Misima. He saw a house with fire in it, a pot, food, wood, water, everything inside. He went under the house and stood up with it on his back and flew with the house to the island. His mother was very happy. She cooked, they ate, made a fire, and slept with a mat. When the water was gone, the bird went to Misima looking for more. Finally he found a stone with water in it and picked it up. It was very heavy—he rested at Liak (a village on Misima). When he picked up the stone again it was very heavy, so he left it behind. His mother said it does not matter. But there are some other things I should say. There is a snake and an octopus around. The octopus is at Lova [on Yele]. The snake stays at Misima, at Segara. The snake is huge. The bird says, "I will see to the snake first." He tells all the birds, "We all go tomorrow and make plenty of noise to draw the snake out." They do this, and the bird sees the snake, then goes to his mother and tells her that tomorrow he will go again. "Put some coconut oil in a bottle. If the oil spills, I am dead. If not, I have killed the snake." The bird blinds the snake, and it thrashes about until it dies. All the birds go down and cut its body to bits. They throw the meat all over to make the islands of the Chain, but by the time they get to Sabarl there is only the head—no meat, only bones. Then he goes to Rossel. The bird says "I'll wait one year until you [the octopus] are big enough to kill." There are four arms under the sea and four in the air. The bird is pulled down and drowns. The feathers float back to his mother. She puts them into a wooden platter [*nohai*] with fresh water inside, and they grow into small birds (black-breasted kites).

The Woman in the Moon (Dedeaulea or Mankalawata)

1. *As told by Bwawelia, of Hebenahine village, Sabarl*
A story. A woman is cooking *mwihe* [a red fruit, unidentified]. She puts the food into her basket [explained as being a rough coconut-frond basket or *kayata*], and the moon goes down, then up, then in [to land] and eats it. The moon finishes eating it, and the next day the woman looks

for the fruit. She comes out and looks everywhere, and eventually she cooks more. The moon comes down and eats it. This happens the next day and the next. The woman hides and spies the moon eating. Taking a stick, she strikes the moon and smashes it to small pieces, which fly into the land-crab holes. An elder woman is going to the garden with her grandchild. She spies a small fragment of moon shining from a hole. She picks up the fragment. As she holds it in front of her eyes, it gives out light. Afterward she returns to the village with the fragment of moon in her "coin purse" basket. The next day she goes to the garden and continues to work until after dark, by the light of the moon. However, her daughter's husband has spied on her and says to his wife, "Your mother gardens at night with the baby. There's something strange about her." The woman is furious with her husband. Learning about the argument, her mother climbs a tall betel-nut tree [the hottest variety of betel nut, *bwahatayova*] to the very top and steps into the moon. Her name is Mankalawata, and she is still there, with her grandchild on her back.

2. As told by Jacinta, of Maho village, Sabarl

One woman had a girl baby. And her child had a girl baby as well, and another. The woman went to the garden with her granddaughters. She said to her granddaughters, "You go first" [you walk ahead of me]. They went ahead, and the woman took one *kepu* [black lip] shell in her basket. She touched it, and it began to shine out—lighting her path. She returned to the village, and the light went out. She stayed and said to her daughter, "I'm going back to the garden again." She went to the garden, and in the night she returned, using the shell torch. She returned to the village, and the light stopped again. Her daughter's husband saw the light and said to his wife, "Maybe your mother is a witch [*waunak*]." She asked her mother, "Do you know *waunak* business? You walk around all the time at night." The woman got very upset. She told her granddaughter, "You stay here, and I'll climb up one *kapoi* tree [unidentified]." Her two granddaughters climbed behind her. She was climbing to the middle of the tree when her daughter arrived. She saw her mother and started climbing too. Her mother told her, "Go back. I'm going to climb right up to the sky." The woman's husband was waiting, and the sun was going down. He went out onto the veranda. The moon was coming up in the west. His wife and her children told him, "Oh, my mother is coming up there." Her child was very sad.

3. As told by Simon Sulei, of Maho village, Sabarl

Truly a long time ago, at the beginning of time. Every day people would go to the bush to take fruit [*mwihe*—see story 1]. They would pick it and break it open and place it in a casual basket (*kayata*—see story 1). After filling it they would dip it in the sea. After three days they would fetch the basket and find it empty and they would ask, "Who keeps stealing our food every day? Whoever it is, we should find out so we can attack him." After a day the moon rises and sets, then travels around toward the northwest. Meanwhile, many strong women gather and wait at the point [where the moon rises over Sabarl]. They wait while the moon rises; they wait and watch as the moon dips into the sea and lights it up. It is looking for the fruit. Then it takes it and eats it. The strong women see it, the thing that always steals their food. After four days they go, take up the basket, and find its contents are gone. They say, "One day after the moon has set we must bar its way." After a time they see the water light up, and they go up and cut the moon to bits. They shatter it and crush it into powder, like sand. But one small fragment shaped like a potsherd [used for cooking sago pancakes] remains. You see it today—it looks like a potsherd [the new moon]. This fragment lands in a crab hole. And seeing it there, the women think, "It serves you right. You're always eating our fruit; now you'll know." The fragment stays inside the hole—nighttime through the middle of the day, it continues to "operate" and grow bigger. Then it leaves the hole, and the sky comes to meet it; it is carried up to the sky [by a *yaluyalu*, or black cloud]. There it stays. People ask, "Where does the moon go?" But in the beginning, we broke it to pieces.

Katutubwai

1. *As told by Jane Muluwa, of Maho village, Sabarl*

One woman approaches a group of people in a canoe. They cut her hands as she tries to get in. She approaches with her things, but they throw her mat out of the canoe. She approaches another canoe, and another. The same thing happens. They are fleeing the island. After they leave, she goes back to the village, then goes out to the water again and enters a giant clamshell. There she gives birth, in the mouth of the clam. Afterward she drinks fresh water, then seawater [a reference to the salt water drinking rituals of nursing mothers] and keeps doing this until her child, a girl, is big. When she is big, the girl makes a house and spears one of Katutubwai's pigs. Katutubwai calls his pigs' names—Kadom and Siyae and Buluka and one other ("name-name"): only four. But the child has speared one, and she continues to eat a pig a week for three weeks. He says, "Oh, already the fish have eaten my pigs." He waits. The girl comes round the point and he says, "Later I will swallow you." The girl says, "Come out then. Come out and eat me." The giant opens his huge mouth. He nearly swallows the girl, but his long hair becomes tangled in a tree, and the tree falls. The girl retreats to her veranda. She takes up her spear, aims it, and throws. She shouts her success, but the spear falls out. She leaps from veranda to veranda, taking the spears stored there and throwing them, but she draws no blood. He remains alive. She keeps trying, chased by Katutubwai with his mouth open. Finally she goes inside her own house. She goes to the hearth and picks up her cooking pot. Katutubwai opens his mouth, and as she overturns the pot she slides in as well, traveling down to his red anus. She shoots out of his anus. She then takes up her ax and cuts his neck. She takes dead coconut fronds and sets them on fire, cutting off half of his long hair and burning the rest away. She finishes him off and goes to sleep. He is truly dead. Then she takes his canoe, goes to his place, and destroys his house. His pots, his shell necklace, his ax blades, his tortoise-shell and wooden ceremonial lime-sticks—all these valuable things she takes, places in a basket, and puts inside his canoe along with food, sugarcane, bananas, and taro. She punts back to her place and tells her mother, "You take this food and cook it and wash it: I have cut down Katutubwai." She cuts off his testicles and throws them away. Then she cuts off his limbs so that she can cook them, giving them to her mother and making a butchering platform. They cook their meat and eat it. Afterward they make a min-iature canoe: the girl whittles one end, then the other end and an out-rigger, and makes its sail and rope. Her guide rope is made from Katu-tubwai's hair. Then she sends it racing along to her maternal uncle's wife, who is washing yams at the shoreline on another island. When she sees the canoe she thinks, "Oh, maybe the woman has eaten Ka-tutubwai." She takes the canoe to show her husband and says, "Maybe we should go see." They go, and there they find the girl festively dressed in a man's pubic leaf: a special decorated one [with incised designs] and a belt from the burnt skin of seagulls' legs. She wears this as well as Katutubwai's ceremonial belt [woven fiber with red shell beads attached]. She wears his shell necklace—crisscrossed. When her uncle and his wife arrive there, she goes down to greet them. They are not tricked and say, "You're not a man but a woman." Then she goes into the house and changes her clothes and returns to cook their food in a pot, and they eat. Afterward she says, "You go back to your place now. I'll stay here with my mother." But her uncle says, "No. Later I'll return with your other uncles." They do, and they dig up the pigs she has killed and buried, which they call Boluka, Kadom, and Siyai. They wait and wait to see if Katutubwai himself will return—the fourth pig. Then they settle down.

2. *As told by Nigeta, of Maho village, Sabarl*

Katutubwai was frightening the people from the place. They went to
Misima and stayed there. But Katutubwai went looking for them, chas-
ing after them. Some of them said they must keep running or Katutubwai would swallow them. One of the women had two brothers. She
folded her mat and prepared it for carrying on her head and went off
with her brothers. She wanted to come aboard the canoe, and one of
her brothers sent her back because the canoe was too small. She went
to another canoe where the other brother was. It was already full. She
told her brothers to go away. "I don't care if Katutubwai comes for me
and attacks me." She went back to the house. She took *kunabwa* [un-
identified—a starch used like sago] with her. She took half. All her
friends were gone. She saw Katutubwai coming. Coming closer and
closer. She didn't say a word. Katutubwai did not see her footprints
(maybe she walked on stilts). She climbed a small hill and stayed there.
He was looking for her everywhere. He returned to his cave, named
Pilili. Meanwhile the woman got pregnant, and the next day she had a
baby, a girl. Maybe from a reef heron. She drank salt water, and the baby
was already sitting up. The next day the girl started to walk. Then all
at once she was an adult. She asked her mother, "You and who else is
staying in this place?" Her mother told her daughter that her uncles
had thrown her out. She said, "My mother. Don't say anything more."
The daughter took an ax and cut down some small trees. (She laid the
sticks on the ground and built the frame in a single day. She put the
walls on right afterward.) Later she killed Katutubwai, and then she
told her mother that they should go back to her brothers. But the
brothers showed up before they could leave. She accused them of leaving her behind. They told her that they would not have come back if
her child had not killed Katutubwai.

3. *As told by Tom Sikarl, of Maho village, Sabarl*

Boiogalagala [a name for Katutubwai when he takes the form of a pig]
lives in a cave at a place called Kolaiwa. He is eating many people there,
so they flee from the place. One woman has no friend [no lover]. She is
a lonely person. She approaches one canoe as the fleet is departing and
tries to climb in, but they cut her finger off. Over and over the same
thing happens. She cries, "My mother, my mother, my fingers." She
goes back to Kolaiwa village when all the canoes have left without her.
Sitting on top of a flat stone she sees a bird [a reef heron]. The reef
heron asks, "Why are you crying?" and she replies, "All my friends are
gone. I'm distraught." The bird says, "You come to me." He takes her
and tucks her under his wing. Then they go walking about together,

passing by Boiogalagala, who says, "Maybe you are hiding a person there?" The heron says, "No, only myself." He opens up his feathers and there is no one visible there. The monster lets him pass. Then he passes a mangrove crab [*haman*—its shell, red from cooking, is used by sorcerers]. The crab says, "Maybe you are hiding someone?" But the heron says no and shows him that there is no one there. He goes on and sees a sea eagle. The same thing happens. Then he comes to a tree called *hapwahapwa* [unidentified] and says, "This is my house." He puts the woman down and tells her to stay there while he goes fishing. The woman becomes pregnant and gives birth to a boy. She looks after her son until he is big. He makes his spear and goes out fishing. Every day he does the same, but his mother warns him not to go far away or the monster or the crab or the eagle will eat him. The next day he spears four fish for Boiogalagala, who comes out and takes it for his family. Another fish he gives to his mother. She says, "You speared fish for the monster. Now when he's looking for fish he'll come and eat us instead." The next day he spears four fish but gives two to his mother. The giant comes out and is furious to see only two. "Which person is living in this place?" I'm the only one here—I've eaten all the people." The crab and sea eagle say, "There are only the three of us here eating people." The next day the son builds a veranda and sharpens spears and puts them there. He prepares his magic oil. He tells his mother, "To-morrow morning you cannot see me. If the lid comes off the bottle of oil, you know I am dead." His mother cries for him. It is nearly daylight when he climbs up onto the *mwamwaki* tree [unidentified] near Boio-galagala's house. He stays there until the monster comes out. The boy picks a fruit and throws it in front of him. "Who's living here and eat-ing fruit? I ate all the people." Then he looks up and sees the boy and shouts up, "I'll eat you." The monster roots around the tree. The boy jumps down and goes to one of the verandas and takes up a spear. He throws many spears, but the monster chases him from veranda to ve-randa. When the boy swims in the sea Boiogalagala swims after him. Then he climbs another veranda and taunts him with a song, throws his spear, and again goes to swim in the sea. Boiogalagala swims after him. This goes on. The boy is thinking, "I have only two spears left, called Kaugamwa [for the stomach] and Kauhate [for the heart]." As he spears the pig—for that is the form of Boiogalagala—he kills him. But it is like he has killed himself. He falls panting. At sunset he awakens and takes the pig and burns it, then cuts it and gives it to his mother. Then he asks her, "Where does this crab stay?" The next day he goes to the bush, climbs a tree [Moraceae: *Ficus myriocarpa*], and looks down to see his own reflection in the fresh water below. The crab is away from his home in the sea, looking for food, and comes to the pool. He comes, sees the reflection of the boy, and says to it, "My friend, why have you come to my home?" He walks into the pool, looking for the boy. When he emerges the boy spears him and carries him home for his mother. The next day he cuts down the tree and builds a canoe from it, making a hole in the center and then plugging the hole with a pointed piece of wood. On the following day he paddles around the point and confronts the sea eagle. The bird says, "I have already killed many people and chased the others away. Now it is only you and I." The bird flies down to the canoe and capsizes it, but the boy dives beneath it and removes the plug. When the bird puts its claw through the hole the boy ties it to the canoe and rights it, drowning the bird, which he carries home to his mother. His mother is pleased. The next day he constructs a toy canoe. He makes the mast from the pig's bone and the sail from the wing of the bird, using the crab shell for a bailer. He tells the canoe to go wherever the rest of the people are living. As it approaches their place, the children playing in the water are the first to spot it, and they shout, "Our canoe, our canoe." The old men say, "Bring that canoe to us." When they do, everyone gathers round to see what it is made of. The old men announce that everyone will leave for home the next day. Meanwhile the boy tells his mother to wash herself and put on a new skirt. He also washes himself and dresses up. As the people arrive, the mother comes down from her house and greets them. She tells them to return to their homes and send two girls to marry her son. They do this, and when they bring the two girls, everyone remains in that place forever—their true home.

4. *As told by Richard, of Hebenahine village, Sabarl*
In the time of Katutubwai, children are playing on the beach. From his cave, Katutubwai hears the sound of their voices. He seeks them out and eats one of them, and the others run away. They go to their elders. They explain that Katutubwai has eaten a child. The elders are furious. Meanwhile Katutubwai goes to his cave to sleep. There is a northwesterly wind [a chill wind] when his anus opens, and as he sleeps the child leaves through the hole. He runs to the elders and they say, "Oh, our child, you're back." The boy [swallowed child] says, "Katutubwai's stomach is full, but there is no child inside him any longer." Waking up, Katutubwai wages war on the people. But the elders take up bush knives, spears, axes, and shell trumpets and beat their drums. The

sound of the drum sends Katutubwai flying back to his cave, where he remains at Panaeve [Kimuta]. If we go there we can hear his noise.

5. *As told by Jane Muluwa, of Maho village, Sabarl*

A Kimuta story. Little children are swimming. Afterward they lie in the sun. One of them falls fast asleep and the others run away [after trying to wake him]. They run to their mothers as Katutubwai approaches the sleeping one and swallows him. He goes back to his cave in the bush. But the boy in his stomach wants to get out. So when Katutubwai goes to defecate, the boy shoots out whole and runs back home to his mother. His body is painted white with *bwan* [explained as being the slimy stuff that covers new babies]. His mother asks, "Where have you been?" He tells her. Katutubwai comes looking for him but cannot find him anywhere.

6. *As told by Dina, of Tagula*

One day I saw one fruit, *gil* [unidentified], growing there on Sudest. It had flowers on it and four fruits. When it was time, the first fruit fell down and became a man. When he grew up, he took his spear and went to look for betel nut. He went to take betel nut and mustard, and Katutubwai followed him. He approached one tree. He climbed up and took one stone with him, leaving it there. Gil went to steal all of Katutubwai's betel nut. Then Katutubwai followed Gil again. He told Gil, "My friend. Today I saw one possum [*lawesi*] there on that big tree. Do you want to come with me to catch it? Gil said, "I'm going to climb up to that possum." Katutubwai sat underneath the tree. Then Gil came back down, and Katutubwai told him that he would climb. Katutubwai climbed up and shook the tree. A stone fell off and struck Gil. Then Katutubwai took Gil and threw him in the rubbish. He returned to his place. The second *gil* fruit fell down and became a man. He took his spear . . . looking for betel nut, etc. Katutubwai followed him. The same thing happened. Same for the third fruit. The tree is called *haiyawa* [Moraceae: *Ficus microcarpa*]. The last fruit fell. The same thing happened, except when Katutubwai climbed the tree he told Gil, "Don't look up." He threw the stone, but it missed Gil. Afterward Gill looked up and said, "You've tricked my brothers. Now I know your way." He continued, "Today is our day, you and I. When Katutubwai wanted to come down he could not, because Gil blocked his path. Then he came down, and Gil struck him. He made a fire and struck Katutubwai. Then he went out to collect insects (red ants and other stinging insects). He threw them on top of his brothers, and his brothers came alive again. They swelled into life.

7. *As told in English by Josephine, head teacher at Maho school in 1977, whose home is Tagula*

Katutubwai had no children. In a nearby village grew one fruit, *hava-huye* [a sweet red fruit, unidentified]. Children from another village would come and steal it. One day five children were standing, one on the other's shoulders, to reach the fruit. The eldest said, "We must not make any noise." But then a crow came to eat the fruit and cried out. They tried to chase him off, but he cried out again and the noise awakened Katutubwai. The children started blaming each other for being noisy. The eldest had the idea of throwing the fruit and luring the giant off—each time, the child on the bottom would run away. Each fruit was thrown farther than the one before until all the children escaped, laughing at how they had tricked Katutubwai.

The Bush Fowl's Legs

The heroic bird is the brown-collared brush turkey (*Talegalla jobiensis*).

1. *As told by Simon Sulei, of Maho village, Sabarl*

In the beginning, in the time of our ancestors, every day two girls, cousins, would sit and talk. One day they talked until morning. One suggested they go fishing the following day. The other said, "Good, let's go." One brought along a wooden platter, the other carried their bush knives. They took along their lime. They found a spot and put their things down, then took off their outer skirts because you can't swim in them. Each put her skirt on the wooden platter. Then they went looking for mangrove crabs. But only one had any luck; the other found nothing. There had been a bird there before them. As they were washing the crabs, the one cousin commented, "My friend, you have many crabs and I have none." They put their things in a basket [large carrying basket] and the two of them set off, the good cousin first and the bad one following behind. They were walking along when they spotted a betel palm. One cousin said, "My friend, you climb up and pick some betel nut." The good cousin asked, "Which of us should climb?" and the other one said, "Not me." And so the good one climbed up. It was a *bwahatayova* tree [a very hot variety] but not very tall. Yet as she climbed it grew taller. She kept climbing toward the betel nut, but the tree kept growing until her arms were growing tired. Her friend, looking up, said, "Keep climbing, keep climbing." The good cousin looked down and shouted, "My cousin, maybe you should climb after me." But her friend said, "Only a little higher." It was growing dark. Finally, looking down, the girl in the tree could no longer see her cousin. While she was climbing, the bad cousin had broken open the crabs, and only the platter remained. She disposed of the shells, then left, leaving her friend in the tree. Her mother said, "Where is your cousin?" She replied, "She took one path, I another." Her mother and father went looking for their child. They came upon the platter, then spotted the discarded shells. They thought, "Where could she be?" then looked up at the tall tree. Meanwhile the bad cousin was back in the village. She was thinking about magic, had drunk salt water and made a potion of hot things [ginger, leaves, etc.] and slept during the day [behaving like a *waunak*]. The next day her [the good cousin's] parents made a feast: they cooked sago pudding, baked sago cakes, and issued an invitation to all the birds of the place. Her father said, "Whichever of you is a strong spirit leader, fly up and see if you can see my child." The birds promised to try hard. One particular bird, a sea eagle, said, "I'll go up." Another large bird said, "I'll go up," and the girl's father tied a pandanus streamer to his leg. The sea eagle got to the top of one of the branches but had to return. All the birds tried and failed. Only the bush fowl had stayed on the ground, waiting. The father asked, "Who are you?" and the bush fowl said, "I am the one who will fly to the top and return." The father replied, "If you bring back my child, I will give you a shell necklace as a reward." Afterward he flew up and up and up, and the girl's parents waited. The other birds were thinking to themselves that he would never make it (so slow and ponderous is the heavy bird), but even as they thought this he had reached the top. Meanwhile the good cousin had married a man [in the form of a reef heron]. He went fishing, and she was sweeping the house. She tossed a basket of rubbish out the door, over the bush fowl, who cried out. Hearing him the girl said, "Oh, a bird from my home." When he said that her parents had sent for her, she rolled up her mat and her things, closed up her house, and climbed into the black rubbish basket. The bush fowl put the basket on his back and carried her back down to her mother and father. They held their child. The bush fowl said, "You see, I can fly if I want to." Then they took hold of the bush fowl's legs and wrapped one side of a red shell necklace round each leg. When you see a bush fowl, his reddish legs look like a shell necklace.

Taviavia

1. *As told by Dominic Wasilolo, of Maho village, Sabarl*
There is a child, Taviavia, who smells because of his weeping sores. The villagers are mending the net, preparing to go fishing on the reef together. They spear a domestic pig, they prepare sago pudding, they

bake sago cakes and cook garden food. The child goes over to where the people are eating, into the midst of them. He smells bad, like the stench of rotting carrion. They tell him to go away, that they don't want him around, and they continue eating. They say they will vomit if he is around. The child cries and goes up to his house. He waits for his father and mother to return from the garden. They return that evening. He tells them, "They had a feast without me." The next day a fleet goes out fishing on the reef. They go to the Manuge reef and fish there all day. But Taviavia and his mother have gone before—their bird [clan] is Maho [the crow is their totemic emblem]. One by one the canoes sink—all four—pulled down by the reef where a *mwadawa* tree [a kind of teak] is growing with all the birds of the world on it. They cry and lure the canoe to the reef, which traps them. Taviavia and his parents have worked their magic. His father marries all the widows.

Miscellaneous

1. *The original story of yams, as told by Manuge, of Hebenahine village, Sabarl*

This is a Tokuna story [on Panatinani] about how yams began at that place. At that time there were two friends and their siblings (same sex) and mothers. They go to the garden. The one friend works, but his food is no good; the other does no work but produces the wonderful yams called *bwoibwoi* [the "parental" yams of the garden]. The one becomes jealous. "Why is your food good when you're so lazy?" Their mothers settle it by saying, "Right. The one who works hard must go, but takes the good food with him." The one who will leave climbs a fruit tree [*tawai*—unidentified], and when he reaches the top of the branches calls down to his mother, "I am going now. I am no longer working for you. Give me the food." He takes *pwanakau* yams [a fine, delicate variety] and departs for Motorina [he flies, using coconut bast for wings]. He rests there, and his mother follows by sea, swimming. She calls out for him to wait, but he replies, "You have one son back home; I am leaving." He goes on to Basilake. He stays, and his mother follows. Afterward he goes to Duau. He waits for his mother, but she never comes. Maybe a fish ate her. That's why Duau and places up that way have *pwanakau* and there are none here.

2. *The story of the reef heron (boi), as told by Dominic Wasilolo, of Maho village, Sabarl*

This is the story of the reef heron. He is fishing, but the mist is obscuring his view; he waits and tries to fish. He asks his mother to wait until he can see. Meanwhile he walks about and climbs a small hill. An elder woman, the owner of the hill, lives there. He approaches her and finds a fire burning. He comes to a tree and climbs it. She stays where she is. Then he takes some of the fruit from the tree and samples it, but throws it away afterward. The woman asks what he is doing: she does not know what kind of bird ate that fruit. Staring, she says, "You're a man." She says, "Come here," and the man comes down from the tree. She takes him into her house. She opens her house and her mat. She spreads open the mat, named Sagieda [a type of pandanus]. Then she shuts the house. She has two grown granddaughters in another house. She says to them, "Stay there [in my house] and I will stay here. Don't come to me for food. You cook, you eat, you sleep, you stay. I don't want food either." One girl becomes pregnant. She gives birth to a male child. She leaves the bush with her child and goes to the sea. She tells the bird to take the child by the hand. He asks, "Where?" She says, "I'll keep him on the land." The bird asks, "What will he do there?" The woman says, "Wait a moment." She takes a piece of wood and rubs her bottom over it. Then she tells the reef heron to try to make fire with it and to put water over it. He does this and drinks the water—his body becomes thoroughly warm. He says, "What a good thing." He brings it to his mother. Then his wife says, "Try cooking food with it." He tries it and it is sweet, and he tells his mother. Afterward he makes a huge fire and hovers over it and becomes warm.

3. *The story of Tobwatobwa, as told in English by Soter Kankan, of Maho village, Sabarl*

There were two boys, cousins, who lived on a reef off Misima. They had no parents. One day one boy spotted smoke coming from the bush on the big island. He said to his cousin, "Let us go and visit those people in the bush." They dried fish, put it in their baskets, and paddled their canoe to the big island. There they pulled the canoe up high on the beach, walked into the bush, and found the house. A girl was sitting on the veranda, and her grandmother [her maternal grandmother] was sweeping under the house. One boy whistled to the girl, but she was frightened that her grandmother would be cross, and she did not reply. The boys approached the grandmother and asked if they could come and live in the house, and she said they could. The girl cooked the fish they had brought together with her garden food, and they all ate together. But they did not know that the girl was already married to a *tobwatobwa* [a stone ax blade]. The ax blade slept on the platform above the hearth. While the elder cousin was thinking about sleeping with the girl, the ax blade crept down and slit her throat. The boys were terrified. They covered her with leaves, ran down to the beach, and hid in their canoe, but the old woman ran after them and found them. She cried, "I fed you. Why did you do this to my grand-daughter?" The first cousin explained what had happened. They all returned to the house. The grandmother told the boys to gather fire-wood. Then they built a very large fire and placed the ax blade in it. When it was very hot, the ax blade exploded from the fire and flew all the way to Duau, where there are many ax blades today. After this had happened, the grandmother put her granddaughter's body in a large wooden platter [*nohai*] and left it for a while. When she looked again, the girl was sitting on top of the dish smiling. [In another version, the girl is cut in pieces after her throat is slit.]

4. *The girl with the snake eel inside, as told by Ludi, of Liak village, Misima*

One end of Liak village is called Kibkib. A *vitvit* tree [Leguminosae: *Inocarpus fagifer*] is there, at the western end of the village. And Man-kalawata [the beautiful girl who shines like the moon] stays at the east-ern end. An old woman lives in the middle of the village. There are five *vitvit* nuts. One drops each day. The first one drops into the creek and is carried out to sea, where a boy breaks out of the shell. The boy is naked, and he looks for a leaf and string to cover himself. He makes a basket, puts everything inside, and starts to go up to the east. [He becomes "a human being" when he does these things.] He doesn't know about the old woman and the girl. He walks up, and as he ap-proaches the old woman calls out to him, "My grandson. Where to?" [A question suggesting a sexual proposition.] He thinks she is so ugly that he cannot bear to answer her. He goes up, then sees the girl and sleeps with her. But when he is inside her an snake eel there eats his penis, and he dies. This happens with his other three brothers. The last boy is named Kaisilili [the name for blisters on the feet that cause one to limp]. The old woman spots him and calls out, "My poor son. Where are you going?" He says, "Up here. Did you see my brothers?" "Yes, all of them. Do you have any betel nut?" He says yes and gladly goes up to her house. She tells him the story about the girl with the eel inside her. He listens carefully. She gives him food, and he follows her into the bush—her gift to him for showing respect. She takes him to the *mwak* tree [like a banana with black juice inside]. She splits open the tree, creating a hole that he walks through. He becomes after this very beautiful. Then she takes him to the breadfruit tree [*biena*], where he sees the red spear-like blossom [*wap*] that preceeds the breadfuit. The old woman says, "Take this, peel it, and use it instead of your penis on the girl." Then she makes a fishnet-string and ties it to the end of the blossom. She tells him to put this inside the girl after foreplay and the snake eel will see it coming and start to eat it. He must then tie the string around its neck and pull it out. The boy does this, but when he pulls the snake eel out the beautiful girl dies. The old woman has told him how to revive her. So he takes a magic broom and hits her with it, and she wakes up and asks, "What happened?" He tells her, "I killed the snake eel." They are very happy, and she takes him for her husband. Then he sweeps his brothers with the magic broom and they come to life again.

Notes

Introduction

1. This study is based on one year of field research in 1976–77, three months in 1979, and two months in 1986. Unless otherwise noted, the "ethnographic present" of the book is 1976–79. Funding for the original research was provided by the William Wyse Fund and the Smuts Memorial Fund (Cambridge University), the Esperanza Trust (Royal Anthropological Institute), and Girton College, Cambridge. Subsequent research was funded by the Wenner-Gren Foundation for Anthropological Research and by Mount Holyoke College.

2. The present study, in line with certain other ethnographies from the Pacific (especially Munn 1986; Parmentier 1987; Strathern 1988; Wagner 1986), is concerned with ethnography-derived models of value production. In theoretical terms, I am taking the position that cultural meaning is essentially realized in practice, through concrete images and exchanges that, more than expressing consensual values, actually construct and convey them. Thus a central element here is the "pragmatical dimension" of Sabarl cultural life, where the meaningfulness of specific cultural acts and their objectifications is taken to reside in a "social reality that is fundamentally symbolic" (Ricouer, in Munn 1986:7). This symbolic approach differs from comparative research methods in that, as Strathern succinctly notes, "theoretical interest [is] directed to the manner in which ideas, images, and values are locally contextualized." In this regard, "The task is not to imagine one can replace exogenous concepts by indigenous counterparts; rather the task is to convey the complexity of the indigenous concepts in reference to the particular context in which they are produced . . . to show the contextualized nature of indigenous constructs by exposing the contextualized nature of analytical ones" (1988:8).

3. In contrast to the view that it is primarily the ethnographer whose pursuit of knowledge is limited by his or her outsider status (cf. LeRoy 1985:11), I take human "being" to exist only in dialogue. "Man," to quote Bakhtin, "has no internal sovereign territory; he is all and always on the boundary; looking within himself he looks *in the eyes of the other or through the eyes of the other*" (1984:311–12; emphasis in original). Of course, there are limits on how far or whether it is possible to represent this dialogue in a written text (as acknowledged at least implicitly by critics of totalizing, objectivist

217

ethnographies, most contagiously Boon 1982; Clifford 1983; the contributors to Clifford and Marcus 1986; Marcus and Fischer 1986; Myers 1988; Strathern 1988; Tyler 1987; and Wagner 1975). Here, however, and if I correctly interpret the movement toward self-other awareness more broadly, the concern is less to produce a stylistically different kind of written object than to generate an awareness of gaps in understanding insofar as these relate to the process of ethnography.

4. A recent critique by Sangren (1988) of the perspectivist claim to counterhegemony considers the problem of whether "postmodern" anthropologists mask their own power goals and their interests in producing and reproducing their own careers with a mystifying and elitist discourse; a discourse that often fails to recognize its own antecedents in more traditional ethnographies—not to mention in cultures that are decidedly not "postmodern." Ethnographic rhetoric is not my subject here. However, I feel compelled to note the failure of Sangren (and it must be said, of many postmodern writers as well) to distinguish postmodernism, a movement with roots in the specifically historical problem of the alienating and fragmenting effects of Western socioeconomic and political influences on other cultures and on individuals' attempts to find meaning (see, for example, Lyotard 1979), from analytic perspectives ("hermeneutic," "deconstructivist," "poststructuralist") that have as their goal respect for indigenous ways of conceiving the cultural reproduction of knowledge that are themselves "perspectivist." The Hegelian question of how pertinent contemporary analytic frameworks can ever be to understanding social phenomena in other times, or in the present case, to understanding other cultures in our own time, must, I believe, be approached with this level distinction in mind and with a critical eye for what is meant by "modern," "postmodern," or any other nonindigenous label indicating periodicity.

5. Later I will return to the subject of cultural artifacts as objectifications of dialectical (and dialogical) social processes. A process-oriented approach has the advantage here of circumscribing differences based on the material properties of objects (for example, "hard" or "soft" wealth) or on formal characteristics. Thus items such as Polynesian fine mats, which are judged too valuable to give away (Weiner 1986), and the carved *malanggan* figures of New Ireland, which are destroyed or disappear intact behind the stage of their public display (Küchler 1987, 1988), convey a sense of permanence and the constructivist inflection of these societies *in the same terms.* At base, we are talking about the relative significance ascribed to human agency in the matter of separation. Weiner's similarly process-based division of wealth into "alienable" and "inalienable," and her presentation of gender correlates, is an important example of the greater sophistication of process-based distinctions. (See also Munn's [1977] discussion of objects as extensions or contractions of the political "reach" of persons and groups and her subsequently published discussion of valuable objects [1986] and Young's [1983] fascinating discussion of the linguistic markers of person/object alienability and inalienability in Kalauna.) This is not to say that property distinctions, which often articulate important cultural notions of substance value (e.g., wealth items = bodily substances), are unimportant or insignificant. Indeed, Sabarl artifacts are discussed in these terms below.

6. I am adopting Gombrich's (1963:8) broad use of the term "representation" to mean a created substitute, which may include the feature of structural equivalence with which, in particularly notable studies of value production from the Pacific, Munn (1973:21 n, 1986:16) and Parmentier (1987:108) are concerned, drawing on the semiotics of Charles Peirce. Aside from the Peircean notion that icons correspond to actual physical referents, the position taken here lies within the pragmatic tradition that stresses the application of representational signs to particular social/historical contexts. In short, I take iconic signs to be the material vehicles of culturally informed existential meanings where the form of the sign structurally resembles what it signifies. As considered here, such signs are vehicles of social relations rather than merely expressing something about them (Battaglia 1983a). When such icons have the status of "generative schema" (Munn 1986:121) or "templates"— what Ardener (1978:106) talks about as "template structures," Parmentier as "diagrammatic icons" (1987:108), and Tyler (1987:105) as "scheme, schema or schemata" (he notes Bartlett's usage and the Aristotelian *schemae* and *figurae,* referring to the rhetorical "making of tropes by fixed formulae")—they tend to emerge as dominant "themes" of ethnographic discourse, which is how I incorporate them here.

7. I shall borrow from Russian formalism to the extent of using "story" (*fabula*) to mean any sequence of actions or events, as distinct from their manifestation and ordering in discourse (verbal or otherwise; see Culler 1981). The term *lihulihu,* "narrative," is translated colloquially as "story" by Sabarl who speak English. The term (from *lihu,* "word") applies to all forms of narrative discourse.

8. I am using Wagner's phrase (1986a) to indicate the concrete immediacy of visual images over verbal metaphors in societies like Barok and Sabarl, where "talk is cheap."

9. Tagula is the common Saisai name for what appears in historical accounts and most published literature as Sudest Island. From her ethnographic research there, Lepowsky calls the island Vanatinai. However, I shall use Tagula throughout the book in deference to the Saisai perspective.

10. Tyler's critique of the visual bias in social studies of memory (1987:135–36), including the tendency to privilege spatial over temporal metaphors (e.g., memory should be seen as the "conservation of time rather than the conservation of an object"), which he links to our own cultural emphasis on writing (narrowly defined), is inappropriate to Sabarl, who grasp time through material embodiments of it. Tyler's warning not to regard memories as being, like objects, "subject to the ravages of entropy. They decay, fade, leave traces—can be stored, retrieved (after being 'lost' or repressed)" (1987:135) is, significantly, very much the Sabarl sense of *paganuwohasik.*

11. Along these lines, Munn (1986:9–10), in developing the subject for Gawa, considers remembering as a "subjective aspect" of space-time and a "constitutive factor" in its formation (cf. Halbwachs 1980). Küchler's analyses of the memory process in northern New Ireland (1987, 1988) offer a comparative picture of the place of memory in exchanges, from a society where recollected internal images, not material objects, are traded and inherited, and without the emphasis on deconstructive agency that is elaborated by Sabarl.

12. I am grateful here and throughout the book for the linguistic assistance of Father Anthony Young, whose nearly thirty years of fluency in Nimowa (a dialect of Saisai) and sensitive concern for the praxis and poetics of translation have been invaluable to this study.

13. Weiner's important earlier study (1976), which details the role of women in Trobriand mortuary practices and their part in social regenesis more broadly, calls attention to the objectification of women's power in the wealth they manufacture. For Sabarl, objectification is a process of endless displacement concentrated in mortuary enactments that incorporate mnemonic objects of various kinds. Here wealth items (food and objects) associated with both sexes focus the process, rather like putting certain figures of speech in italics within a text. However, masculine wealth is written in boldface. As I argue in chapter 7, the masculine inflection qualifies the strength of regeneration as a cultural theme. Therefore Weiner's reference to this aspect, as quoted here, reflects the Trobriand but not the Sabarl emphasis.

14. Kapferer's definition of "performance" as a "unity of text and enactment, neither being reducible to the other" (1986:192), takes a narrower definition of "text," so that although my approach to performance is in the spirit of Kapferer's (see Schieffelin's excellent work on Melanesian performance [1976]; also Schechner 1985; Turner 1982), it remains outside the dramaturgical tradition with its foundation in role theory. In the Sabarl case it is more appropriate to take "writing" (inscription or impression making) as an orienting framework, while acknowledging the "illocutionary force" (Bloch 1974) of dramatically enacted texts.

15. As opposed to the nonsignifying complexes of natural phenomena, "texts" are "coherent complexes of signs" (Bakhtin), or more exactly, complexes of images, considered here as distinct from the stories they manifest.

16. I am using Jauss's phrase in reference to an understanding of genre as a "preconstituted horizon of expectations . . . (the rules of the game)" that "orient the reader's (public's) understanding and . . . enable a qualifying reception" of each new textual concretization. In the case of *segaiya*, the "continuity formative of [the] genre" lies in the thematic structure of commemorative enactments, where performance is the "dominant" in the relational system of the *segaiya* intertext but is not the only generic aspect (Jauss 1982:79–81). Thus I include wealth objects, certain narratives, notions of the physical and spiritual person, and memorial artifacts generally as component texts, without concern for mixing genres.

17. In 1976 no other anthropologist had worked in the Calvados Chain area. Armstrong was on Yele (Rossel) in the mid-1930s, and Liep was there in 1969; Berde worked on Panaeati in 1970. Lepowsky would subsequently work on Tagula.

18. The process of self formation inferred by the notion of relational personhood is taken from William James, who defined the "empirical me" in general as all that a person "can call his": his or her body, traits, and abilities; material possessions; friends and enemies and family; vocations and avocations. Borrowing Favret-Saada's terminology (1980), I shall refer to these elements of self as the "domain" of the person.

19. See Lithgow (1976). For details of cognate counts, see Sebeok (1971).

20. Sabarl also recognize ties of origin and trade to the Deboyne and Ren-

ard islands and to Misima to the north, kept alive through tenuous exchange relationships.

21. Breadfruit (*Artocarpus altilis*), mango (*Mangifera indica*), and a nutty legume called *vitvit* (*Inocarpus fagifer*) are plentiful, as are palm grubs (*gubgub*). Men also hunt opossums, flying foxes, fruit bats, and bush fowl (*Talegalla jobiensis*) all year round.

22. These included octopus (*huita*), which could entangle the baby within the womb or snarl it up on the way out; crayfish (*huyabo*), which could clamp onto the mother's backbone and keep the child inside; and land crabs (*kibkib*), which themselves preferred to stay inside their holes. Pregnant women also abstained from eating coconut cream, which spoils quickly and could leave a polluting smell on the baby, and hot things, for fear of scalding or scorching the fetus (and causing stretch marks): for example, hot varieties of betel nut, hot water, and very hot foods. Sturgeon (*tuitui*), and trevally (*habewa* or *woiywoiya*) were considered too greasy, as was sea turtle, which bleeds to death in butchering.

23. Already in 1976 there were lapses in the "ancestral" practice of abstaining from sex while one child was still nursing, and such lapses were far more frequent by 1986.

24. It is worth noting a letter to the special commissioner for British New Guinea from Henry Forbes, acting deputy commissioner, written on 11 December 1885, regarding the punitive expedition then headed for Panatinani (Joannet). The expedition followed in the wake of violence against the captain of the ketch *Emily*, who reportedly gave a rifle he had promised one man to his mortal enemy instead. The letter mentions that Sabarl and Sudest islanders lent canoes to the Panatinani to allow those of them who were in captivity "aiding with inquiries" to escape. A number of the local people were severely wounded or killed when the punitive expedition "soldiers" pursued them and fired into the area where they were camped. Villages were burned to the ground on Joannet. Forbes writes: "Few people who are not personally acquainted with the . . . untraversable nature of such islands as Joannet and Sabari with their thousand loopholes of escape and places of concealment, can realize the difficulty of capturing rebel natives, following them up narrow paths set with spear points (as the Joannet Is. paths were) where all the odds are heavily against the pursuers." "I regret to have to draw your Excellency's attention to the inhumanitarian feeling among the traders themselves, by continuing to barter on the most friendly terms with the very men whose hands are fresh dripping with the blood of one of their rivals. On this account I have assumed the responsibility . . . of prohibiting the erection of all stations on, and the cessation of all trade with, Joannet, Grassy, Pig and SudEst islands" (British New Guinea Annual Report 1986b).

25. The information comes from the report by F. I. Middleton (Australia Patrol Report 1944–45). Government documents of the "Motorina cargo cult" contain material that indicates the amount of mayhem described in statements from officers in the Australia New Guinea Administrative Unit, delivered to Sidney Smith, P.O., on 20 February 1943. An example is this one from A. C. Maipu of Orokolo: "I went with all the other police and lay for about three hours behind Hebenahine village on Sabari Is. About 3 or 4 o'clock in the morning we heard canoes being pushed into the water, we sang out to the

people not to run away but they took no notice and all tried to escape. We rushed down to the beach to catch the Bagaman man [an island in the western Chain]. All the women and men were mixed up. I saw one man with a scrub knife so I tried to catch him. When I got up the track a little he came out from behind a big piece of limestone. I went to catch him and he made a slash at me with his knife. I jumped back. I made another attempt to catch him and he nearly cut me through the shoulder. I then shot him through the body and killed him." Other statements describe the death of a woman on the same occasion, and subsequently of a boy on Panatinani (dated 11 March 1943).

26. Maho village received a 40,000 gallon water tank (at a cost to the local government council of $9,000 several years ago), but its catchment collapsed in the first big wind, and the pump broke shortly afterward. Money for repair of the tank was allocated in 1977; in 1986 work had yet to begin on the project. There is also a nonfunctional 500 gallon tank at Hebenahine village and a well whose salinity increases over two-week cycles.

27. On one very unlucky day, the men of Maho village brought in about 130 kilograms of fish. The men were paid 20 toya (about 20 cents U.S.) per kilo on the spot. The Department of Primary Industries at Samarai purchased the catch for 1 kina (K1) per kilo (about $1 U.S.) for "line fish" (e.g., kingfish) and 55 toya per kilo for "net fish" (e.g., mullet). This had been a bad year, and the total catch for the Chain islands was expected to be in the vicinity of 6,000 kilos, compared with the previous year's 10,000 plus.

28. People I asked considered 1984–85 to be a typical year in terms of income for Sabarl residents. A sample of forty-seven Maho village men revealed an average income of K30.50, and the average was K4.18 for a sample of forty-five women. Figures included all sources, but 98 percent of Sabarl income derives from the single source of the government fisheries. Both men and women dive for trochus, black lip, and clam, and those with access to dinghies may also search for bêche-de-mer. During that year, the fisheries boats stopped four times at Sabarl. However, in 1985–86, for example, the boats came only twice. Average income was K15.00 for men and K2.00 for women; that is, taxes were 67 percent of male incomes that year and took 100 percent of the income of women.

29. Rectangular houses were introduced to the area in 1947, possibly by men returning from Port Moresby after their imprisonment. Old-style houses (*pwalago*) had rounded thatch roofs with a center ridgepole and were raised on pilings made of *Intsia bijuga* (*kivi*), an exceedingly hard wood associated with the strength of affines and "red inside like a person." The last such house disappeared from the area in 1964. At one time a pig was killed for every *kivi* post cut and one for every post erected, and each post was carved and painted with totemic "handmarks" of the affinal male contributing it. *Kivi* is said to make the house "too heavy" for the average man—a way of saying that the price is oppressive to anyone who is not well connected. It is traditionally reserved for leaders' houses. The church at Maho was supported entirely by *kivi* posts.

Chapter One

1. Sabarl narrative genres are not linguistically marked, though they tend to be divided into two categories. The first includes stories that are taken as

historically "true" (*lihulihu suwot*)—stories that are believed to be situated in time and that, having the status of records of historical events, are objects of interest mainly to the politically inclined. The second includes stories "from the first time" (*sauga tawa lelei*) or "the time of the ancestors" (*hetutubumai wali sauga*), which are model tales on moral and cultural themes, taken as allegories. These narratives have the status of "custom" (*paga*), and they are taken very seriously as "objects of and for remembering," embodying what Burke (1969:439–40) has termed the "logical essence of primary moral relationships." (Notably, Parmentier [1987] develops a similar distinction between them in his discussion of "signs in history" versus "signs of history" on Belau, and LeRoy [1985] does so in his analysis of Kewa narrative.)

Though Sabarl in general regarded allegorical narratives as *essentially* more important than histories and legends, it tended to be the intellectuals who talked about the Katutubwai "stories for children" (*bwebwesa lihulihuina*) as the "most important" allegorical tales. However, it should be noted that "stories" from the Catholic Bible, some of which has been beautifully translated by Anthony Young into the local language, were in 1986 more popular than Sabarl tales and were heard more regularly.

2. The fragments of a belief in the recycling of human substance are discernible when we look more closely. It is widely held that ambergris, which floats across the sea in waxy blocks (called *muho*), is in fact discarded fat from human bodies consumed by sorcerers and witches at faraway spirit feasts. I will discuss this later in connection with the importance of *muho* in gardening rituals. But the image of congealed "father's blood" adrift on the sea and headed toward the shores of the living is suggestive. The saltwater environment is also significant, for as clear water (*bwai*) is intrinsically "cool" and clarifying, salt water (*soga*) is thought of as "hot," and heat is considered conducive to conception. I know of no one who consciously links conception with *muho*. Nonetheless, any trace of interest in the symbolic recycling of paternal substance is worth noting in a matrilineal society, for not only does it indicate a central position for males in societal reproduction (cf. Weiner 1980), it likewise cues us to look for analogues in the realm of economic productivity and in the management of wealth and human energies.

3. Munn (1986:60) discusses the "subjective potential" of "food-giving acts" for Gawa, though not the gift of preparation and display, which has (in the local view) as its wider audience the ancestors as well as those specific living persons whose minds one seeks to turn in one's favor.

4. I discuss this process of reversible androgyny more fully in a forthcoming chapter, (Battaglia in press) in connection with ambivalence in Sabarl leadership models.

5. It is relevant here to put this tale in perspective by returning to the image of Enak, the original androgyne, embodiment of masculine and feminine productivity unviolated (unseparated), which produces an additional being, Katutubwai, who is not androgynous (not a duplicate or a reproduction—not in the image of the Creator) but rather the violent aspect of the original. The child-monster that issues from Enak at once adds something to the world and lacks something essential from which he/she has become separated. This same logic informs the mythical heroine's violent transformation in the story just told—the birth of her masculine aspect—and the requirement

that it be reversed. She must, that is, separate from this violent part of herself if she is not to become what she kills.

Chapter Two

1. Lutz's discussion of Ifaluk personhood, and in particular of the self as an "undivided entity" where "thought/emotion" (*nunuwan*) and "will/emotion/desire" (*tip-*) are encompassed in the notion of "our insides" (1985:46–52) and often refer to the same phenomena, helps make the important point that it is not a contrast with Western concepts of person and self that is at issue here so much as distinctions across even other Pacific cultures. Sabarl distinguish "mind" and "emotion" linguistically without denying the intersubjective nature of operationalizing the distinction in social practice. It follows that Sabarl do not "act" out "roles" of social persons (compare, for example, Baining personhood as discussed by Fajans 1985), far less recognize the possibility of experiencing themselves as "social objectivities" (as Errington and Gewertz 1987 argue for the Chambri). Rather, a sense of self and of person (the self as a social significance) are taken as ongoing processes, comprising, as Munn has observed for Gawa (1986:60–61), acts of reconstituting oneself in the mind of the other by means of "subjective acts" (such as acts of "remembering" social connections by giving food or material objects, or ultimately one's own substance in the production of a new person), and alternatively, in the Sabarl context, of deconstituting oneself by officially "forgetting" connections that inhibit or stall self-development (e.g., breaking off ties of exchange with trading partners, or of affinity with the dead and their representatives among the living, and so forth). Although certain cultural performances, and *segaiya* especially, are representational of this process, participation constitutes the participants as social persons and as "self-others" rather than merely depicting them as such.

The range of approaches to the study of Pacific personhood, all taking as their premise the person as a sociocultural construct, is represented in the work of Errington and Gewertz (1987), Leenhart (1979), Mosko (1985), Wagner (1986a), the contributors to White and Kirkpatrick (1985), and Young (1983), to name a significant few.

2. For a detailed discussion of the etymology of the gift in another Massim society, see Young (1983).

3. I have seen, for example, a man invest his wealth in his own child instead of his nephew and heir, behaving "like" a maternal clansperson rather than the child's mother's husband—giving out of sentiment, against the rules of matrilineality. I have watched as a Maho village leader "in a mood" after an argument with his wife, spontaneously withdrew from a collective venture involving several villages. Since he was the organizer, the venture "unraveled" (the Sabarl image) and people went home—and this behavior was tolerated without a negative word to him. I was told that men of influence are also sometimes unpredictable, and one ought to show respect for their decisions. Of course this "undoing" is precisely what keeps the rules fresh in mind, as people constantly renegotiate, redefine, contest, and sneak around them.

During a visit in 1986, my Trobriand field assistant, Silipokapulapola Digim'rina, was moved to comment on how "careful" people were with one another (Sabarl were amused by the seemingly "hard" tone of the exchanges between him and his friendly Trobriand hosts, then teaching at Maho school). I have several times heard Europeans remark that being among Sabarl was a "softening" experience, and I have felt the same way. In fact I was never able to reconcile this with the fierceness that some of these same people were capable of turning on outsiders in times of war and that was so much a part of Sabarl's image to their neighbors (though Maho villagers remark with amusement that the Sabarl of Nigahau typically use a very "hard" style of speech in their trade negotiations). This finely tuned regard for feelings is a salient cultural feature of Sabarl islanders.

4. I myself was another example. It seemed to my teachers that I was incredibly slow to learn "Sabarl *haningalia*," the Sabarl "speech" they regarded as so much simpler than English. This problem was attributed to my failure to ingest enough Sabarl water (the partly saline *yeluyelu*) "to clear my mind for it"—as if the clarity were a transmittable property of the water and an artifact specifically of the "homeplace." In other words, I needed to internalize the "place/object of and for remembering"; without it I was unable to organize and retain fundamental knowledge. And just as water (salty followed by fresh) was at one time drunk by warriors in rituals to heighten their senses before a battle and is still used today to "transform and clarify" (*didigana*) a lover's appearance and to remove impurities from a nursing mother's system, so people continued to hope that time and more water would one day improve my language skills.

5. In a provocative discussion of an analogous concept (*kaa*) from Yele (Rossel Island), Liep (n.d.a) explores the effecting presence of image in this area in terms of its affinities with the Polynesian concept of *hau*—what Mauss called the "spirit in the gift."

6. Following Charles Peirce, I am using "belief" to refer to a kind of loosely articulated state of nondoubt.

7. Catholicism has had some effect on the practice of malevolent magic and on the use of fear to control other people in the eastern Calvados Chain. For example, more people were denying rather than boasting about their experiences at spirit feasts and their skills as sorcerers in 1986 than in 1976, and public announcements were being made about giving up human "pig"—"because I am Catholic"—although I never heard of anyone giving up the role of seer, the use of protective magic, or the knowledge of poisons. And though fear of sorcery and witchcraft remained almost tangibly part of the neighboring Tagula culture and far more salient as an everyday concern of people there, in 1986 serious illness was still invariably dealt with in the Saisai area as if the victim and his or her group were physically under attack by malevolent spirits.

8. In one technique that I learned of, the *bibiloia* tied charmed *siniho* leaves (Myrtaceae: *Syzygium branderhorstii*) to his ankles, the number of leaves determining the distance he could "walk"—one or two to Nimowa, three or four to Sidea, five or six to the New Guinea mainland. As he uttered the magic words, I was assured that he would vanish from the spot and his body would instantly materialize at his destination.

9. A *saksak* (male *waunak* leader) is typically also a sorcerer with a reputation for practicing the most lethal forms of magic—those that kill the vic-

tim instantly, without illness. The magical techniques are legend (though as recently as 1979, witnesses to one of these sent a Tagula man to prison under the terms of the Sorcery Act of 1979). For example, there is the deadly "match-box magic": the box with a hole in one end is filled with "hot" substances and flicked in the direction of the victim while a sorcerer utters magic words. In another technique, the sorcerer looks into a mirror as he utters deadly words, then flashes the mirror in the victim's eyes. Rarely are gestures alone sufficient to commit the foul deed; magic words are needed to direct the force. However, in at least one method of sorcery, even the motions can kill. This technique involves the use of an especially thin and valuable stone ax blade—the *popo-sisi* (or *pepa ston*), which is still the only appropriate fee for a sorcerer assassin. The stone is taken to a tidal pool to be infused with the water's heat for several days, then baked in the sun and afterward sprayed with hot substances, such as ginger or sassafras root. It is then fitted into a ceremonial handle, and the sorcerer shoulders the ax and walks to a spot deep in the bush. By this time the blade is so hot and powerful that if its shadow (*kanukanunu-*) were to cross the sorcerer's own, it would kill him instantly. Once inside the bush, he names a tree for his victim, then calls out the names of the victim's body parts, strik-ing the tree each time he does so. My consultant had practiced on a dog, and the dog had "exploded" instantly. Such sorcerers are also believed to have the power as *waunak* to manifest themselves as dangerous animals or to manipu-late animals for nefarious purposes. Snakes, for example, are never killed in-side the house, for fear that their spirits or those of their *waunak* masters will take revenge there. Whatever his methods, the skill of a *saksak* sorcerer is never deemed to be "innate" (*yapewa*): he must always acquire it from a living adept.

10. There are several ways of stealing a *kanukanunu-*. A reflection may be snatched away as someone looks into a mirror or a pool of water, a photo-graph stolen from the house, a shadow bespelled, a name trapped within a crab shell red from cooking (the image of a person can be seen in the creases of these shells when they are held to the light).

11. As far as I could determine, "sleeping with leaves" is a simple matter of speaking magic words into *puwoga* leaves (Moraceae: *Ficus*) while drying them over a fire, then tucking the leaves under a mat or pillow and either sleeping and dreaming or having a vision while only partly awake. During my first period of fieldwork on Sabarl I tried repeatedly to persuade someone to show me the method for flying—at one point becoming positively obsessed by the idea (I now regard this a a quirk of youth). But my potential tutors were firmly opposed and refused to take responsibility for teaching me. Their fear was that I was still too ignorant of the geographic terrain for my spirit image to find its way back to Maho village by "dead reckoning" and that I would never awake from my sleep.

12. Favret-Saada (1980) schematically represents witchcraft in the Bocage in terms surprisingly similar to Sabarl, where the elements of the "personal domain" define the self that is under attack to the extent of rendering the individual vulnerable if bespelled.

13. For discussion of the cultural labeling of death as "good" or "bad," see Bloch and Parry (1982). In talking about death in these terms, Sabarl tend

to focus less on the way of dying than on how a death is observed by survivors, and its consequences for them.

Chapter Three

1. In 1986 Sabarl still preferred black twist tobacco to store-bought cigarettes, though the latter could be obtained at a cost and among some of Sabarl's neighbors were considered far more prestigious. A Trobriand schoolteacher commented that Sabarl "died" for tobacco the way Trobrianders "died" for betel nut.

2. This is a classic instance of food as well as wealth mediating relations as part of the system of "tracing out blood relations" (Strathern 1984).

3. Note that the pudding and ax blades given as part of a "father's" gift of "bones" are thus what I have termed "anticipatory symbols," of which there are many in connection with *segaiya*. What we are seeing, arguably, is a cultural process of "prospective imagination."

4. If things actually go otherwise and the "father" dies before the cousin "child," or if a "father-child" relationship is never established or for some reason lapses, the "fatherless" person will be assigned a "father" posthumously, often as a way of paying off some unrelated debt to patrilateral kin.

5. When I was on Sabarl in 1976, the harvests were unusually rich, many feasts were scheduled, and there were twenty-six domestic pigs in Maho village—a huge number by local standards. In 1986 there were eight, two of them piglets, and this was more usual. Readers familiar with the numbers of pigs and quantity of pork consumed in exchange feasts in the Highlands of Papua New Guinea or even on Misima will find the quantity of pigs in the Saisai area almost unbelievably small. Yet the importance of pigs as a feast food essential is no less great.

Chapter Four

1. According to the data supplied by my assistant, Silipokapulapola Digim'rina, in a gardening study conducted in 1986, taro, yams, and bananas commonly fail in the drier, clayey red soil. Black soil, which is also clayey but moister, was found primarily in the valleys and along the sides of creeks and is thought to be alluvial. In alluvial grounds, topsoil ranged from 10 to 30 centimeters deep before the color changed, indicating the next layer of soil. Elsewhere the range was from 2 to 10 centimeters.

2. Standard yam baskets (*rorokeri*) hold about ten single yams about 15 centimeters long and 7–9 centimeters wide.

3. Although metaphysical disciplines seem always to have been important in the garden, between 1976 and 1986 much thought was being devoted to what form these procedures should take. On the one hand, in 1986 more middle-aged and older people were beginning to use holy water and prayers in place of traditional substances and magic words. On the other, some younger people were rediscovering an interest in "custom" as the meaning of national slogans of pride in "roots" and "self-reliance" trickled out to the Saisai.

4. The use of *muho* raises some interesting questions about magic words, as opposed to magic substances. Among the Sabarl it is often the case that magical efficacy is seen to reside primarily in the latter, while words as it were

give the magician finer aim—are the accompaniment but not the central "performative" vehicle (see Bloch 1971; Philsooph 1971; and Tambiah 1968, 1973 for discussion of the performative value of words). In this context it is interesting to note Gell's comment that "where the 'bias' of the system is away from spells (Trobriand-type) and toward substances (Zande-type) we will find a corresponding increase in the importance of the *olfactory* element in magic" (1977:26). More recently, papers by Tuzin (delivered in Philadelphia at the American Anthropological Association meetings, 1986) and Küchler (delivered in Phoenix at the American Anthropological Association meetings in 1988), have explored the subject further in other Melanesian societies.

5. The ritual was restaged for the cameras of Malone-Gill Productions in 1979 and appears in parts within the Commanding Sea series, broadcast on British television the following year.

6. The notion of increment as I have developed it here within the Melanesian context is not unlike Derrida's broader philosophical concept of supplement, a "plenitude enrichening another plenitude, the fullest measure of presence" (1977:144–45).

Chapter Five

1. My translation of *-logugui* as "direct" derives from the sense the term conveys of "guiding" or "morally authoritative words" (hence its use in translation for "sermon"). A "leader," *tologugui*, is someone who employs words effectively to move the minds and hearts of persons to action that is beneficial to them, as self-others.

2. It is interesting that as their world expands to include more opportunities for young people to leave the island in search of work or education or training, and as there is some reduction in the distrust of off-island strangers, the "trick" of *tubu* marriages is increasing. In fact, such marriages seem to have been revalued upward as a hedge against the insecurities that increased out-migration brings to those who remain behind.

Chapter Six

1. In a Panaeati myth, a red seed that is born of a woman grows into the first *mwadawa* (or *malauwi*) tree and is magically transformed into the first canoe. "If you look at the inside of the *malauwi* tree, you will find blood from the woman who gave birth to it. They gave the woman's name to the canoe" (Berde 1974).

2. Munn, in a classic article (1977), discusses the subject from the vantage point of canoe manufacture on Gawa.

Chapter Seven

1. I have drawn selectively from major psychological sources for this chapter, including Piers (1953) and Singer (1953), Nathanson (1987a,b), Wurmser (1981, 1987), Lewis (1981, 1987), and Broucek (1982).

2. Noting that this list is far from exhaustive, important anthropological sources from the Pacific include Poole (1985), Rosaldo (1984), White and Kirkpatrick (1985), Lutz (1985), Ito (1985), Fajans (1985), Schieffelin (1985), Myers (1986), and Epstein (1984).

3. This is not to suggest that Sabarl is a "shame culture" (as profiled by Benedict 1946 and succinctly critiqued by Singer 1953, among others). However, shame, as a relational complex is pervasively present and elaborated in certain cultural practices that are central to Sabarl social process.

4. A version of this syndrome is evident in the psychoanaltyic literature concerning "maturation," where the idealized "other" is discussed as the omnipotent parental (or other kind of) authority figure who represents the sum of positive identifications for the self, *as well as later identifications and potentialities* (emphasis mine) (Piers 1953:13–15). The insights of Nathanson (1987) and Broucek (1982) are particularly useful on this subject.

5. A slightly different slant on the problem is evident in Schieffelin's perception that for Kaluli, "a person's face is thus not located on the person himself but is diffusely located in the flow of events in the encounter, since it depends to some extent on the other participants" (1985:178). However, it is still self-image, not the projection of a self-other unity, that Schieffelin sees as the issue, although the element of "below par performance" (Ito 1985:322 n.10) is evident in both cases.

6. It should be mentioned that women and men are equally vulnerable to shame and have the same recourse to justice; they also have the same responsibility to pay penalty fees or to settle, using the same forms of durable wealth. There is, in short, an ideology of equality in these matters that may help account for the absence among Sabarl of drastic shame-related redressive or revenge measures such as murder or suicide, which in other Pacific societies are usually gender linked.

7. People describe the *hivi* of ancestral times as crossed ax handles with a helmet-shell "head" wedged in the crotch of the X: a skull-and-crossbones warning to trading partners not to look for valuables in that hamlet. A pig's jawbone hanging from the handles signaled that pigs could not be taken from that hamlet. One encounters *hivi* of this type less often today, but the rules remain.

8. Belshaw (1955) notes that *pan leau* in the Ware language means "trade partner" in commercial exchanges, as well as in the ceremonial exchanges known as *kune.* Indeed, traditional Sabarl *leau* somewhat resembles a type of exchange between Ware and Misima, in a circuit that Belshaw calls *kune* type I, a "straight link between Ware and Misima, possibly with Sudest sometimes brought in" (1955:27). Extensive research by Macintyre (1983) has thrown a great deal more light on the subject and cast doubt on the notion of rings of exchange as separate as Belshaw suggests, as well as on the separateness of "ceremonial" and "commercial" exchange in the southern Massim.

9. Portions of this section are taken from a paper presented to the workshop on Big Men and Great Men in Melanesia, 21–23 July 1987, under the sponsorship of the Maison de la Science de l'Homme in Paris. The points of Sabarl history and culture that I raise here permit comparison in terms of the "big man/great man" typology developed (notably) by Maurice Godelier (1986) and others. This is generally depicted in the literature as a difference between highlands societies, featuring secular "big man" polities, clan-based organization, large populations,the mediated exchange of substances and incremental exchange of wealth, and lowland societies, featuring "great man" leadership,

"inward-turning" initiation cults and moiety organization, smaller communities, and unmediated exchanges of vital substances. Regionalism aside, my purpose here is to show how strikingly ambivalent attitudes toward leadership in the southern Massim can be explained by reference to a gender-linked paradigm of the big and the great from the "root period" of Sabarl settlement and the masculine nature of the notion of increment that underlies asymmetries within this model.

10. Males of enemy groups engaged in skull exchanges in the southern Massim area (see Lepowsky 1983; Berde 1974), but the Sabarl seem never to have been directly involved in this.

11. It is interesting to note the words of Administrative Officer McLeod in his 1953–54 Misima area Annual Report, under the section "Status of Women": "Generally comparable to other sophisticated areas of Papua with the noted exception of the women of the Calvados Chain and Deboyne Lagoon. These females are truly amazons. They can handle canoes, fish, clear timber, swim for trochus, etc. as well as most of their men. In conference their opinions are loud and sustained on matters of community interest regardless of whether the Administrative Officer is there or not."

12. For more on the subject of siblings in Oceania, see Marshall (1979). Also see Berde (1974) for Panaeati terminology.

13. As Strathern (1984) points out, the circulation of "labor" or "name" in the Massim area has been the subject of recent studies with regard to its embodiment in valuables and indicates "interesting possibilities for the creation of debt relations."

14. This was a source of exasperation to the government officer-in-charge (a notoriously uncaring figure in most other respects), who complained to me: "Make more than one or two gardens, you die from sorcery. Make your house too large, you die. Get a big canoe, it's the same." He judged the situation extreme by his own Sepik standards. But in 1986 other forces were at work on the indigenous process of leadership, coming, ironically, from a national government that has as its motto "self-reliance." What I observed in the space of ten years was the nominal eclipse of the triad of clan leaders by government, church, and school representatives—albeit "strong" men from the three major clans. As a consequence, villagewide meetings had proliferated to organize village-based work as never before. Beyond the formerly infrequent calls to community net-fishing expeditions, villagers were being summoned weekly for Sunday readings from the catechism, as well as for "community work" and "school work" that required whole days of building, repairing, and tidying up public space and structures. This concern with appearances put a noticeable strain on persons raised within the *saisai* ethos to value a nonconformist work style and personal initiative, and there was great discontent: What time was left for gardening? For fishing or gathering shells for money? For making sago? More and more people were talking about breaking away in defiance and "guiding themselves" along the "two paths" of traditional and national development. Yet the nonindigenous "path" to leadership holds two obvious attractions. One is the lure of a prefabricated following; another is a position where "standing out" is dictated and (to an extent) validated by a higher authority—with the result that the risk of doing so is displaced. In these circumstances (though not only these circumstances) self-serving motivation can masquerade

as public service, and responsibility for striving can be laid on an amorphous national leadership. Knowledge of government, church, or school procedures thus supplies the protective coating individuals feel they require to survive standing out.

Chapter Eight

1. For roughly contemporary descriptions and analyses of mortuary events in other Massim societies, see Munn (1986), Berde (1974), Weiner (1976), and Lepowsky (n.d.); also, see the unpublished papers (including Lepowsky's) of the conference on Massim Internal Exchange, convened at the University of Virginia in 1981 under the auspices of the Wenner-Gren Foundation for Anthropological Research.

2. The latter case merits some elaboration. In large part, children who die are given the honor of commemorative feasts as extensions of their parents. Thus, notable persons with extensive resources are more likely to honor their children with the full set of mortuary feasts than are less well-connected parents, who tend to abbreviate these events. *Segaiya*, for children, honors their "memory potential" as predicated on the social reach of the parents, gathering together the social relations that might have been developed through them.

However, in the final analysis the scale and spacing of all *segaiya* are contingent on natural more than social variables. Apart from the funeral, feasts tend to cluster regionwide in good garden years. (My initial fieldwork was conducted in one such year.) Shortages of money are insignificant by comparison but are linked, in that bad weather, drought, and so forth, restrict money-making activities and lead to greater spending on rice and other store-bought staples.

3. In addition to baby powder, a basil wand (*pedidi*—Labiatae: *Ocimum basilicum*) is waved over the body as a deodorant and fly whisk. The branch is called *babaloma wali dude*, the "spirits' digging stick." In some places basil is also used to dig small drainage holes in the bottom of the grave before the body is lowered into it. Along with the strong smell of decay, emissions (*gulolu*) are escaping from the body's orifices that the dead man is thought to be controlling and bestowing selectively as a gift on those who mourn him.

4. I witnessed a death on Panabarli where a local woman from the dead man's clan applied the wrong design. After much discussion and no hard feelings, the face was repainted by a woman from the widow's clan, who was expert in these matters. However, most people remained uncertain, and indeed, about the meaning of all face painting designs there is much confusion.

5. *Daperli*, pieces of red lip shell in pandanus wrappers, are in common use on Tagula and Yeina and in Bwailahine village on Panatinani as low-value currency (one bundle is roughly equivalent to two kina). Sabarl profess not to use them, although they are sometimes presented to a young widow's group member during Moni as a small gesture of "giving something" to repeal his or her taboo.

6. Common substances are the ginger or sassafras root used by sorcerers as spirit spears, and such things as soap and sugar—signs that covetousness for European things was behind a death.

7. It is said that in ancestral times graves were L-shaped, and I have seen

such graves for children in places where the earth is not too sandy to support them. People speak of these graves as places where the dead can "sleep" without the earth's disturbing them.

8. The ostentatious destruction of the house called to my mind the destruction of masks in other Melanesian societies.

In this connection it should be noted that the remnant of a masquerade tradition, already removed from its original mortuary context to the realm of special-occasion theater for outsiders, exists on Sabarl today. It is the dance of Binapalo, the coconut spirit, represented by a coconut-bast mask (*geba*). Traditionally, the dance took place near the grave immediately following a burial and involved luring out Binapalo spirits from nearby palms and spearing them. After the performance the mask was thrown into the bush. The dance was last performed in context in 1972. Another dance, depicting various stories about the child-eating monster Katutubwai, is similarly performed on special occasions by skilled men in the senior generation. This once involved a perishable mask but is now danced with a "masked" face, frozen of expression.

9. The timing of Hanyalogi is variable. Depending on the season, it may be postponed until fish are schooling, in which case it is usually combined with the feast of Hanlekeleke. For a combination feast, a village the size of Maho will typically plan on preparing some thirty pots of garden produce (2 to 5 kilograms per pot) and twenty-five pots of rice (50 kilos), as well as three pots of fish or turtle, twenty-five pots of sago pudding (about fifty double bundles and one hundred coconuts), and ten large and small sago cakes (about another one hundred double bundles and another fifty coconuts)—plus three mature pigs.

10. In 1976 and still in 1986, certain phases of commemoration were often combined into one feast, no matter how notable the deceased or his survivors and regardless of significant fluctuations in food surpluses between those years. In other words, we are seeing the signs of abbreviations in the feasting timetable that have nothing to do with garden yield, following a trend that has led—for example, in the Misima area—to "concise" versions of the mortuary sequence as a whole. This seems mainly to be a result of absenteeism owing to wage labor increases in those areas where feasting has shrunk most noticeably: people condense their obligations into whatever time they have off from jobs elsewhere.

11. Among the people I spoke with there was contradiction on the matter of names, beyond that of the leading ax, known as Thunder. Some listed interment services, such as "assembling the coffin" (*waga hamham*), "grave digging" (*heliwaga pwepwai*), "rolling up the mat" (*lam golgol*); others stressed preparation of the body, including "black face paint" (*seaku hunhun*), "white face paint" (*pwakau hunhun*), "cutting the hair" (*kaununa lamwana*), and "scented oil" (*bebaewa*).

12. I was given a sample spell of the type whispered into the premasticated ginger. It goes: "Where do you come from? Where from? Open. There it is. It's appeared, opened. Its place." I was told that the ginger "opened the eyes of the ax blade leader so that he can see his friends and beckon them to join him on the path."

13. Amelie Rorty's insight that "the measure and scope of the person, his powers, lie in his ability to transform the lives of those around him" (1976:312) is pertinent here.

14. The classic discussion of visible shame—shame "on the skin" of Mount Hageners (A. Strathern 1977; M. Strathern 1979), displayed as a kind of social cosmetic masking what may be shameless inner feelings—is a case in contrast to the "confessional" nature of displays of shame among Sabarl. Whether exposure to Roman Catholic doctrine has anything to do with this I was unable to determine.

15. A typical *gogomwau* count for a notable man or woman is thirty-five ax blades, two wooden ceremonial limesticks, one long shell necklace (two "sides" of 2 meters each) and K100: that is, thirty-eight wealth items.

Chapter Nine

1. The repetition of forms of *segaiya* rituals and exchanges *as if they were exact repetitions* of past forms of *segaiya*—as it were, in the name of *segaiya*—renders verbal or even graphic accounts superfluous. Myerhoff (1974) has suggested that the unique power of ritual in situations of anxiety and impotence is that by its repetitive character it provides a message of pattern and predictability—that is, it gives an illusion of control and continuity. This works, as Geertz (1973) puts it, by dramatizing abstract, invisible conceptions—by making ideas and wishes palpable. More recently, Bloch has discussed the repetition in ritual by noting that in the context of Merina circumcisions, where no ideas have been added or taken away over the course of two hundred years, "we are dealing with continuous repetition . . . of two kinds: either different symbols with the same significance are used . . . or there may be simple repetition of exactly the same acts and songs" (Bloch 1986:165). Although I do not have the historical data to argue the case here for Sabarl rituals, it is important to recognize that we are dealing here with repetition in the less literal sense of action referencing repetition in the past—that is, in an instance of symbolic action standing for itself (Wagner 1986b)—in order to close off further repetition.

2. Bourdieu's gloss is "habitus" (1977), basically the same concept that Charles Peirce talks about as "habit" or "conduct": the readiness to "act in a certain way under given circumstances and when actuated by a given motive" (Peirce 1931–35, 5:480); likewise Giddens's use of "conduct" (1979).

3. The Sabarl system shares some attributes with both the Trobriand and Muyuw systems (and with the Tubetube, who differ in other ways from all three; see Macintyre 1983). For example, like Muyuw, Sabarl do not distinguish cross-cousins by gender. They also expressly prohibit cross-cousin marriage. Like Trobrianders, they feature women's wealth in mortuary exchanges and emphasize the asymmetrical father-child relationship symbolically. Indeed, asked why mortuary feasts are so important to them, Sabarl, like the Trobrianders Weiner spoke with, say, "We feed our father." However, there are significant differences also. For a note on some of these see Battaglia (1985).

4. Forge (1972) some time ago suggested that women are in an ultimate sense the source of inequality between men as wife givers and as wife takers. The Sabarl concern to keep widows within the lineage is a specific instance of this, although we must be aware of the dangers of discussing the matter outside the context of colonial history. That penalties for contravening the widow descent rule seem to have remained quantitatively stable, despite increased monetization and other forms of colonial intervention, allows for some discussion here. Of course the unanswered question is what certain quantities and certain

objects mean in the context of the penalty, and whether the penalty payment can be viewed as substituting for women in the same sense as bridewealth. This is especially pertinent in cases of unmediated sister-exchange marriages.

5. Bourdieu's position is worth quoting more fully. He writes: "When a society lacks both the literacy which would enable it to preserve and accumulate in objectified form cultural resources it has inherited from the past, and also the educational system which would give its agents the aptitudes and dispositions required for the symbolic reappropriation of those resources, it can only reserve them in their incorporated state. Consequently, to ensure the perpetuation of cultural resources which would otherwise disappear along with the agents who bear them, it has to resort to systematic inculcation, a process which ... may last as long as the period during which the resources are actually used" (Bourdieu 1977:186–87). His point is that the project of "preserving" and (more appropriately) "perpetuating" cultural resources operates in and through certain "structural exercises" based on the Platonic notion of mimesis or "mimicry," "practical reactivation mobilizing all the resources of a 'pattern of organized actions' ... for mnemonic purposes in an act of affective identification" (Bourdieu 1977:236 n. 41, quoting Eric Havelock).

6. See especially Errington (1974), Wagner (1986), Munn (1977, 1986), Clay (1986), Campbell (1983), Küchler (1987, 1988), and Scoditti (1982) for pertinent analyses of nonverbal imagery and value in island Papua New Guinea.

7. Young's analysis (1983) of "lived myth" in Kalauna society might be interpreted in this sense, that is, as a study in telescoping values and model behaviors into contemporary life through narrative "memories."

8. Lienhardt (1961) notes somewhat the same phenomenon of a present, active memorial agency for Dinka: "What Western man would call a 'memory,' related to a past experience, Dinka [in Africa] conceive as an exterior agency still potent to act upon them. Where the individual in Western culture encapsulates his personal past within himself, Dinka experience what Western man would regard as interior, psychic phenomena as features of a timeless external world."

9. Goody (1962) depicts the gradual disentanglement of the dead from the affairs of the living in his major study of LoDagaa property transfers, which has come to represent this view in the mortuary literature. More recently the "repair" approach, based upon the Durkheimian (1965) premise that religious action is aimed at returning survivors to a whole and coherent social life (see also Mauss 1954; Hertz 1960), has provided the analytic strategy for several major studies of mortuary practice in Indonesia and Oceania as well (notably Weiner 1976; Traube 1986; De Coppet 1982; Metcalf 1982). Jackson (1977) was the first to suggest the importance for anthropologists of recognizing that especially in small-scale societies, death is a central part of the "business of life" rather than a threat to it. Other critics (especially Mosko 1985; Munn 1986; Wagner 1986a) see mortuary practices as acts of deconstructing social relations, returning actors to a prerelational state vis-à-vis the dead. I would argue that the implicit constructivist orientation in the image of a fabric with holes may well be appropriate in those cases where it is employed (see Introduction) as compared with societies where deconstructive agency is emphasized in cultural practice and imagery. In the present study, as I have noted in the text,

deconstruction is taken as integral to construction (in a way, Jackson was suggesting this perspective from a pre-perspectivist perspective).

10. What I am describing here has the deconstructionist quality of a temporary composition that "leads necessarily to a double reading: that of a fragment perceived in relation to its text of origin; that of the same fragment as
incorporated into a new whole, a different totality" (quoted by Ulmer 1983:88,
from Collages 34–35).

References

Ardener, E. 1978. Some outstanding problems in the analysis of events. In *Yearbook of symbolic anthropology*, ed. E. Schwimmer. London: C. Hurst.

Aristotle. 1973. *De sensu* and *De memoria*. Trans. G. R. T. Ross. New York: Arno Press.

Austin, J. L. 1962. *How to do things with words*. London: Oxford University Press.

Australia Patrol Report. 1943. Misima subdistrict file 14.4, Native Labour and Recruiting, Pre-war box 491. Bwagaoia: Misima.

———. 1944–45. Report 5. Misima subdistrict file 18.8, Pre-war box 491. Bwagaoia: Misima.

Bakhtin, M. 1984. Toward a reworking of the Dostoevsky book. In *Problems of Dostoevsky's poetics*, ed. and trans. C. Emerson. Minneapolis: University of Minnesota Press. Originally published 1976.

———. 1986. The problem of the text in linguistics, philology, and the human sciences: An experiment in philosophical analysis. In *M. M. Bakhtin: Speech genres and other late essays*. ed. C. Emerson and M. Holquist, trans. V. W. McGee. Austin: University of Texas Press.

Battaglia, D. 1983a. Projecting personhood in Melanesia: The dialectics of artefact symbolism on Sabarl Island. *Man*, n.s., 18:289–304.

———. 1983b. Syndromes of ceremonial exchange in the eastern Calvados: The view from Sabarl Island. In *The Kula: New perspectives on Massim exchange*, ed. J. W. Leach and E. R. Leach. Cambridge: Cambridge University Press.

———. 1985. "We feed our father": Paternal nurture among the Sabarl of Papua New Guinea. *American Ethnologist* 12(3): 427–41.

———. 1986. *"Bringing home to Moresby": Urban gardening and ethnic pride among Trobriand Islanders in the national capital*. Special Publication 11. Boroko: Institute of Applied Social and Economic Research.

———. n.d. Punishing the yams: Leadership and gender ambivalence on Sabarl Island. In *Big men and great men: The development of a comparison in Melanesia*, ed. M. Godelier and M. Strathern. Cambridge: Cambridge University Press. In press.

Bayldon, F. 1925. Voyage of Luis Vaez de Torres from the New Hebrides to the Moluccas, June to November 1606. *Journal of the Royal Austrian Historical Society* 11:158–94.

Belshaw, C. S. 1955. *In search of wealth.* Memoir 80, vol. 57 (no. 1, part 2). Washington, D.C.: American Anthropological Association.

Benedict, R. 1946. *The chrysanthemum and the sword.* New York: World Press.

Berde, S. 1974. Melanesians as Methodists: Economy and marriage on a Papua New Guinea Island. Ph.D. diss., University of Pennsylvania.

———. 1976. Political education in the rural sector: A comparison of two Papua New Guinea island communities. *Journal of the Polynesian Society* 85(1): 76–94.

Blauner, R. 1966. Death and social structure. *Psychiatry* 29:378–94.

Bloch, M. 1971. *Placing the dead: Tombs, ancestral villages and kinship organization in Madagascar.* London: Seminar Press.

———. 1974. Symbols, song, dance and features of articulation. *European Journal of Sociology* 15:55–81.

———. 1986. *From blessing to violence: History and ideology in the circumcision ritual of the Merina of Madagascar.* Cambridge Studies in Social Anthropology 61. Cambridge: Cambridge University Press.

Bloch, M., and J. Parry, eds. 1982. *Death and the regeneration of life.* Cambridge: Cambridge University Press.

Boon, J. 1982. *Other tribes, other scribes: Symbolic anthropology in the comparative study of cultures, histories, religions, and texts.* Cambridge: Cambridge University Press.

Bougainville, L. A. 1772. *Lewis de Bougainville: A voyage around the world performed by order of His Most Christian Majesty, in the years 1766, 1767, 1768 and 1769.* Trans. J. R. Forster. London.

Bourdieu, Pierre. 1977. *Outline of a theory of practice.* Trans. R. Nice. Cambridge: Cambridge University Press.

British New Guinea Annual Report. 1886a. File G9. 188/86. Papua New Guinea National Archives, Port Moresby.

———. 1886b. File G9.192/86. Papua New Guinea National Archives, Port Moresby.

Broucek, F. 1982. Shame and its relationship to early narcissistic developments. *International Journal of Psychoanalysis* 65:369–78.

Bruner, E. M., and P. Gorfain. 1984. Dialogic narration and the paradoxes of Masada. In *Text, play and story: The construction and reconstruction of self and society,* ed. E. M. Bruner. Washington D.C.: American Ethnological Society.

Burke, K. 1969. *A grammar of motives.* Berkeley: University of California Press.

Campbell, S. 1983. Kula in Vakuta. In *The Kula: New perspectives on Massim exchange,* ed. J. W. Leach and E. R. Leach. Cambridge: Cambridge University Press.

Casey, E. S. 1987. *Remembering: A phenomnological study.* Bloomington: Indiana University Press.

Clay, B. J. 1977. *Pinikindu: Maternal nurture, paternal substance.* Chicago: University of Chicago Press.

———. 1986. *Mandak realities: Person and power in central New Ireland.* New Brunswick, N.J.: Rutgers University Press.

Clifford, J. 1983. On ethnographic authority. *Representations* 1(Spring): 118–46.

Clifford, J., and G. Marcus, eds. 1986. *Writing culture.* Berkeley: University of California Press.

Corris, P. 1968. Blackbirding in New Guinea waters, 1883–84. *Journal of Pacific History* 3:85–105.

Culler, J. 1981. *The pursuit of signs: Semiotics, literature, deconstruction.* Ithaca: Cornell University Press.

Damon, F. 1983. Muyuw kinship and the metamorphosis of gender labour. *Man,* n.s., 18:305–26.

De Coppet, D. 1982. The life-giving death. In *Mortality and immortality,* ed. S. Humphreys and H. King. New York: Academic Press.

Derrida, J. 1977. *Of grammatology.* Trans. G. C. Spivak. Baltimore: Johns Hopkins University Press.

———. 1980. The law of genre. In *On narrative.* Chicago: University of Chicago Press.

———. 1981. *Dissemination.* Trans. B. Johnson. Chicago: University of Chicago press.

Durkheim, Emile. 1965. *The elementary forms of the religious life.* New York: Free Press. Originally published 1912.

D'Urville, D. 1833. *Voyage de la corvette L'Astrolabe . . . pendant les années 1826–1829: Histoire du voyage.* Vol. 5. Paris.

Edholm, F., O. Harris, and K. Young. 1977. Conceptualizing women. *Critique of Anthropology* 3:101–30.

Epstein, A. L. 1984. *The experience of shame in Melanesia: An essay in the anthropology of affect.* Occasional Paper 40. London: Royal Anthropological Institute of Great Britain and Ireland.

Errington, F. 1974. *Karavar: Masks and power in a Melanesian ritual.* Ithaca: Cornell University Press.

Errington, F., and D. Gewertz. 1987. *Cultural alternatives and a feminist anthropology: An analysis of culturally constructed gender interests in Papua New Guinea.* Cambridge: Cambridge University Press.

Fajans, J. 1985. The person in social context: The social character of Baining "psychology." In *Person, self, and experience: Exploring Pacific ethnopsychologies,* ed. G. M. White and J. Kirkpatrick. Berkeley: University of California Press.

Favret-Saada, J. 1980. *Deadly words: Witchcraft in the Bocage.* Trans. C. Cullen. Cambridge: Cambridge University Press.

Firth, R. 1965. *Primitive Polynesian economy.* 2d ed. London: Routledge and Kegan Paul.

Forge, A. 1972. The golden fleece. *Man,* n.s., 7:527–40.

Fortune, R. 1932. *Sorcerers of Dobu.* London: Routledge and Kegan Paul.

Geertz, C. 1973. Religion as a cultural system. In *The interpretation of cultures.* New York: Basic Books.

Gell, A. 1975. *Metamorphosis of the cassowaries.* London School of Economics Monograph 51. Atlantic Highlands, N.J.: Humanities Press.

―――. 1977. Magic, perfume, dream. In *Symbols and sentiments*, ed. I. Lewis. London: Academic Press.

Giddens, A. 1979. *Central problems in social theory: Action, structure, and contradiction in social analysis.* London: Macmillan.

Gillison, G. 1980. Images of nature in Gimi thought. In *Nature, culture and gender*, ed. C. MacCormack and M. Strathern. Cambridge: Cambridge University Press.

Godelier, M. 1986. *The making of great men: Male domination and power among the New Guinea Buruya.* Cambridge: Cambridge University Press.

Goffman, E. 1967. *Interaction ritual.* Garden City, N.Y.: Anchor Books.

Gombrich, E. 1963. *Meditations on a hobby horse.* London: Phaidon.

Goody, J. 1962. *Death, property and the ancestors: A study of the mortuary customs of the LoDagaa of West Africa.* Stanford: Stanford University Press.

―――. 1987. *The interface between the written and the oral.* Cambridge: Cambridge University Press.

Gough, K. 1958. Cults of the dead among the Nayars. *Journal of American Folklore* 71:446–78.

Gregory, C. 1982. *Gifts and commodities.* New York: Academic Press.

Halbwachs, M. 1980. *The collective memory.* New York: Harper and Row. Originally published 1950.

Hertz, R. 1960. *Death and the right hand.* Trans. C. Needham and R. Needham. New York: Free Press. Originally published 1907.

Huntington, R., and P. Metcalf. 1979. *Celebrations of death: The anthropology of mortuary ritual.* Cambridge: Cambridge University Press.

Huxley, T. H. 1935. *T. H. Huxley's Diary of the Voyage of H.M.S. Rattlesnake.* Edited from unpublished manuscript by J. Huxley. London: Chatto and Windus.

Ito, K. 1985. Affective bonds: Hawaiian interrelationships of self. In *Person, self, and experience: Exploring Pacific ethnopsychologies*, Berkeley: University of California Press. ed. G. M. White and J. Kirkpatrick.

Jackson, M. 1977. The identity of the dead. *Cahiers d'Etudes Africaines* 66–67(2–3): 271–97.

Jauss, H. R. 1982. *Toward an aesthetic reception.* Minneapolis: University of Minnesota Press.

Kahn, M. 1986. *Always hungry, never greedy: Food and the expression of gender in a Melanesian society.* Cambridge: Cambridge University Press.

Kapferer, B. 1986. Performance and the structuring of meaning and experience. In *The anthropology of experience*, ed. V. W. Turner and E. M. Bruner. Urbana: University of Illinois Press.

Kelly, C., ed., trans. 1966. *La Austrialia del Espiritu Santo: The Journal of Feray Martin de Munilla, O.F.M., and other documents relating to the voyage of Pedro Fernandez de Quiros to the South Sea (1605–1606) and the Franciscan missionary plan (1617–1627).* Cambridge: Hakluyt Society at Cambridge University Press.

Kirkpatrick, J., and G. M. White. 1985. Exploring ethnopsychologies. In *Person, self, and experience: Exploring Pacific ethnopsychologies*, ed. G. M. White and J. Kirkpatrick. Berkeley: University of California Press.

Kristeva, J. 1969. *Sémiotike: Recherches pour une sémanalyse.* Paris: Seuil.

———. 1980. *Desire in language: A semiotic approach to literature and art.* New York: Columbia University Press.

Küchler, S. 1987. Malangan: Art and memory in a Melanesian society. *Man,* n.s., 22:238–55.

———. 1988. Malangan: Objects, sacrifice and the production of memory. *American Ethnologist* 14(4): 625–37.

Leach, J. W., and E. R. Leach, eds. 1983. *The kula: New perspectives on Massim exchange.* Cambridge: Cambridge University Press.

Leenhart, M. 1979. *Do Kamo: Person and myth in the Melanesian world.* Trans. B. M. Gulati. Chicago: University of Chicago Press. Originally published 1947.

Lepowsky, M. 1983. Sudest Island and the Louisiade archipelago in Massim exchange. In *The Kula: New perspectives on Massim exchange,* ed. J. W. Leach and E. R. Leach. Cambridge: Cambridge University Press.

———. 1984. Food taboos, malaria and dietary changes: Infant feeding and cultural adaptation on a Papua New Guinea island. *Ecology of Food and Nutrition* 15:116–28.

———. n.d. Death and mortuary ritual on Vanatinai (Sudest Island). Paper presented at the Conference on Internal Exchange in the Massim, University of Virginia, 1981.

LeRoy, J. 1985. *Fabricated world: An interpretation of Kewa tales.* Vancouver: University of British Columbia Press.

Lewis, H. B. 1981. Shame and guilt in human nature. In *Object and self: A developmental approach,* ed. S. Tuttman, C. Kaye, and M. Zimmerman. New York: International Universities Press.

———. 1987. Shame and the narcissistic personality. In *The many faces of shame,* ed. D. L. Nathanson. New York: Guilford Press.

Lienhardt, G. 1961. *Divinity and experience.* Oxford: Oxford University Press.

———. 1985. African representation of self. In *The category of the person,* ed. M. Carrithers, S. Collins, and S. Lukes. Cambridge: Cambridge University Press.

Liep, J. 1983. Ranked exchange in Rossel Island. In *The Kula: New perspectives on Massim exchange,* ed. J. W. Leach and E. R. Leach. Cambridge: Cambridge University Press.

———. n.d.a. Gift exchange and the construction of identity. Paper presented at the Symposium on Culture and History in the Pacific, University of Helsinki, January 1987

———. n.d.b. The day of reckoning on Rossel Island. Paper presented at the Conference on Internal Exchange in the Massim, University of Virginia, 1981.

Lindenbaum, S. 1987. The mystification of female labors. In *Gender and kinship: Essays toward a unified analysis,* ed. J. F. Collier and S. J. Yanagisako. Stanford: Stanford University Press.

Lithgow, D. 1976. Austronesian languages: Milne Bay and adjacent islands (Milne Bay Province). In *New Guinea area languages and language study,* vol. 2, ed. S. A. Wurm. Pacific Linguistics, ser. C, no. 39, Research School of Pacific Studies. Canberra: Australian National University.

Lutz, C. A. 1985. Ethnopsychology compared to what? Explaining behavior and consciousness among the Ifaluk. In *Person, self, and experience: Exploring Pacific ethnopsychologies*, ed. G. M. White and J. Kirkpatrick. Berkeley: University of California Press.

———. 1988. *Unnatural emotions: Everyday sentiments on a Micronesian atoll and their challenge to Western Theory*. Chicago: University of Chicago Press.

Lynd, H. M. 1958. *On shame and the search for identity*. New York: Science Editions.

Lyotard, J.-F. 1979. *La condition postmoderne: Rapport sur le lavoir*. Paris: Minuit.

Macintyre, M. 1983. Warfare and the changing context of kune on Tubetube. *Journal of Pacific History* 18:11–34.

———. 1987. Flying witches and leaping warriors: Supernatural origins of power and matrilineal authority in Tubetube society. In *Dealing with inequality: Analysing gender relations in Melanesia and beyond*, ed. M. Strathern. Cambridge: Cambridge University Press.

Malinowski, B. 1922. *Argonauts of the western Pacific*. New York: Dutton.

———. 1935. *Coral gardens and their magic*. Vol. 1. New York: Dover.

Marcus, G., and M. Fischer. 1986. *Anthropology as cultural critique*. Chicago: University of Chicago Press.

Marshall, M., ed. 1979. *Siblingship in Oceania: Studies in the meaning of kin relations*. Ann Arbor: University of Michigan Press.

Mauss, M. 1954. *The gift*. Trans. I. Cunnison. London: Cohen and West. Originally published 1925.

Metcalf, P. 1982. *A Borneo journey into death: Berawan eschatology from its rituals*. Philadelphia: University of Pennsylvania Press.

Mosko, M. 1985. *Quadripartite structures: Categories, relations and homologies in Bush Mekeo culture*. Cambridge: Cambridge University Press.

Munn, N. 1973. *Walbiri iconography: Graphic representation and cultural symbolism in a central Australian society*. Ithaca: Cornell University Press.

———. 1977. The spatiotemporal transformations of Gawa canoes. *Journal de la Société des Océanistes* 33:39–51.

———. 1983. Gawan Kula: Spatio-temporal control and the symbolism of influence. In *The Kula: New perspectives on Massim exchange*, ed. J. W. Leach and E. R. Leach. Cambridge: Cambridge University Press.

———. 1986. *The fame of Gawa: A symbolic study of value transformation in a Massim (Papua New Guinea) society*. Cambridge: Cambridge University Press.

Myerhoff, B. 1974. A death in due time: Construction of self and culture in ritual drama. In *Rite, drama, festival, spectacle: Rehearsals toward a theory of cultural performance*, ed. J. J. MacAloon. Philadelphia: Institute for the Study of Human Issues.

Myers, F. 1986. *Pintupi country, Pintupi self: Sentiment, place, and politics among western desert aborigines*. Washington, D.C.: Smithsonian Institution Press.

———. 1988. Siting ethnographic practice: Romance, reality and politics in the Outback. *American Ethnologist* 15(4): 609–24.

Nathanson, D. L. 1987a. A timetable for shame. In *The many faces of shame,* ed. D. L. Nathanson. New York: Guilford Press.

———. 1987b. Shaming systems in couples, families, and institutions. In *The many faces of shame,* ed. D. L. Nathanson. New York: Guilford Press.

Nelson, H. 1976. *Black, white and gold: Goldmining in Papua New Guinea, 1878–1930.* Canberra: Australian National University Press.

Parmentier, R. 1987. *The sacred remains: Myth, history, and polity in Belau.* Chicago: University of Chicago Press.

Peirce, Charles S. 1931–35. *Collected papers of Charles Sanders Peirce.* Vols 1–6. Ed. C. Hartshorne and P. Weiss. Cambridge: Harvard University Press.

Philsooph, H. 1971. Primitive man and mana. *Man* 6:182–203.

Piers, G. 1953. Shame and guilt: A psychoanalytic study. In *Shame and guilt,* ed. G. Piers and M. B. Singer. Springfield, Ill.: Charles C. Thomas.

Pizzey, F. 1986. *A field guide to the birds of Australia.* Princeton: Princeton University Press.

Poole, F. J. P. 1985. Coming into social being: Cultural images of infants in Bimin-Kuskusmin folk psychology. In *Person, self, and experience: Exploring Pacific ethnopsychologies,* ed. G. M. White and J. Kirkpatrick. Berkeley: University of California Press.

Read, K. E. 1965. *The high valley.* New York: Charles Scribner's Sons.

Rorty, A. 1976. A literary postscript: Characters, persons, selves, individuals. In *The identities of persons,* ed. A. Rorty. Berkeley: University of California Press.

Rosaldo, M. 1980. *Knowledge and passion: Ilongot notions of self and social life.* Cambridge: Cambridge University Press.

———. 1984. Toward an anthropology of self and feeling. In *Culture theory: Essays on mind, self, and emotion,* ed. R. A. Shweder and R. A. Levine. Cambridge: Cambridge University Press.

Sangren, P. S. 1988. Rhetoric and the authority of ethnography. *Current Anthropology* 29(3): 405–35.

Schechner, R. 1985. *Between theatre and anthropology.* Philadelphia: University of Pennsylvania Press.

Schieffelin, E. 1976. *The sorrow of the lonely and the burning of the dancers.* New York: St. Martin's Press.

———. 1985. Anger, grief, and shame: Toward a Kaluli ethnopsychology. In *Person, self, and experience: Exploring Pacific ethnopsychologies,* ed. G. M. White and J. Kirkpatrick. Berkeley: University of California Press.

Schwimmer, E. 1979. Reciprocity and structure: A semiotic analysis of some Orokaiva data. *Man,* n.s., 14:271–85.

Scoditti, G. 1977. A Kula prowboard: An iconological interpretation. *L'Uomo* 1(2): 199–232.

———. 1982. Aesthetics: The significance of apprenticeship on Kitawa. *Man,* n.s., 17:74–91.

Sebeok, T., ed. 1971. *Current trends in linguistics.* Vol. 8. Linguistics in Oceania. The Hague: Mouton.

Seligman, C. 1910. *The Melanesians of British New Guinea.* Cambridge: Cambridge University Press.

Singer, M. B. 1953. Shame cultures and guilt cultures. In *Shame and guilt*, ed. G. Piers and M. B. Singer. Springfield, Ill.: Charles C. Thomas.

Slater, P. 1970. *A field guide to Australian birds: Non-passerines*. Edinburgh: Scottish Academic Press.

Stevens, H., ed. 1930. *New light on the discovery of Australia*. London: Hakluyt Society at Cambridge University Press.

Strathern, A. 1977. Why is shame on the skin? In *The anthropology of the body*, ed. J. Blacking. London: Academic Press.

Strathern, A., and M. Strathern. 1971. *Self-decoration in Mount Hagen*. London: Duckworth.

Strathern, M. 1976. An anthropological perspective. In *Exploring sex differences*, ed. B. Lloyd and J. Archer. New York: Academic Press.

———. 1979. The self in self-decoration. *Oceania* 49(4): 241–57.

———. 1980. Culture in a netbag: The manufacture of a sub-discipline in anthropology. *Man*, n.s., 16:665–88.

———. 1981a. Self-interest and the social good: Some implications of Hagen gender imagery. In *Sexual meanings*, ed. S. Ortner and H. Whitehead. Cambridge: Cambridge University Press.

———. 1981b. Subject or object? Women and the circulation of valuables in highlands New Guinea. Paper presented at Australian Anthropological Society conference, August, Canberra, Australia.

———. 1984. Marriage exchanges: A Melanesian comment. *Annual Review of Anthropology* 13:41–73.

———. 1987a. Increment and androgyny: Reflections on recent developments in the anthropology of Papua New Guinea. Paper presented at the New Guinea workshop, convened by the Centre for Australian and Oceanic Studies, Catholic University, Nijmegen, The Netherlands, 24–26 February 1987.

———. 1987b. Producing difference: Connections and disconnections in two New Guinea highlands kinship systems. In *Gender and kinship: Essays toward a unified analysis*, ed. J. F. Collier and S. J. Yanagisako. Stanford: Stanford University Press.

———. 1988. *The gender of the gift: Problems with women and problems with society in Melanesia*. Berkeley: University of California Press.

Tambiah, S. J. 1968. The magical power of words. *Man*, n.s., 3:175–208.

———. 1973. The form and meaning of magical acts. In *Modes of thought: Essays on thinking in Western and non-Western societies*, ed. W. R. C. Horton and R. Finnegan. London: Faber and Faber.

Todorov, T. 1981. *Introduction to poetics*. Minneapolis: University of Minnesota Press.

———. 1984. *Mikhail Bakhtin: The dialogical principle*. Trans. W. Godzich. Theory and History of Literature 13. Minneapolis: University of Minnesota Press.

Traube, E. G. 1986. *Cosmology and social life: Ritual exchange among the Mambai of East Timor*. Chicago: University of Chicago Press.

Turner, V. 1982. *From ritual to theatre: The human seriousness of play*. New York: Performing Arts.

Tuzin, D. 1972. Yam symbolism in the Sepik: An interpretative account. *Southwestern Journal of Anthropology* 28:230–54.

Tyler, S. A. 1986. Post-modern ethnography: From document of the occult to occult document. In *Writing culture: The poetics and politics of ethnography,* ed. J. Clifford and G. Marcus. Berkeley: University of California Press.

————. 1987. *The unspeakable: Discourse, dialogue, and rhetoric in the postmodern world.* Madison: University of Wisconsin Press.

Ulmer, G. L. 1983. The object of post-criticism. In *The anti-aesthetic: Essays on postmodern culture,* ed. H. Foster. Port Townsend, Wash.: Bay Press.

Vance, E. 1979. Roland and the poetics of memory. In *Textual strategies: Perspectives in post-structuralist criticism,* ed. J. V. Harari. Ithaca: Cornell University Press.

Wagner, R. 1972. *Habu: The innovation of meaning in Daribi religion.* Chicago: University of Chicago Press.

————. 1975. *The invention of culture.* Englewood Cliffs, N.J.: Prentice-Hall.

————. 1977. Analogic kinship: A Daribi example. *American Ethnologist* 4:623–42.

————. 1978. *Lethal speech: Daribi myth as symbolic obviation.* Ithaca: Cornell University Press.

————. 1986a. *Asiwinarong: Ethos, image and social power among the Usen Barok of New Ireland.* Princeton: Princeton University Press.

————. 1986b. *Symbols that stand for themselves.* Chicago: University of Chicago Press.

Watson, J. 1982. Of flesh and bones: The management of death pollution in Cantonese society. In *Death and the regeneration of life,* ed. M. Bloch and J. Parry. Cambridge: Cambridge University Press.

Weiner, A. 1976. *Women of value, men of renown: New perspectives in Trobriand exchange.* Austin: University of Texas Press.

————. 1977. How to read Trobriand objects of exchange, or What are yams made of. Paper presented at the 150th Anniversary of the Australian Museum, Conference on Exchange in the Pacific, 22–25 August.

————. 1980. Reproduction: A replacement for reciprocity. *American Ethnologist* 7(1): 71–85.

————. 1986. Inalienable wealth. *American Ethnologist* 12(2): 178–83.

————. 1987. *The Trobrianders of Papua New Guinea.* New York: Holt, Rinehart and Winston.

White, G. M., and J. Kirkpatrick. 1985. *Person, self, and experience: Exploring Pacific enthnopsychologies.* Berkeley: University of California Press.

Wurmser, L. 1981. *The mask of shame.* Baltimore: Johns Hopkins University Press.

————. 1987. Shame: The veiled companion of narcissism. In *The many faces of shame,* ed. D. L. Nathanson. New York: Guilford Press.

Young, M. 1983. *Magicians of Manumanua: Living myth in Kalauna.* Berkeley: University of California Press.

Index